CONFIGURING SALES ORDER MANAGEMENT WITHIN DYNAMICS AX 2012

BY MURRAY FIFE

© 2015 Blind Squirrel Publishing, LLC, All Rights
www.dynamicsaxcompanions.com

ISBN-10: 1514161281

ISBN-13: 978-1514161289

Preface

What You Need For This Guide

All the examples shown in this blueprint were done with the Microsoft Dynamics AX 2012 virtual machine image that was downloaded from the Microsoft Customer Source or Partner Source site. If you don't have your own installation of Microsoft Dynamics AX 2012, you can also use the images found on the Microsoft Learning Download Center or deployed through Lifecycle Services. The following list of software from the virtual image was leveraged within this guide:

* Microsoft Dynamics AX 2012 R3

Even though all the preceding software was used during the development and testing of the recipes in this book, they may also work on earlier versions of the software with minor tweaks and adjustments, and should also work on later versions without any changes.

Errata

Although we have taken every care to ensure the accuracy of our content, mistakes do happen. If you find a mistake in one of our books—maybe a mistake in the text or the code—we would be grateful if you would report this to us. By doing so, you can save other readers from frustration and help us improve subsequent versions of this book. If you find any errata, please report them by emailing editor@blindsquirrelpublishing.com.

Piracy

Piracy of copyright material on the Internet is an ongoing problem across all media. If you come across any illegal copies of our works, in any form, on the Internet, please provide us with the location address or website name immediately so that we can pursue a remedy.

Please contact us at legal@blindsquirrelpublishing.com with a link to the suspected pirated material.

We appreciate your help in protecting our authors, and our ability to bring you valuable content.

Questions

You can contact us at help@blindsquirrelpublishing.com if you are having a problem with any aspect of the book, and we will do our best to address it.

Table Of Contents

CONFIGURING ORDER CHARGES (Ctd.)

INTRODUCTION

The Sales and Marketing area within Dynamics AX not only allows you to manage and track all of the customer contact information and marketing activities, but it also allows you to manage all of your sales order activities within your organization. It is where you can configure your sales hierarchies, which allow you to organize all of your products into more manageable groups, and it is also where you can initiate sales orders, manage the changes to the orders, and also manage all of your standard pricing and discount masters. All of these transactions then feed down into the Accounts Receivable module, making the whole sales cycle seamless.

Setting up the Sales Order Management details are not hard either and this guide is designed to give you step by step instructions to show you how to set up the Sales area, and also show you how most of the base components of the module work so that you can get you up and running and taking sales orders.

CONFIGURING SALES ORDER MANAGEMENT CONTROLS

Before we start taking Sales Orders there are a few codes and controls that we need to set up to make our life a little easier. Some of these include the configuration of codes to be used within the orders themselves like the **Sales Origin**, **Delivery Terms**, and **Modes of Delivery**, and others are just configurations that will make you order entry process even easier. Like the **Order Search** feature and the **Event Tracking** feature.

Configuring the Accounts Receivable Parameters for Sales Order Management

The very first thing that we need to do though is to make a small tweak to the **Accounts Receivable** parameters, so that we can create Sales Orders, and also so that the system will track our prices and discounts on the sales order.

Configuring the Accounts Receivable Parameters for Sales Order Management

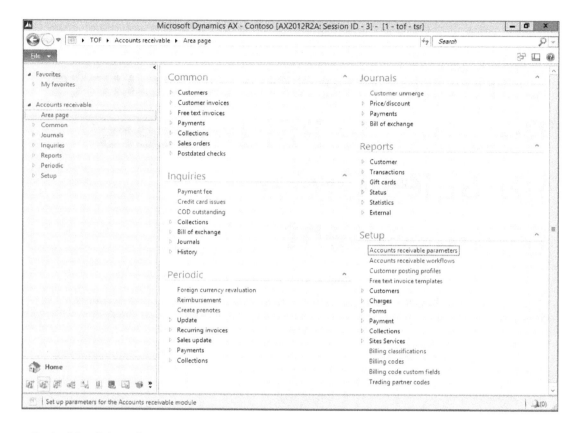

To do this, click on the **Accounts Receivable Parameters** menu item within the **Setup** group of the **Accounts Receivable** area page.

Configuring the Accounts Receivable Parameters for Sales Order Management

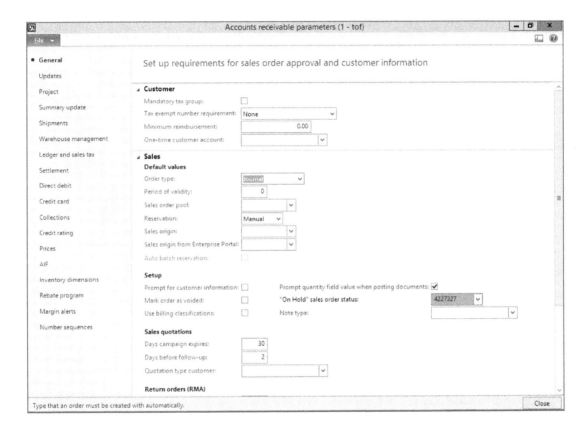

When the **Accounts Receivable Parameters** form is displayed, click on the **General** page link on the left hand side of the form.

Configuring the Accounts Receivable Parameters for Sales Order Management

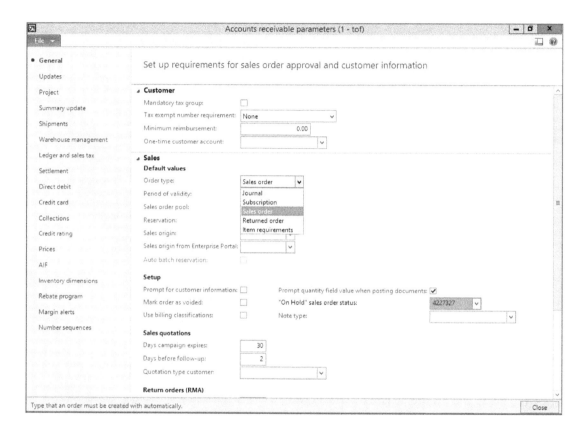

Click on the **Order Type** dropdown list and change the value to **Sales Order**.

Note: This will tell the system that it should create an Order of type **Sales Order** rather than **Journal**. Journals do not have the picking and invoicing option, so this is a very important tweak to make.

Configuring the Accounts Receivable Parameters for Sales Order Management

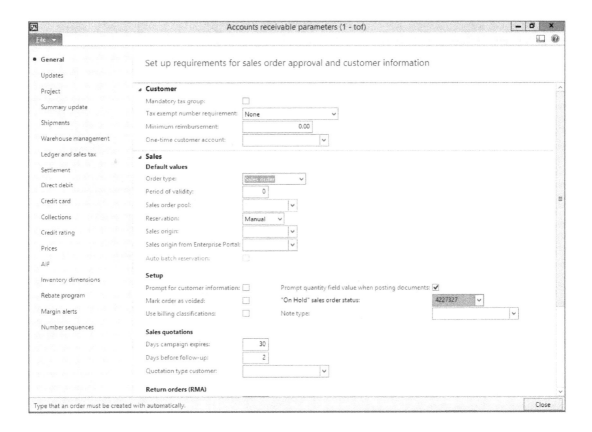

Configuring the Accounts Receivable Parameters for Sales Order Management

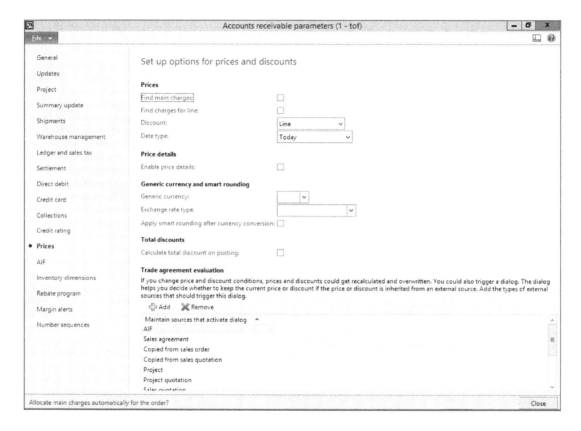

Next switch to the **Prices** page in the parameters form.

Configuring the Accounts Receivable Parameters for Sales Order Management

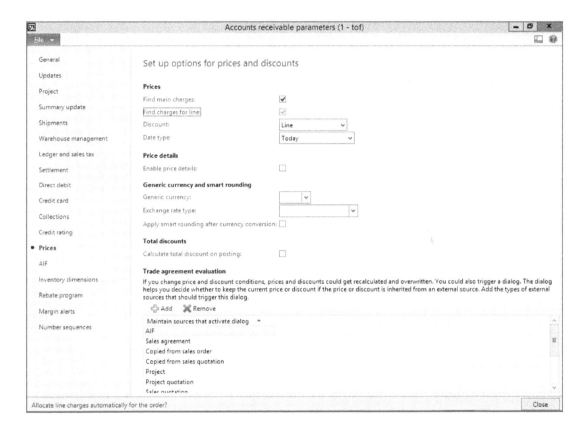

Within the **Prices** field group, check both the **Find Main Charges** checkbox which will allow the system to find header level charges, and also the **Find Charges For Line** which will allow the system to find automatic charges at the line level. We will discuss how these work later on in this book.

Configuring the Accounts Receivable Parameters for Sales Order Management

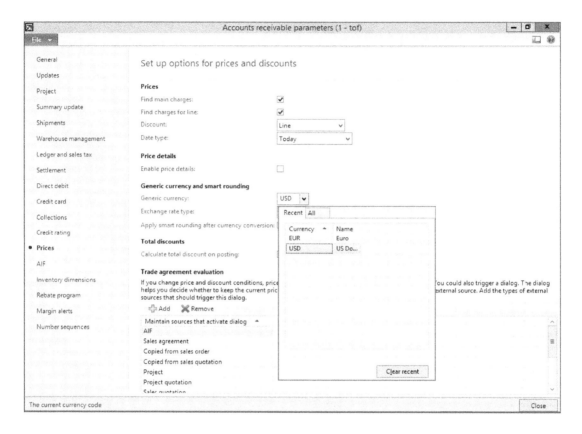

Now click on the dropdown list for the **Generic Currency** field and select the main currency that you want to use on your pricing routines. In this case we will want to select the **USD** option.

Configuring the Accounts Receivable Parameters for Sales Order Management

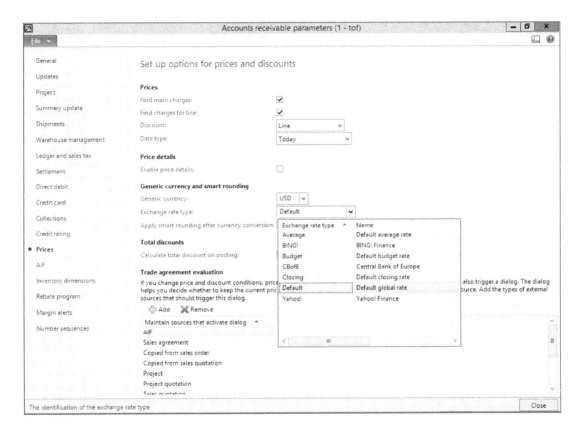

Then click on the **Exchange Rate Type** dropdown list and select the currency exchange rate that you want to use in the case that prices are maintained in different currencies. In this example we will select the **Default** Exchange Rate Type.

Configuring the Accounts Receivable Parameters for Sales Order Management

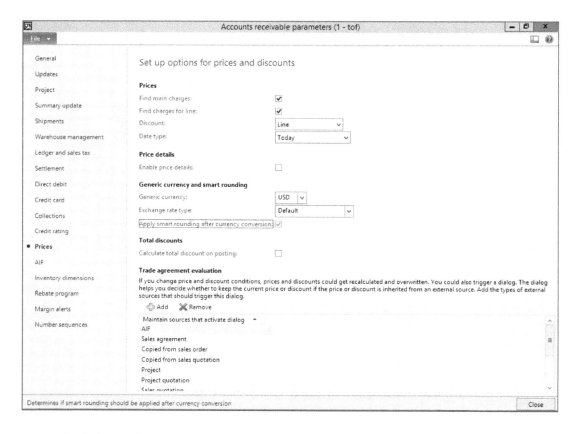

Now check the **Apply Smart Rounding After Currency Conversion** so that when we do use the smart rounding feature, it will round on the final nmber.

Configuring the Accounts Receivable Parameters for Sales Order Management

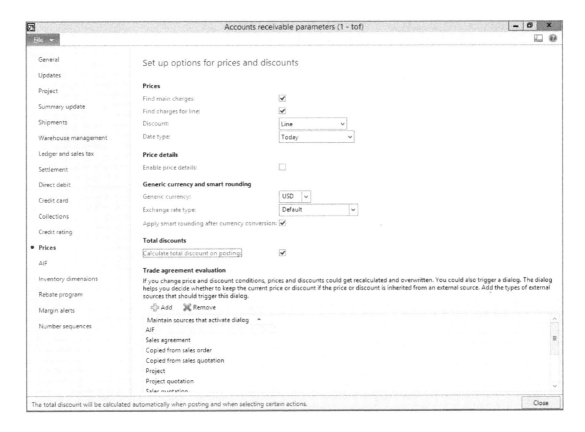

And finally, check the **Calculate Total Discount On Posting** option so that the total discounts will be calculated at the end of the order process.

Once you have made these small tweaks, click on the **Close** button to exit out of the form.

Configuring Customer Reason Codes

Next we will want to set up a few additional reason codes which we will be able to use within the Order Management process.

Configuring Customer Reason Codes

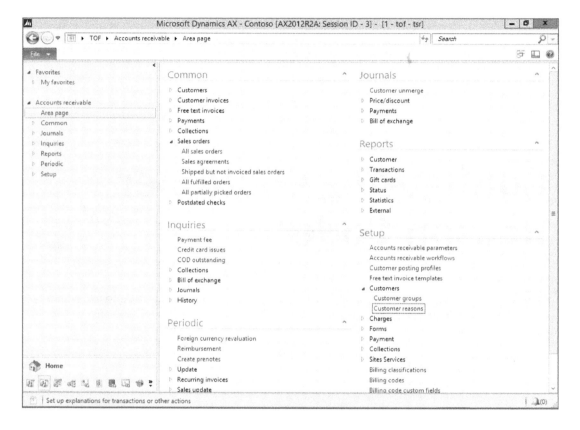

To do this, click on the **Customer Reasons** menu item within the **Customers** folder of the **Setup** group within the **Accounts Receivable** area page.

Configuring Customer Reason Codes

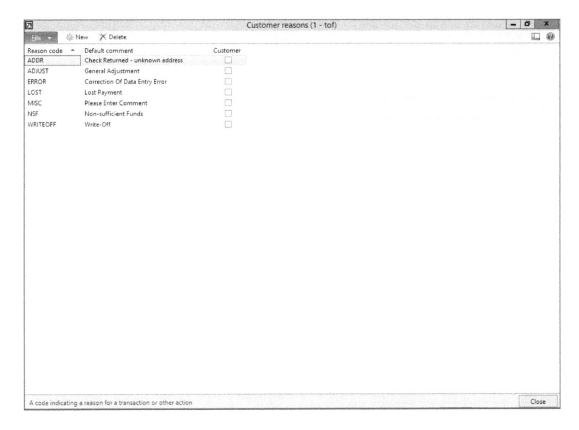

When the **Customer Reasons** maintenance form is displayed, you will notice that there are existing reason codes that have been entered in during the setup of the other modules.

Configuring Customer Reason Codes

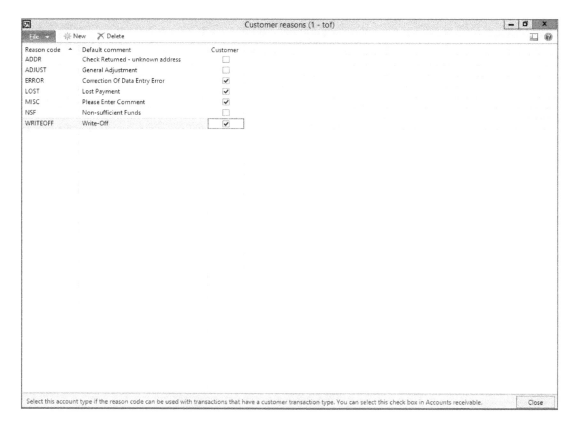

Check the **Customer** flag for the **ERROR**, **LOST**, **MISC** and **WIRTEOFF** reason codes to reuse them within the order management area.

Configuring Customer Reason Codes

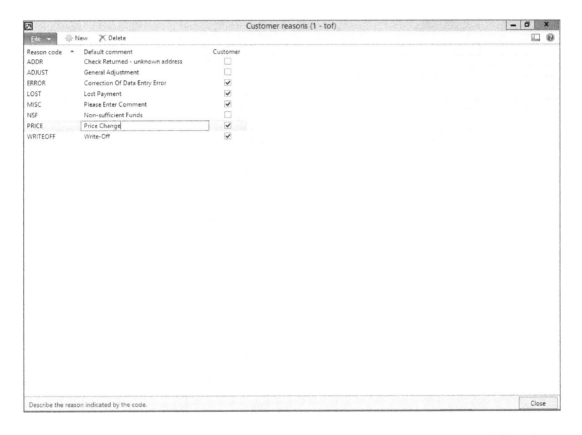

Now we will add a few more reason codes that are specific to Order Management. Click on the **New** button in the menu bar to create a new record, set the **Reason Code** to **PRICE**, the **Default Comment** to **Price Change** and check the **Customer** flag to enable it for use against the customer.

Configuring Customer Reason Codes

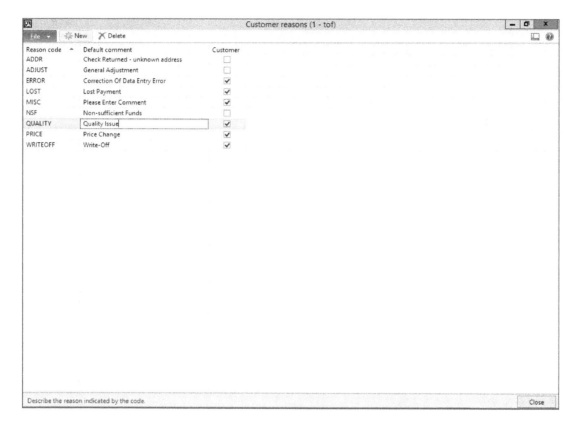

Click on the **New** button in the menu bar to create another record, set the **Reason Code** to **QUALITY**, the **Default Comment** to **Quality Issue** and check the **Customer** flag to enable it for use against the customer.

After you have done that, just click on the **Close** button to exit from the form.

Configuring Delivery Terms

Next we will configure a few **Delivery Terms** codes that we will be able to use within our Sales Orders.

We will configure some of the common **Incoterms**. For more information on these click here:
http://en.wikipedia.org/wiki/Incoterms#EXW_.E2.80.93_Ex_Works_.28named_place.29

Configuring Delivery Terms

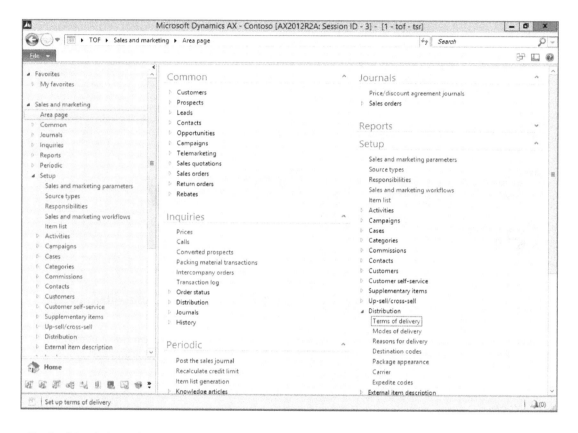

To do this, click on the **Terms Of Delivery** menu item within the **Distribution** folder of the **Setup** group within the **Sales and Marketing** area page.

Configuring Delivery Terms

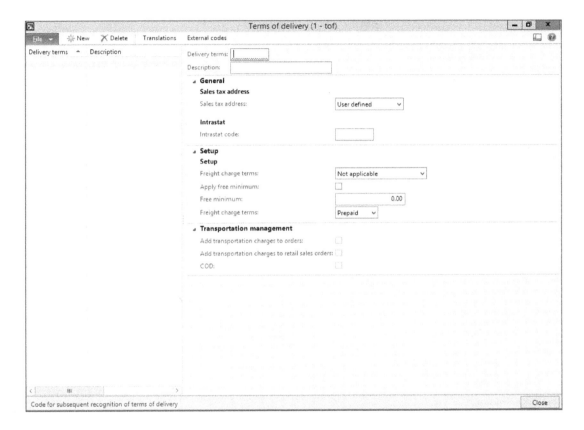

When the **Terms of Delivery** maintenance form is displayed, click on the **New** button in the menu bar to create a new record.

Configuring Delivery Terms

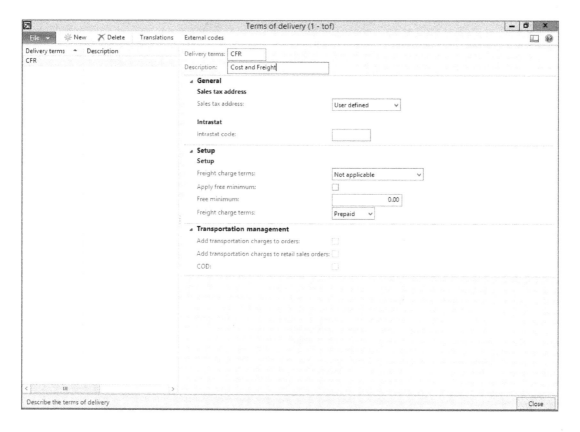

Then set the **Delivery Terms** code to **CFR** and the **Description** to **Cost and Freight**.

Configuring Delivery Terms

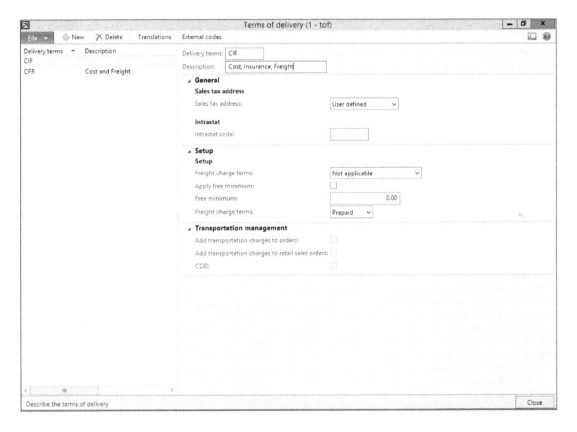

Click on the New button to add another record and then set the **Delivery Terms** code to **CIF** and the **Description** to **Cost, Insurance, Freight**.

Configuring Delivery Terms

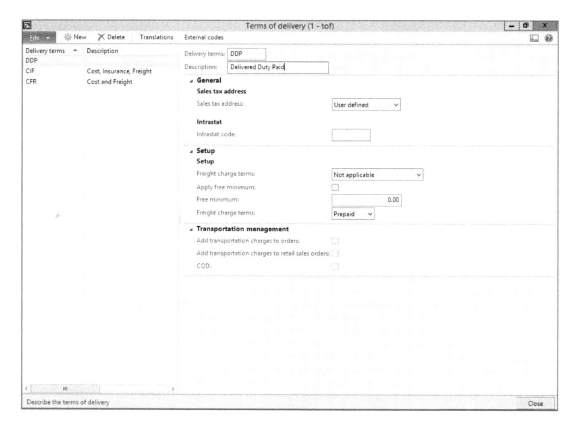

Click on the New button again to add another record and then set the **Delivery Terms** code to **DDP** and the **Description** to **Delivered Duty Paid**.

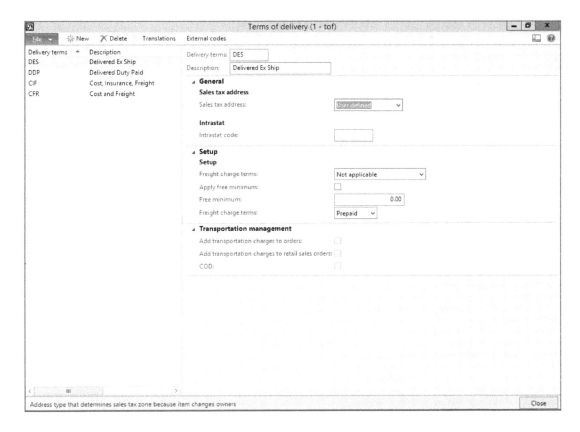

Click on the New button again to add another record and then set the **Delivery Terms** code to **DEX** and the **Description** to **Delivery Ex Ship**.

Configuring Delivery Terms

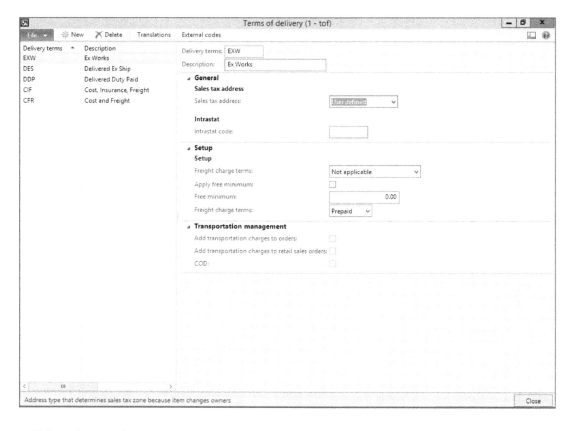

Click on the New button again to add another record and then set the **Delivery Terms** code to **EXW** and the **Description** to **Ex Works**.

Configuring Delivery Terms

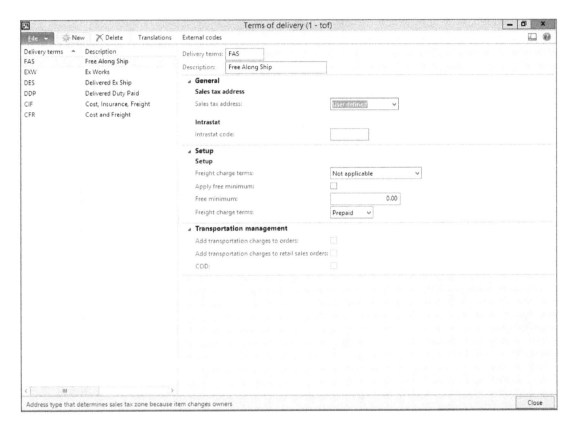

Click on the New button again to add another record and then set the **Delivery Terms** code to **FAS** and the **Description** to **Free Along Ship**.

Configuring Delivery Terms

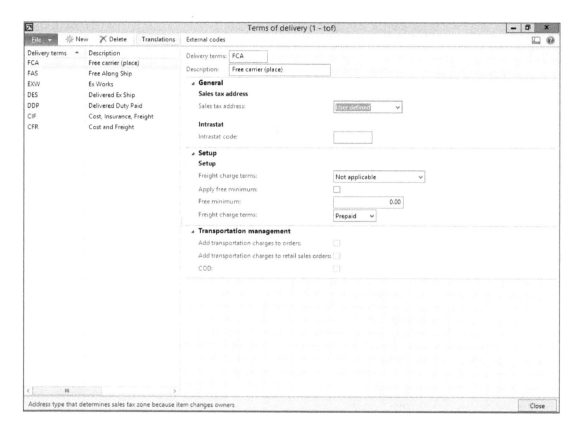

Click on the New button again to add another record and then set the **Delivery Terms** code to **FCA** and the **Description** to **Free Carrier (Place)**.

Configuring Delivery Terms

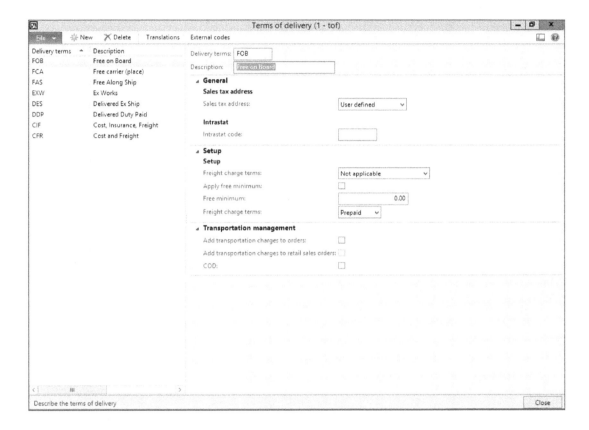

Click on the New button again to add the final record and then set the **Delivery Terms** code to **FOB** and the **Description** to **Free On Board**.

Configuring Modes Of Delivery

Next we will want to configure some default **Modes Of Delivery** that we can assign to our Customers and Sales Orders which we will use to indicate how the products are going to be delivered.

Configuring Modes Of Delivery

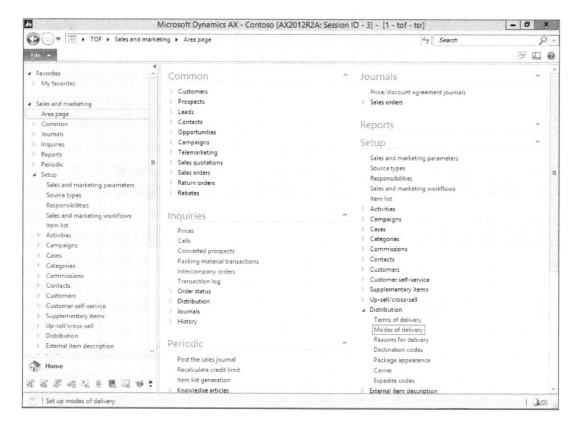

To do this, click on the **Modes of Delivery** menu item within the **Distribution** folder of the **Setup** group within the **Sales and Marketing** area page.

Configuring Modes Of Delivery

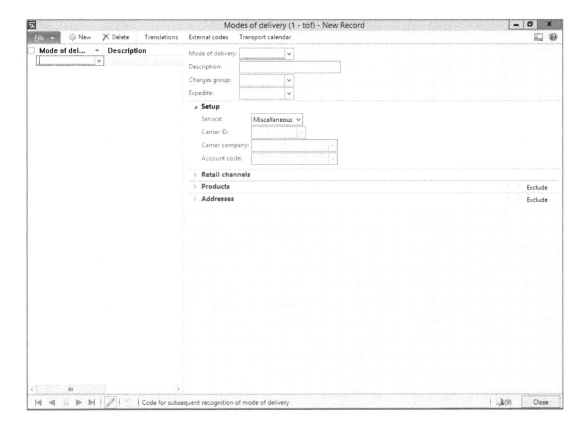

When the **Modes of Delivery** maintenance form is displayed, click on the **New** button in the menu bar to create a new record.

Configuring Modes Of Delivery

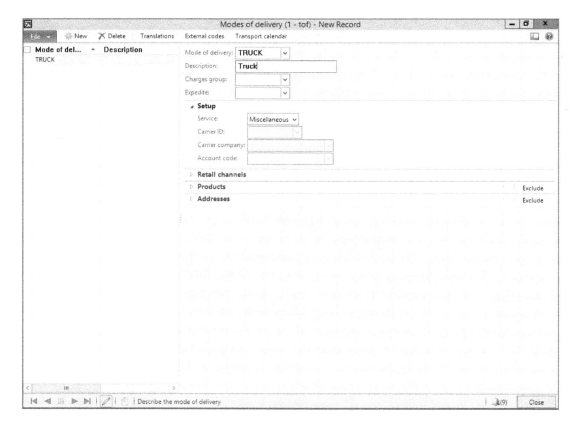

Set the **Mode of Delivery** code to **TRUCK** and the **Description** to **Truck.**

Configuring Modes Of Delivery

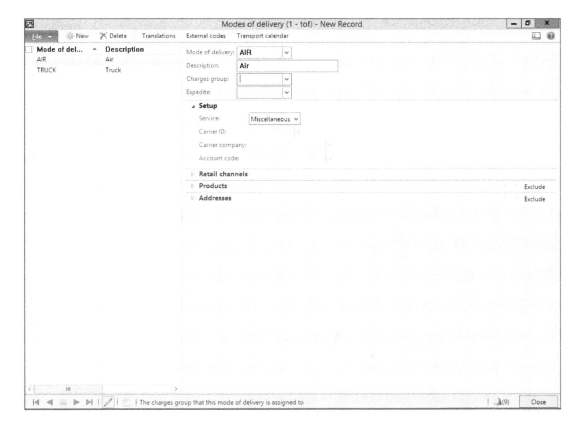

Click on the **New** button in the menu bar to create a new record and then set the **Mode of Delivery** code to **AIR** and the **Description** to **Air.**

Configuring Modes Of Delivery

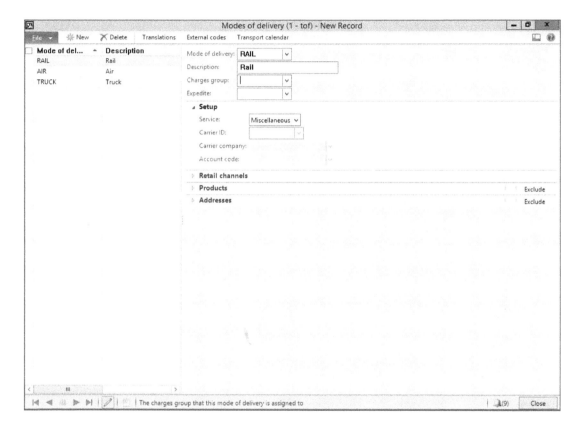

Click on the **New** button in the menu bar again to create a new record and then set the **Mode of Delivery** code to **RAIL** and the **Description** to **Rail**.

Configuring Modes Of Delivery

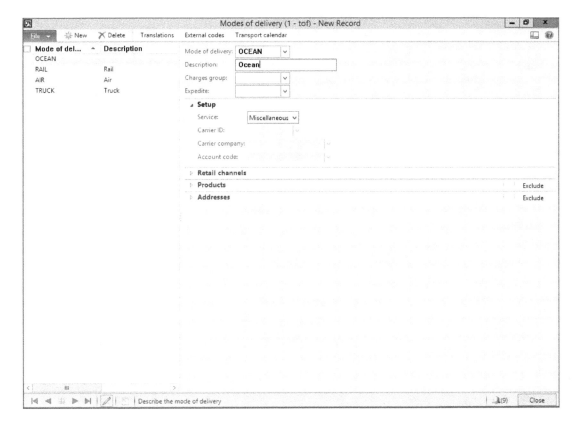

Click on the **New** button in the menu bar again to create a new record and then set the **Mode of Delivery** code to **OCEAN** and the **Description** to **Ocean.**

Configuring Modes Of Delivery

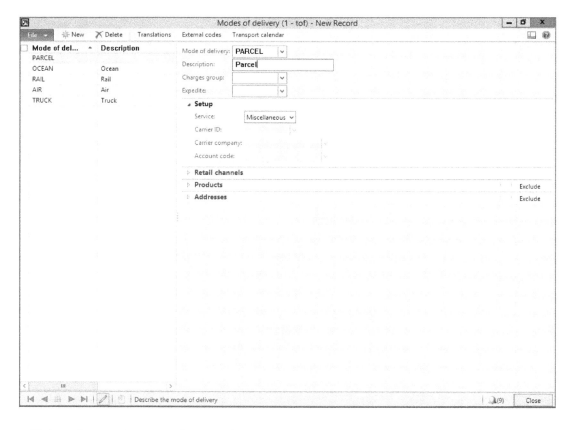

Click on the **New** button in the menu bar again to create a new record and then set the **Mode of Delivery** code to **PARCEL** and the **Description** to **Parcel.**

Configuring Modes Of Delivery

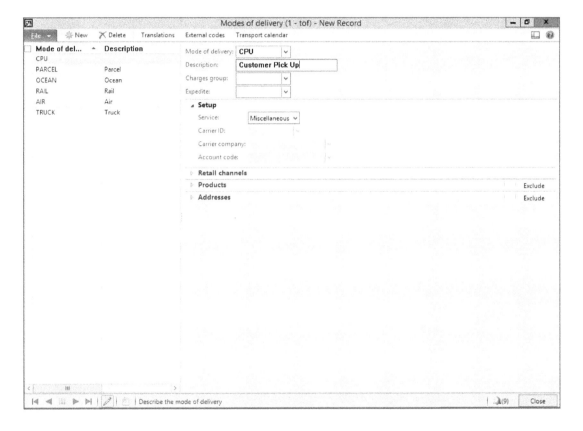

Click on the **New** button in the menu bar again to create the final record and then set the **Mode of Delivery** code to **CPU** and the **Description** to **Customer Pick Up.**

Configuring Sales Order Origin Codes

Now we will configure some **Sales Origin Codes** which we will use to indicate how the order was received. This is a great way to segregate out our orders into different order channels so that we can see what is the most active ordering method.

Configuring Sales Order Origin Codes

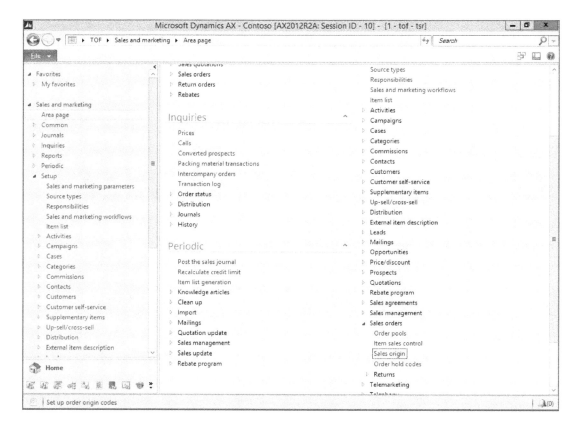

To do this, click on the **Sales Origin** menu item within the **Sales Orders** folder of the **Setup** group within the **Sales and Marketing** area page.

Configuring Sales Order Origin Codes

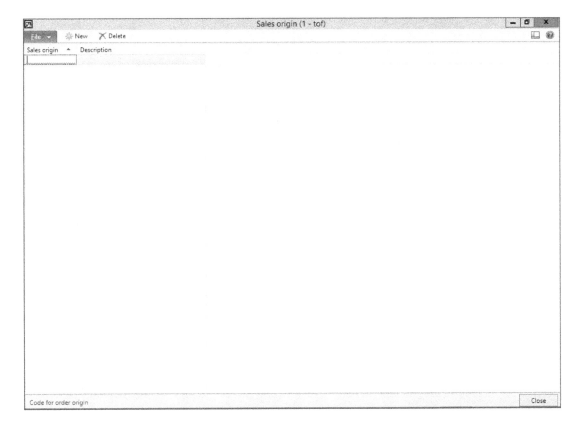

When the **Sales Origin** maintenance form is displayed, click on the **New** button to create a new record.

Configuring Sales Order Origin Codes

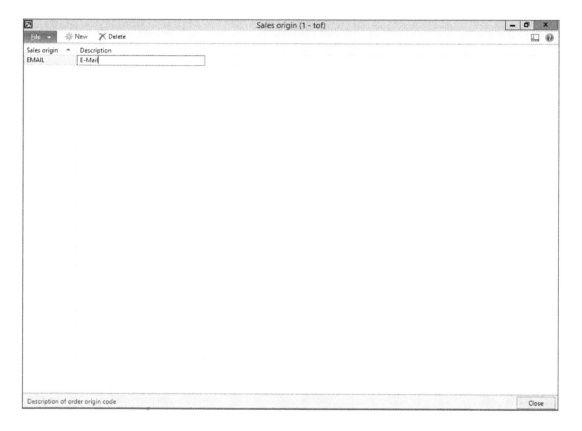

Then set the **Sales Origin** code to **EMAIL** and the **Description** to **E-Mail**.

Configuring Sales Order Origin Codes

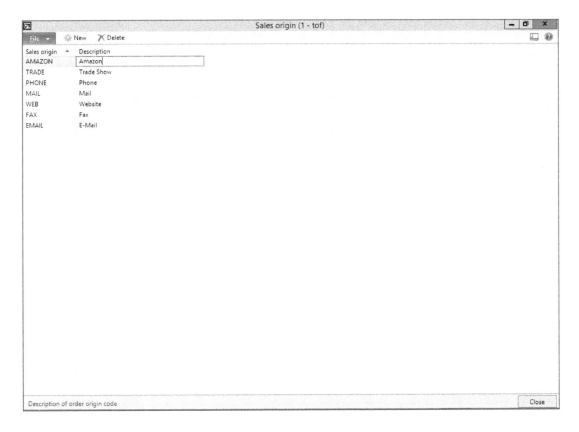

Repeat the process for all of the other methods that you acquire your orders. Here are a few more examples:

AMAZON	Amazon
TRADE	Trade
PHONE	Phone
MAIL	Mail
WEB	Website
FAX	Fax

When you have done that, just click on the **Close** button to exit out of the form.

Enabling Order Event Tracking

Now we will turn on a few features related to order management, starting with the **Order Event Tracking** which will allow you to see all of the changed that are made to Sales Orders.

Enabling Order Event Tracking

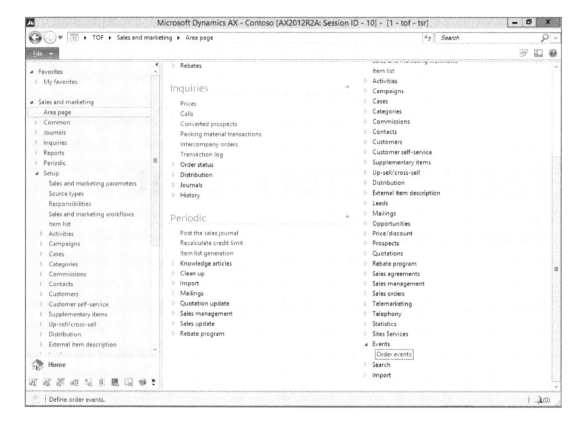

To do this, click on the **Order Events** menu item within the **Events** folder of the **Setup** group within the **Sales and Marketing** area page,

Enabling Order Event Tracking

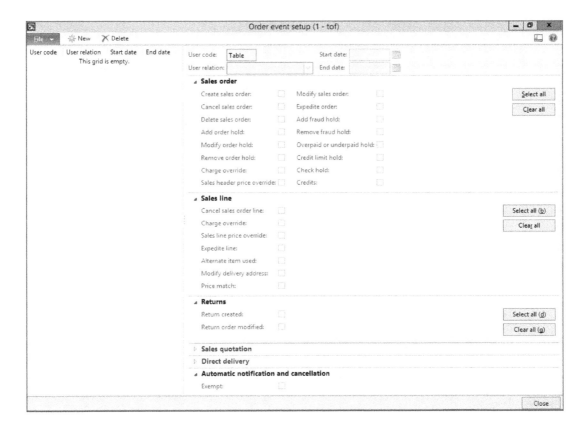

When the **Order Event Setup** maintenance form is displayed you can expand out all of the fast tabs within the form and see all of the different events that you can track.

Enabling Order Event Tracking

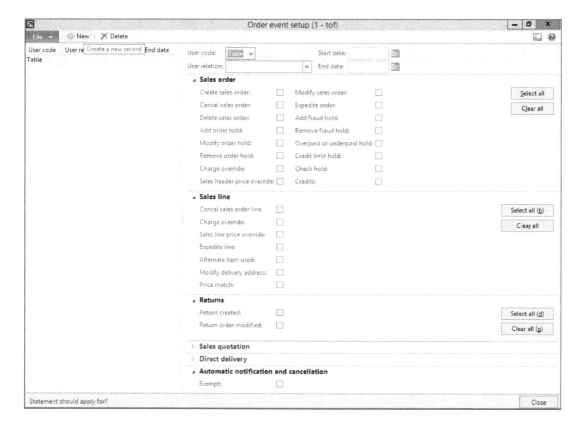

To enable event tracking, click on the **New** button in the menu bar to create a new record.

Enabling Order Event Tracking

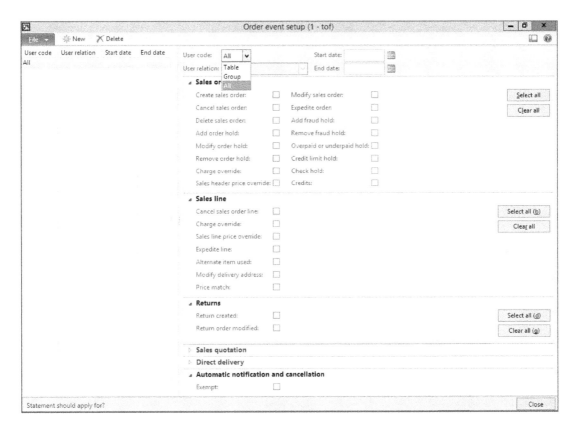

Click on the **User Code** dropdown list and change the value from **Table** to **All** to create a rule that tracks all order changes regardless of the user that made the change.

Note: This feature allows you to track order events for everyone (**All**), for a group of users (**Group**) or even the changes that are made by just one user (**Table**) if you want to be super suspicious.

Enabling Order Event Tracking

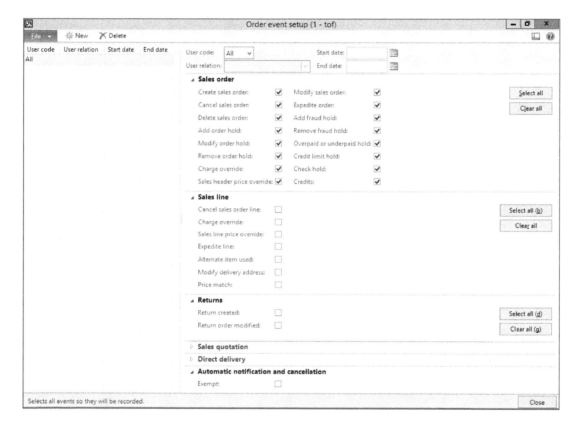

Although you can track individual event types, it is simpler just to click on the **Select All** button to select all of the different event types within the fast tab. So start off by clicking on the **Select All** button within the **Sales Order** fast tab.

Enabling Order Event Tracking

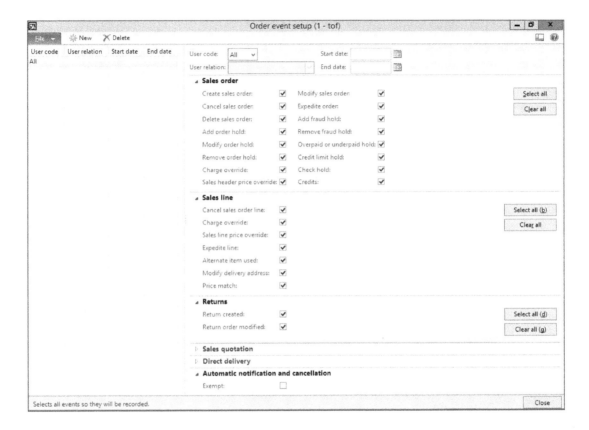

Then click on the **Select All** button within the **Sales Lines** fast tab and also the **Returns** tab.

When you have done that, click on the **Close** button to exit from the form.

Configuring Order Search Parameters

Another very useful feature to enable within Order Management is the **Order Search**. This will allow you to search on multiple fields within the Products and Customers at the time of order entry, and it will return back either the only matching record, or a list of records that match. Before we configure how the search works, we just want to enable it.

Configuring Order Search Parameters

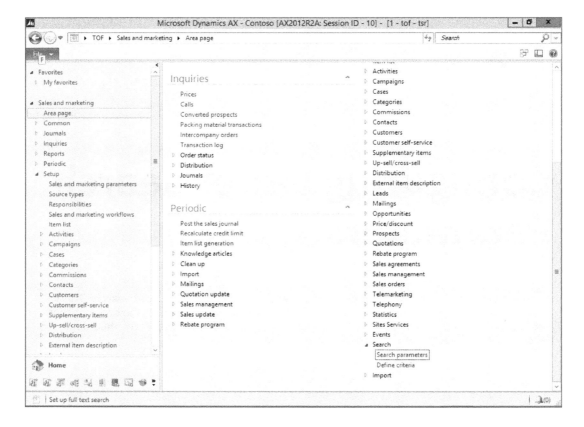

To do this, click on the **Search Parameters** menu item within the **Search** folder of the **Setup** group within the **Sales and Marketing** area page.

Configuring Order Search Parameters

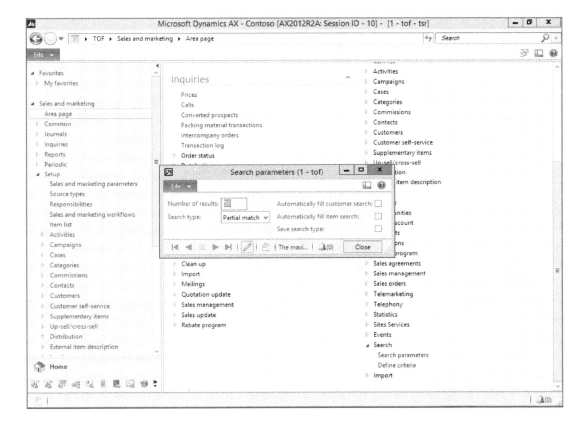

This will open up the **Search Parameters** dialog box.

Configuring Order Search Parameters

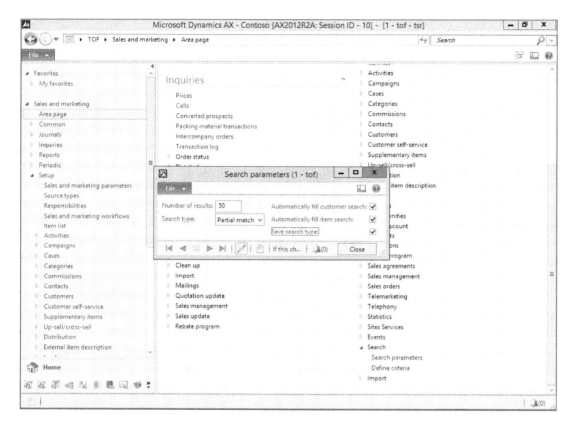

All we need to do here is check the **Automatically Fill Customer Search**, the **Automatically Fill Item Search** and the **Save Search Type** flags.

When you are done, just click on the **Close** button to exit from the form.

Configuring Search Criteria

Now we will need to configure the search feature and tell it what we would like to search on when it is looking for customers and products.

77

Configuring Search Criteria

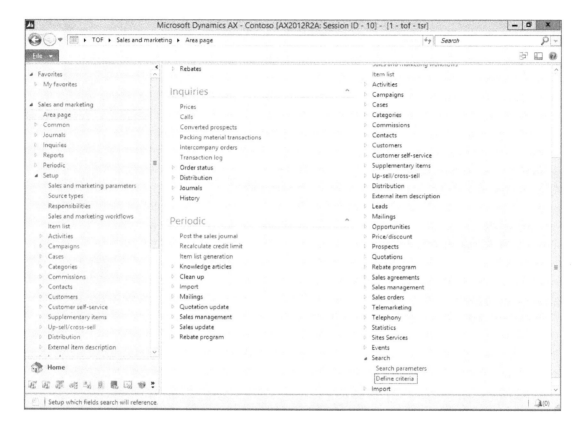

To do this click on the **Define Criteria** menu item with in the **Search** folder of the **Setup** group within the **Sales and Marketing** area page.

Configuring Search Criteria

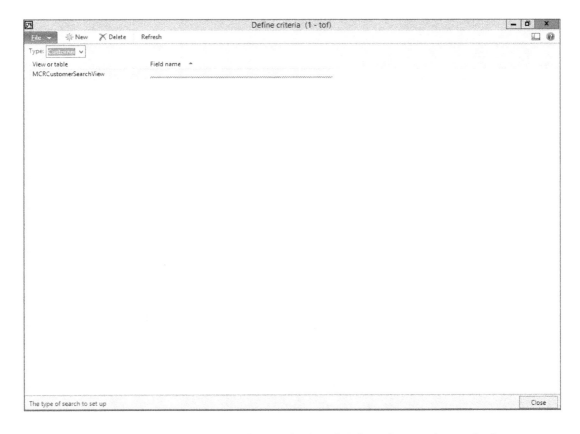

When the **Define Criteria** maintenance form is displayed click on the **New** button in the menu bar to create a new record.

Configuring Search Criteria

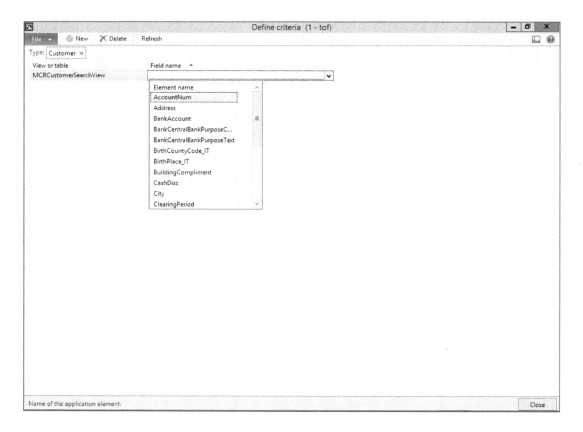

Then click on the **Field Name** dropdown list and you will see all of the different fields that you can search on.

Configuring Search Criteria

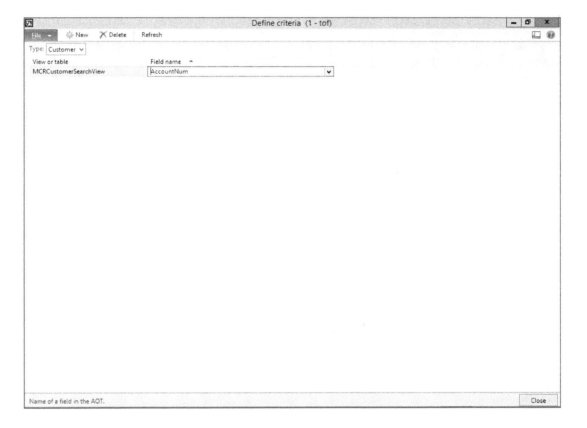

Select the **AccountNum** field to search based on the customers account number.

Configuring Search Criteria

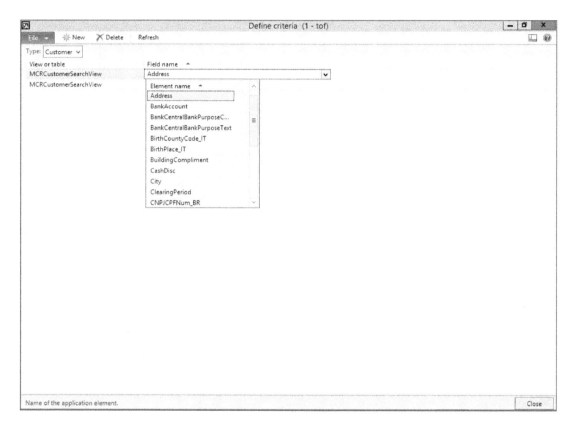

Then click on the **New** button again to create a new search option, click on the **Field Name** dropdown box and select the **Address** field so that we can search based on the customers address.

Configuring Search Criteria

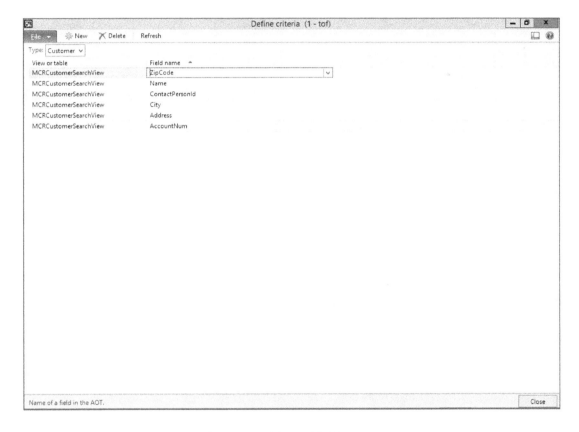

Repeat the process and add the following additional fields:

City
ContactPersonID
Name
ZipCode

Configuring Search Criteria

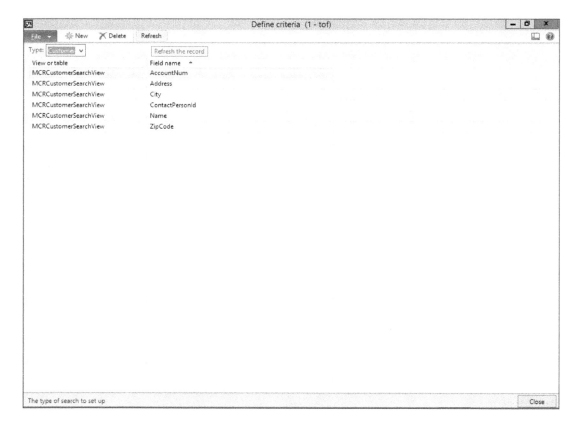

There is one more step that we need to perform before the Customer Search will work, and that is to click on the **Refresh** button in the menu bar.

Configuring Search Criteria

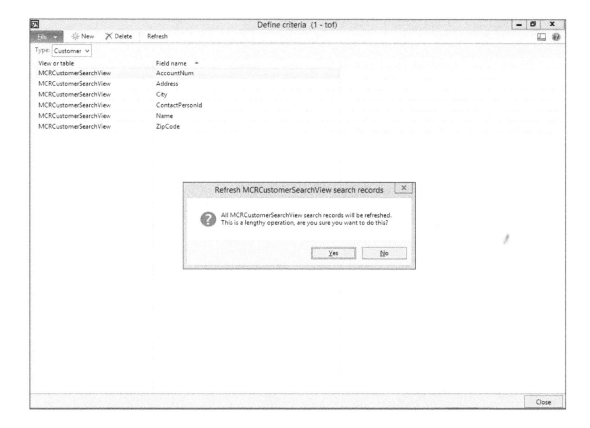

This will open up a warning message telling you that you are about to change the search – just click **Yes**.

Configuring Search Criteria

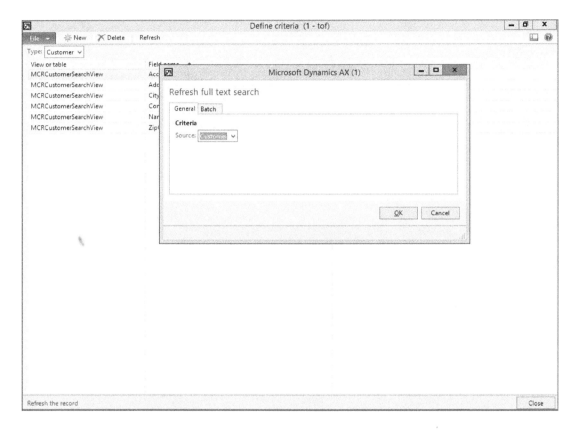

This will take you to the **Refresh Full Text Search** dialog box. All you need to do is click on the **OK** button.

Configuring Search Criteria

Now that we have configured the customer search, we will want to configure the **Item** search next. To do this, click on the **Type** dropdown list and select the **Item** option.

Configuring Search Criteria

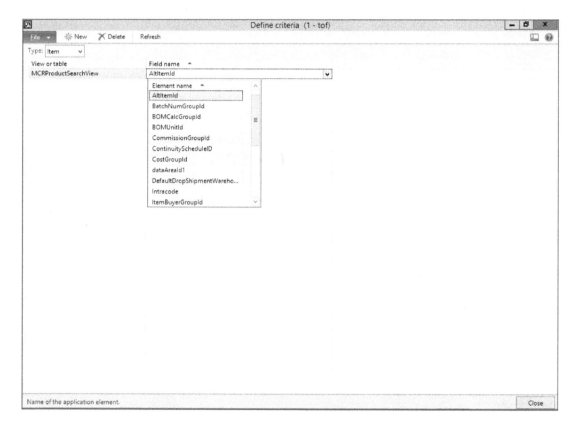

This will open up a new search criteria list. Click on the **Field Name** dropdown list and select
the **AltItemID** field.

Configuring Search Criteria

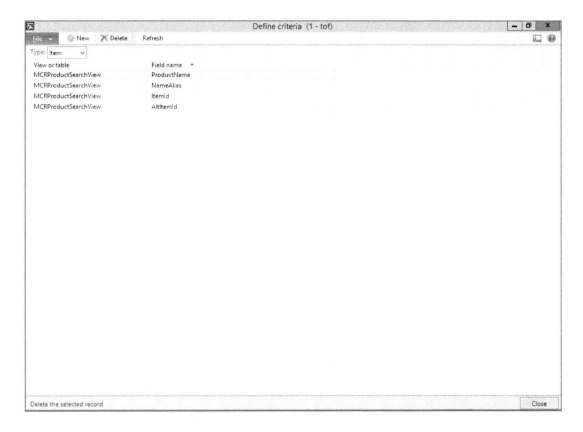

Repeat the process and add in the following additional fields:

ItemId
NameAlias
ProductName

Configuring Search Criteria

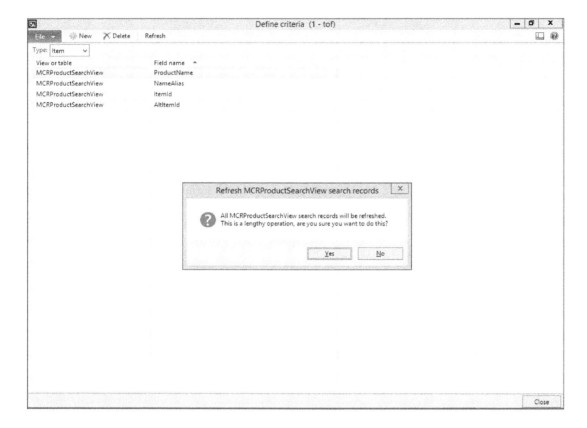

When you have done that, click on the **Refresh** button in the menu bar and then click **Yes** on the warning dialog box.

Configuring Search Criteria

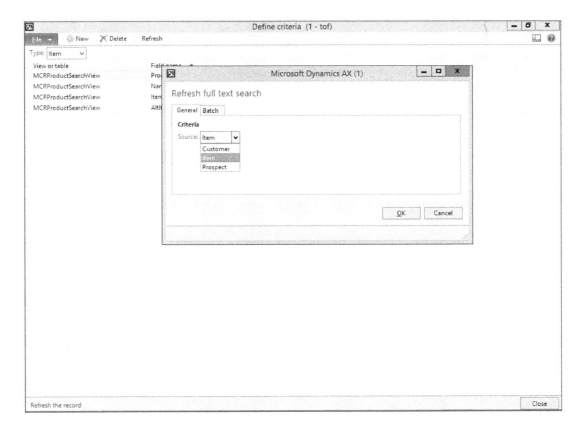

When the **Refresh Full Text Search** dialog box is displayed, click on the **Source** dropdown list and select the **Item** option to tell the system to refresh the items and not the customers.

Configuring Search Criteria

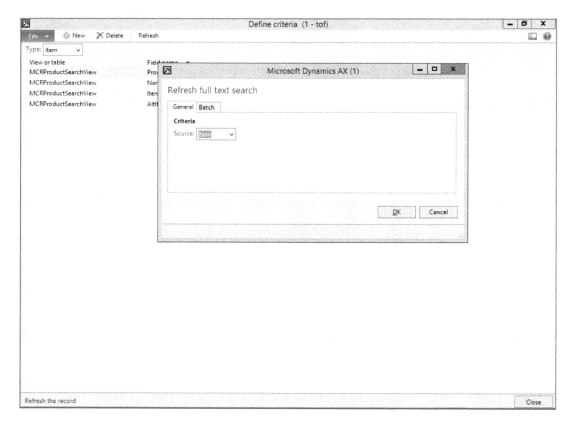

Then click on the **OK** button to refresh the full text search.

Configuring Search Criteria

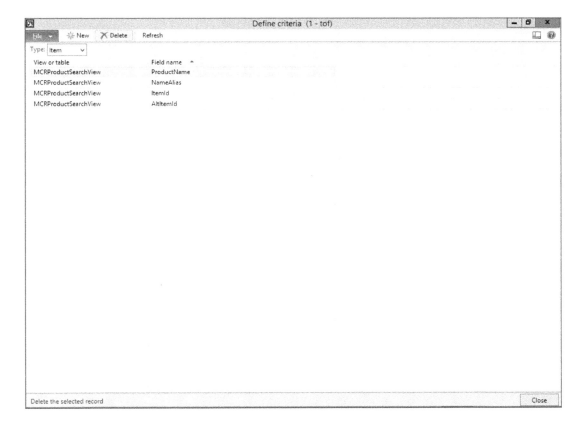

After you have done that you can just click on the **Close** button to exit from the form.

CONFIGURING SALES CATEGORIES

Just like Procurement, Sales also have the ability to set up the **Categories** which will allow you to segregate out your products and easily find them within the ordering process. In this chapter we will show you how you can set them up and link them with you Products.

Configuring Category Hierarchies

To start off we need to create a product **Category Hierarchy** that we will use to group the products together.

Configuring Category Hierarchies

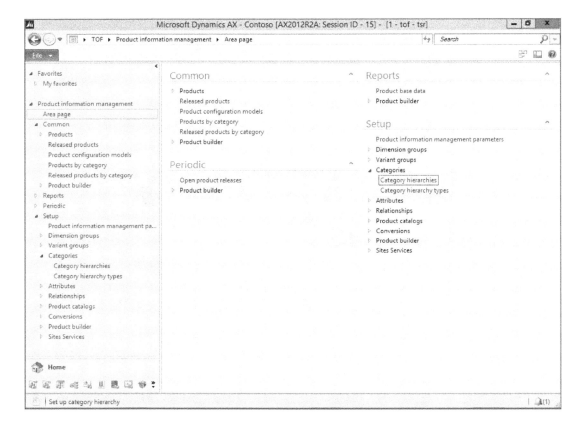

To do this, click on the **Category Hierarchies** menu item within the **Categories** folder of the **Setup** group within the **Product Information Management** area page.

Configuring Category Hierarchies

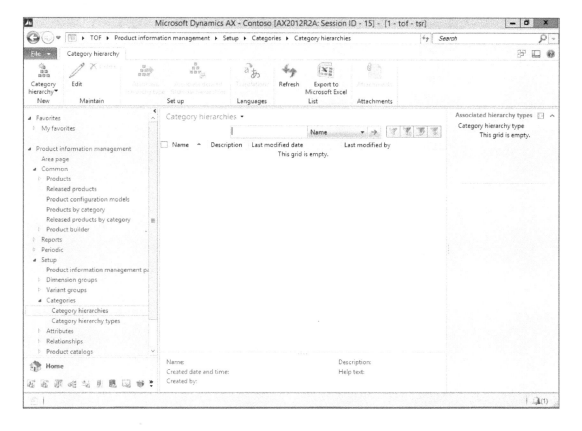

This will open up the **Category Hierarchies** list page.

Configuring Category Hierarchies

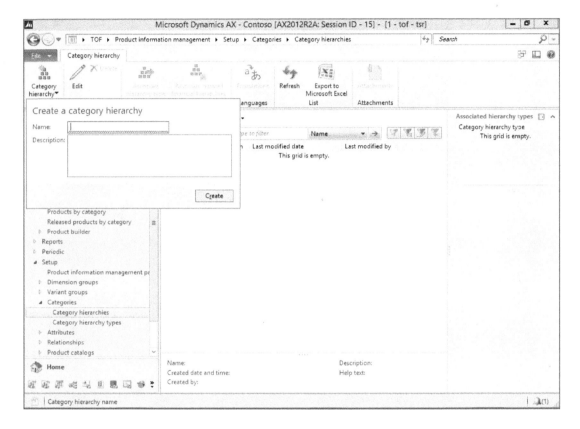

Click on the **Category Hierarchy** button within the **New** group of the **Category Hierarchy** ribbon bar which will open up a quick add window.

Configuring Category Hierarchies

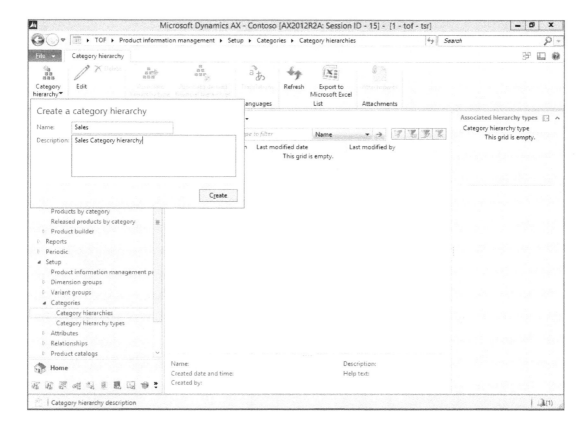

Set the **Name** to **Sales** and the **Description** to **Sales Category Description**. Then click on the **Create** button.

Configuring Category Hierarchies

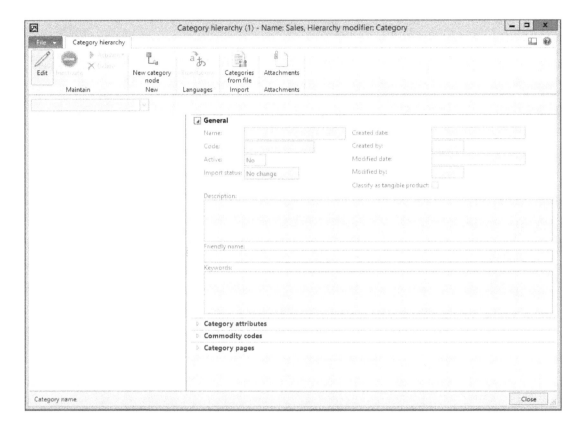

This will open up a new **Category Hierarchy** maintenance form.

Configuring Category Hierarchies

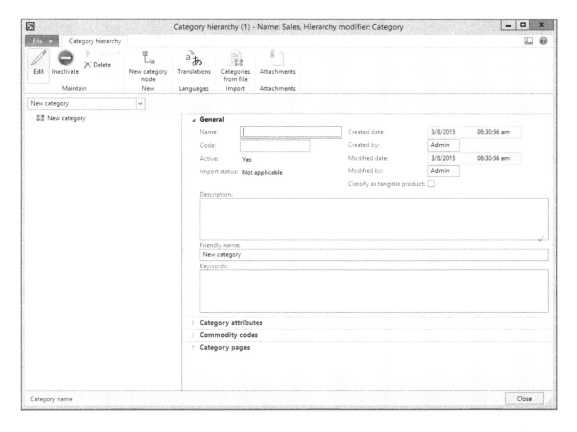

To start building your hierarchy, click on the **New Category Node** button within the **New** group of the **Category Hierarchy** ribbon bar.

Configuring Category Hierarchies

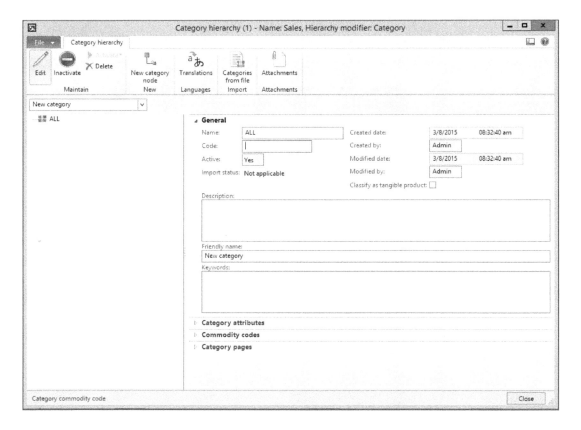

For the first level of the hierarchy set the **Name** to **ALL**.

Configuring Category Hierarchies

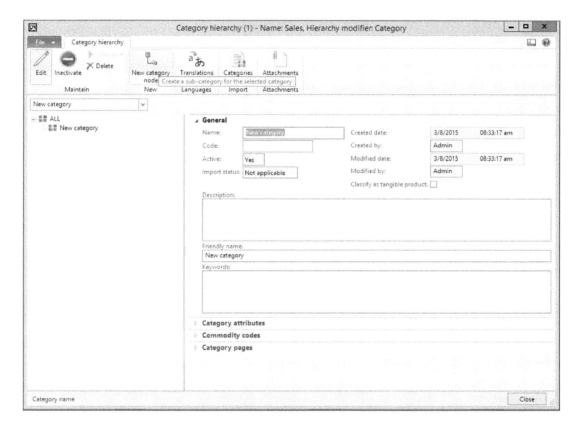

Then click on the **New Category Node** within the **New** group of the **Category Hierarchy** ribbon bar to create a child caregory.

Configuring Category Hierarchies

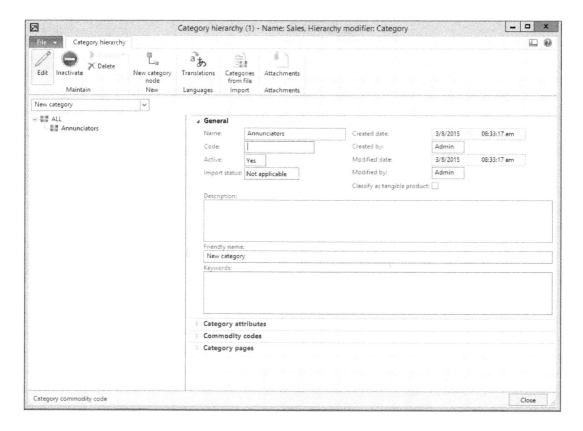

Set the **Name** to **Annunciators**.

Configuring Category Hierarchies

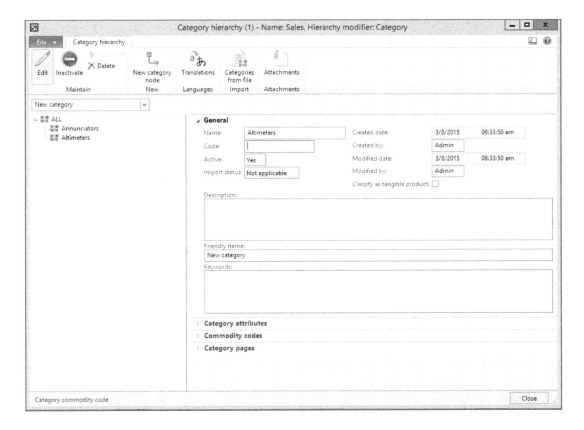

Keep on adding additional **Categories** to the **Category Hierarchy** and when you are done, click on the **Close** button to exit from the form.

Configuring Category Hierarchy Types

Next we want to link the **Category Hierarchy** that we just created to the **Sales** module so that we can use it to set up the product details.

Configuring Category Hierarchy Types

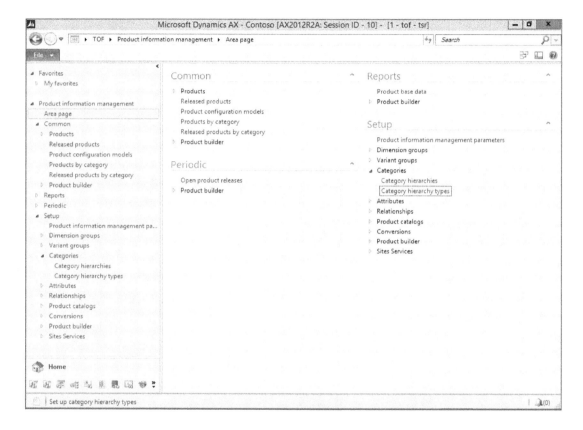

To do this, click on the **Category Hierarchy Types** menu item within the **Categories** folder of the **Setup** group within the **Product Information Management** area page.

Configuring Category Hierarchy Types

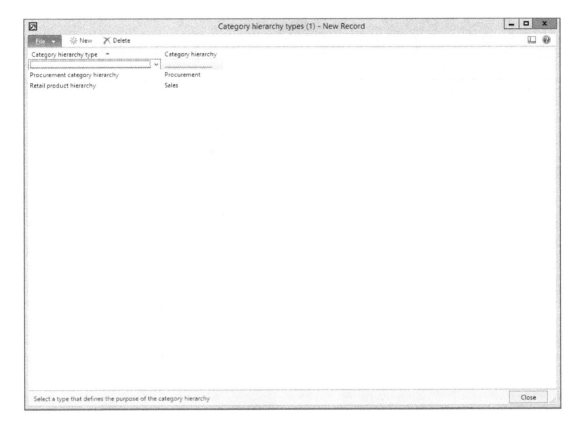

When the **Category Hierarchy Types** maintenance form is displayed, click on the **New** button to create a new record

Configuring Category Hierarchy Types

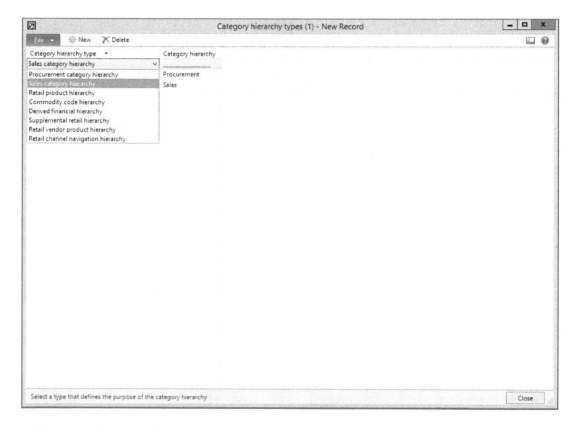

Click on the **Category Hierarchy Type** dropdown and select the **Sales Category Hierarchy** option.

Configuring Category Hierarchy Types

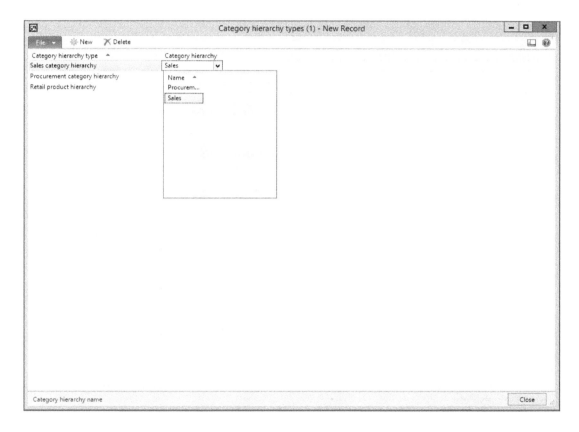

Then click on the **Category Hierarchy** dropdown list and select the **Sales** category that you just created.

Configuring Category Hierarchy Types

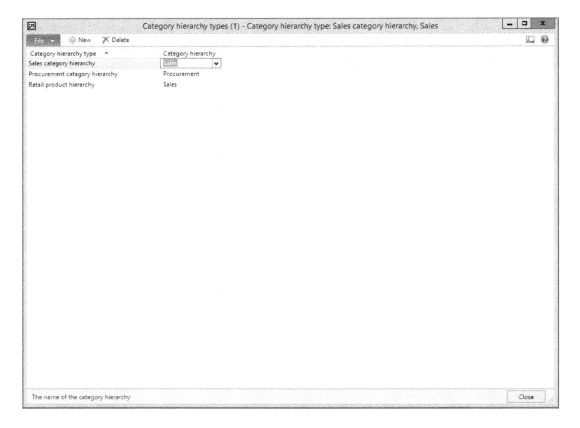

After you have done that click on the **Close** button to exit from the form.

Configuring Sales Categories

Once you have created your hierarchy and associated it with the **Sales** area, you can polish up the data a little by accessing the **Sales Categories**.

Configuring Sales Categories

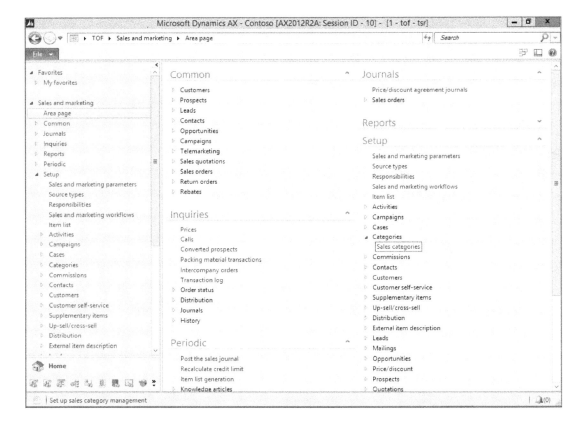

To do this, click on the **Sales Categories** menu item within the **Categories** folder of the **Setup** group within the **Sales and Marketing** area page.

Configuring Sales Categories

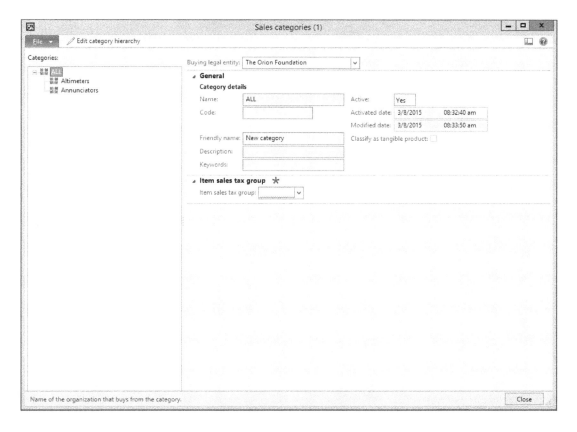

When the **Sales Categories** form is displayed you will notice that the same hierarchy that you configured within the **Product Information Management** area is displayed. To make changes to the hierarchy, click on the **Edit Category Hierarchy** link in the menu bar.

Configuring Sales Categories

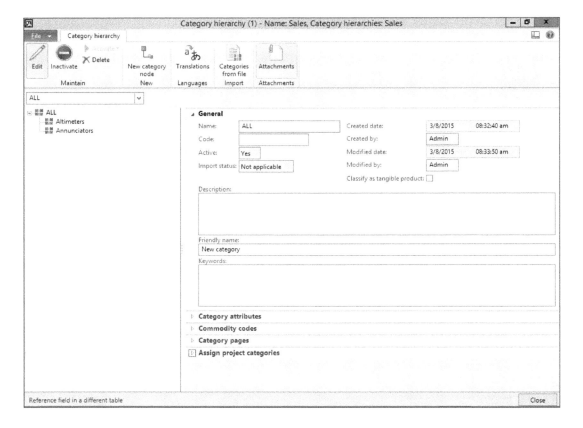

This will open up the **Category Hierarchy** editor.

Configuring Sales Categories

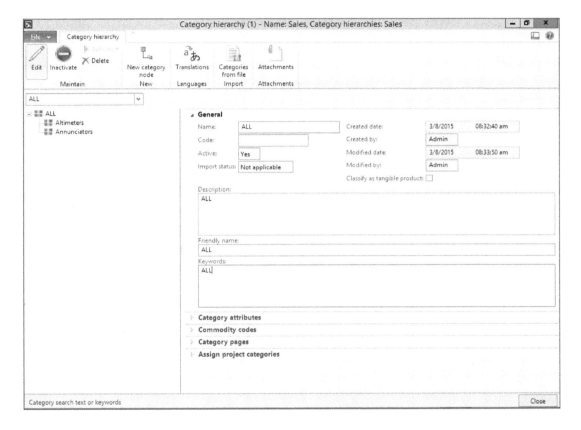

Select the **ALL** node and then update the **Description**, the **Friendly Name** and **Keywords** on the node.

Configuring Sales Categories

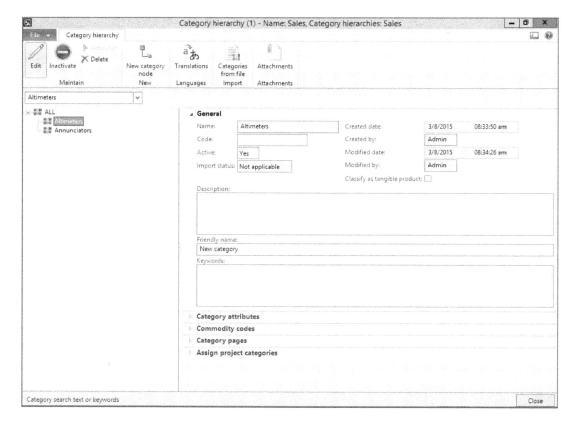

Now select the **Altimeters** node.

Configuring Sales Categories

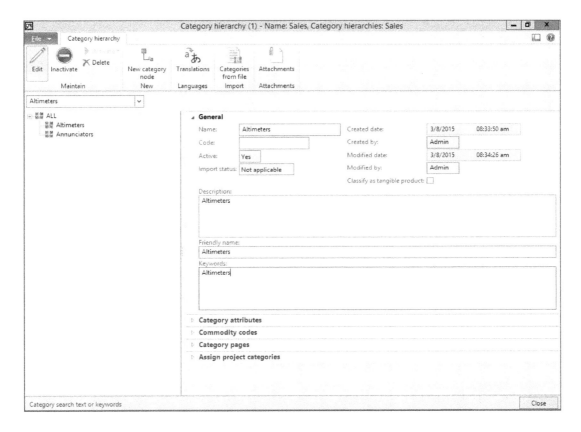

Update the **Description**, the **Friendly Name** and **Keywords** on that node as well.

Configuring Sales Categories

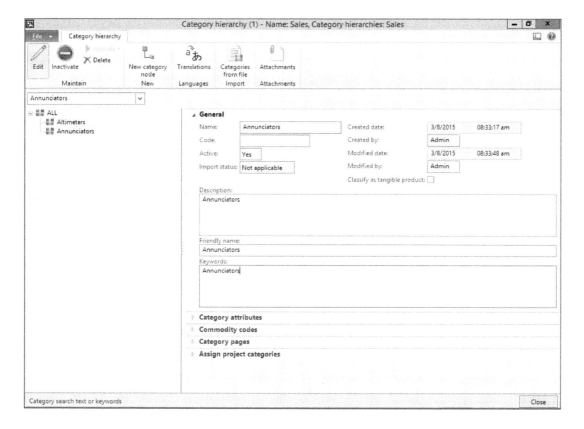

Keep on repeating the process for all of the nodes and when you are done, just click on the **Close** button to exit from the form.

Assigning Products To Sales Categories

One thing that you may have noticed on the **Sales Categories** form is that there was no place to update the products that are associated with the category itself. Don't worry, there is an easy way to link the products to the categories.

Assigning Products To Sales Categories

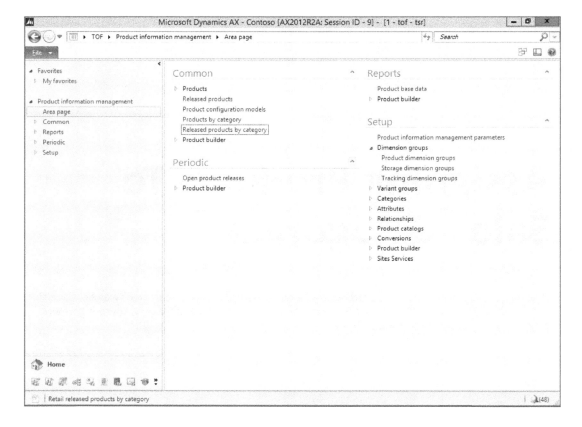

To do this, click on the **Released Products By Category** menu item within the **Common** group of the **Product Information Management** area page.

Assigning Products To Sales Categories

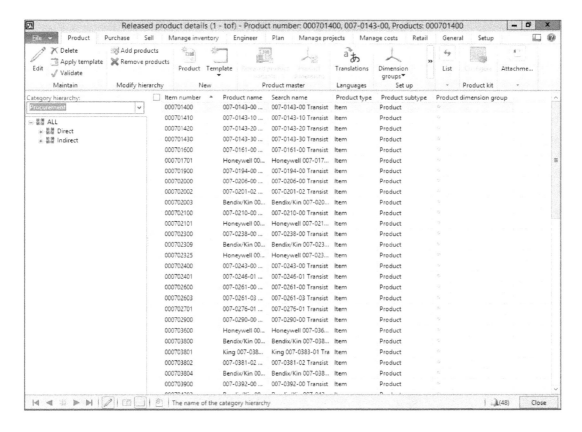

This will open up a variation of the product maintenance form which allows you to filter by category.

Assigning Products To Sales Categories

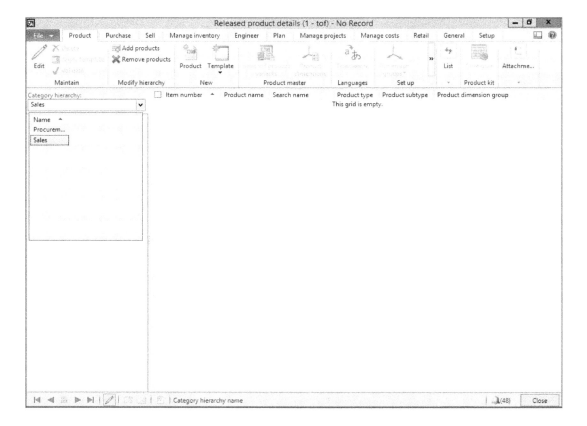

Click on the **Category Hierarchy** dropdown list and select the **Sales** hierarchy.

Assigning Products To Sales Categories

This will show you the new hierarchy that you just created, but there are no product associated with the hierarchy.

Assigning Products To Sales Categories

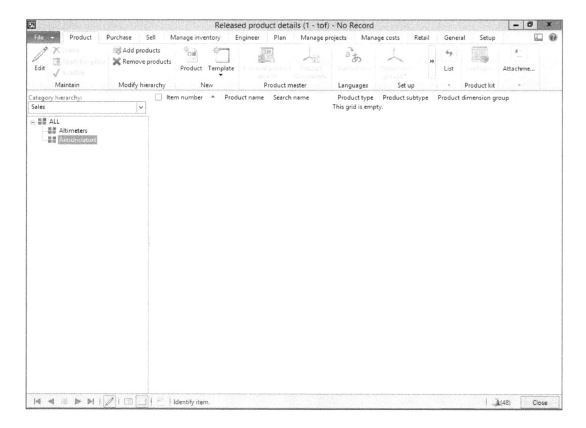

Select the **Annunciators** node, and then click on the **Add Products** button within the **Modify Hierarchy** group of the **Product** ribbon bar.

Assigning Products To Sales Categories

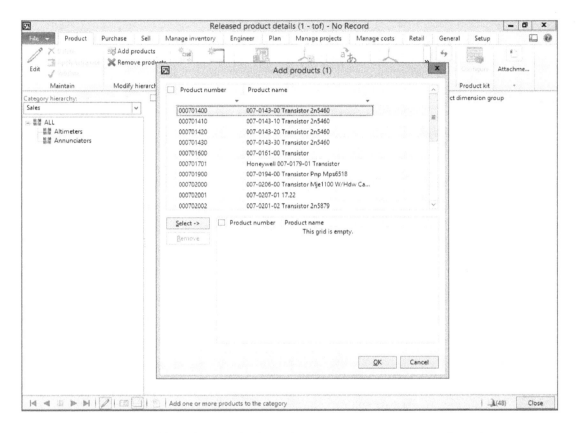

This will open up the **Add Products** dialog box where you can select your products that you want to add to the category.

Assigning Products To Sales Categories

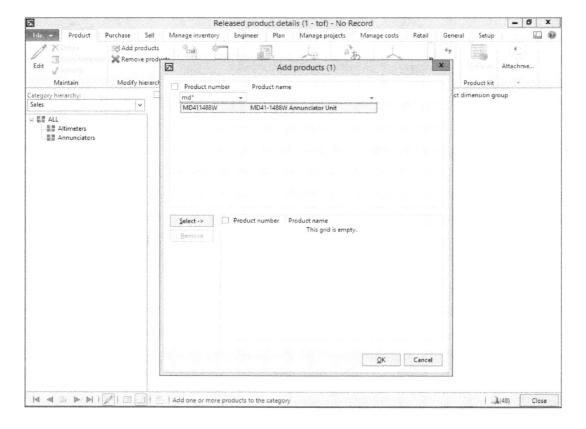

You can filter out the list of products that are shown through the filter box in the header of the grid.

Assigning Products To Sales Categories

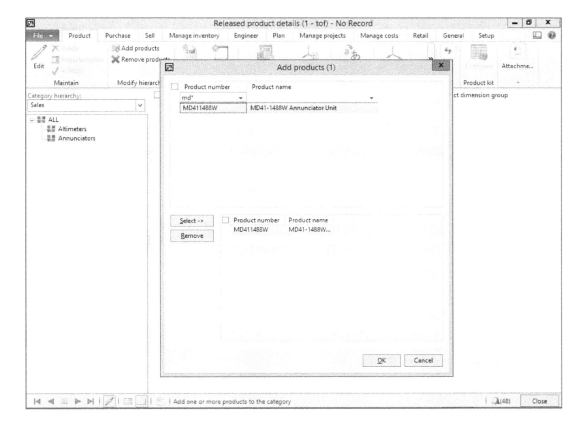

All you need to do is then select the product(s) that you want to add to the category and click on the **Select** button.

After you have selected all of the products that you want to add, just click on the **OK** button.

Assigning Products To Sales Categories

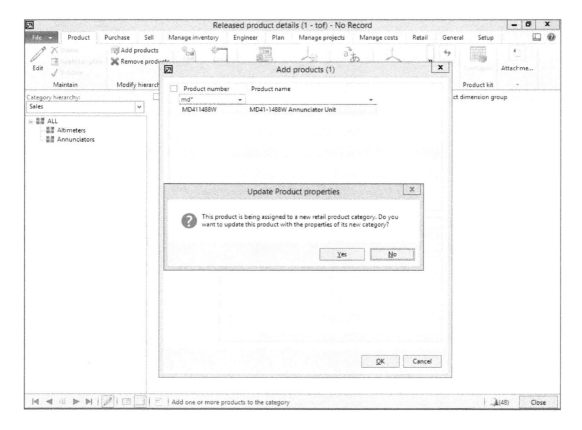

If you have default properties associated with the category then you will be asked if you want to copy them to the products that you have selected to make them consistent. Press **Yes**.

Assigning Products To Sales Categories

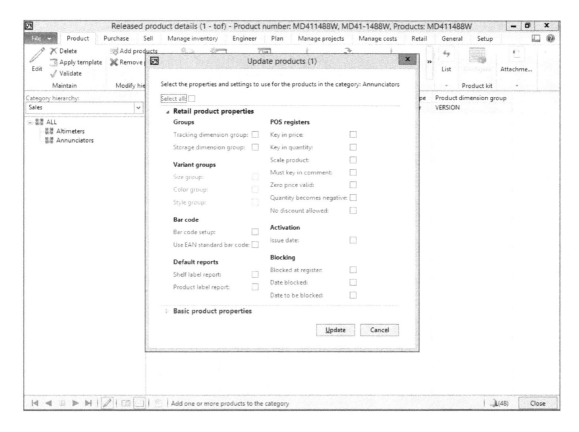

This will open up an options panel that will show you all of the defaults that you can overwrite. Don't select any at this time and then click on the **Update** button.

Assigning Products To Sales Categories

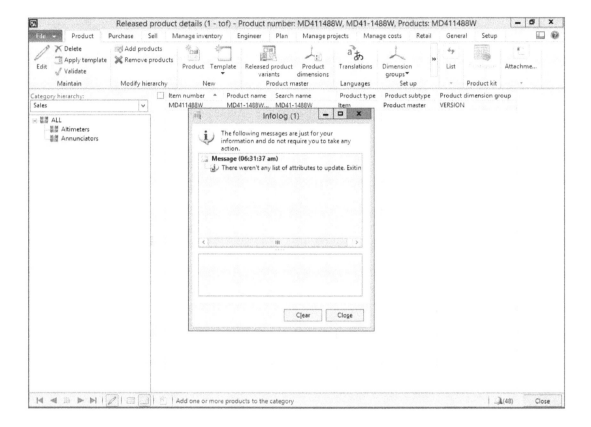

When the Infolog is displayed, just click on the **Close** button.

Assigning Products To Sales Categories

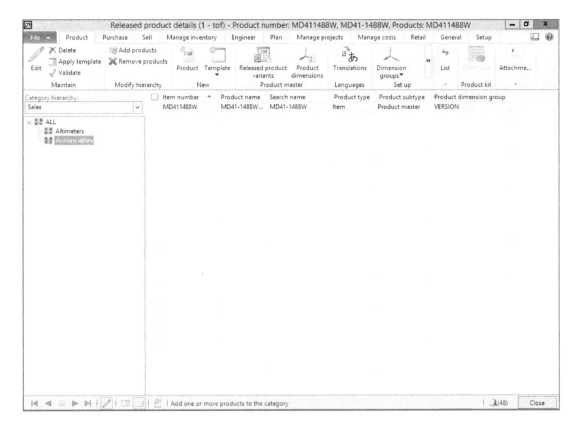

Now you have assigned your product to the category. You can keep on adding additional products if you like and when you are done, just click on the **Close** button to exit from the form.

PROCESSING SALES ORDERS

Now that we have all of the codes and controls set up we can start creating **Sales Orders**, ship them and then create our Receivable Invoices so that we can get money.

Configuring Base Sales Prices For Products

Before we start though we just need to check on one important item, and that is to make sure that we have a base sales price assigned to our product.

Configuring Base Sales Prices For Products

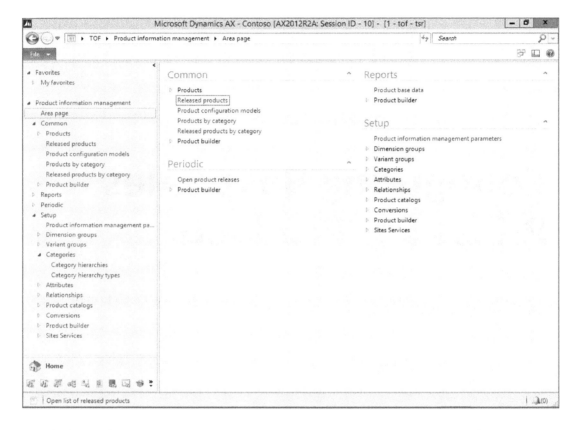

To do this, click on the **Released Products** menu item within the **Common** group of the **Product Information Management** area page.

Configuring Base Sales Prices For Products

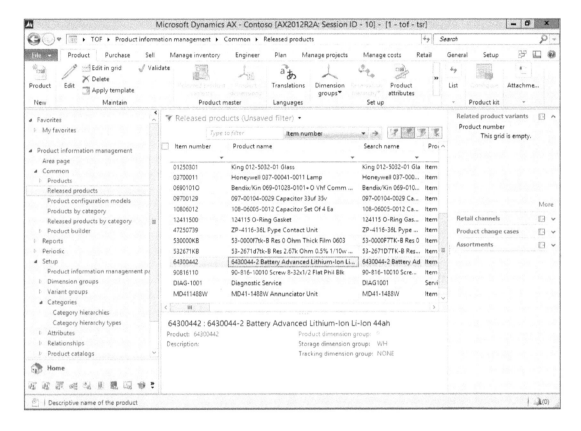

When the **Released Products** list page is displayed, find the product that you want to sell, and click on the **Edit** button within the **Maintain** group of the **Product** ribbon bar.

Configuring Base Sales Prices For Products

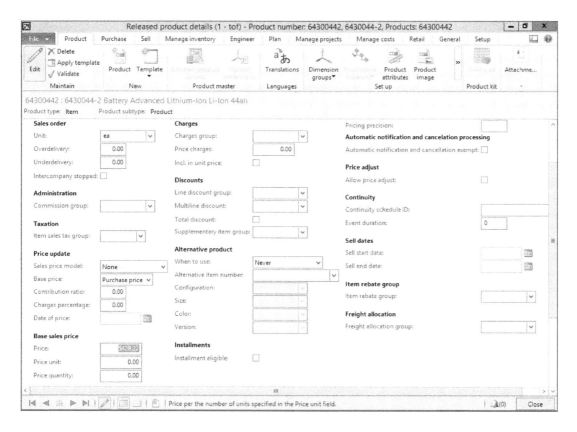

When the **Released Product** detail form is displayed, scroll down to the **Sales Order** fast tab, and make sure that there is a **Price** field has a sales price value set.

When you have finished checking your products, just click on the **Close** button to exit from the form.

Creating a New Sales Order

Now we are set and we can start entering in Sales Orders.

Creating a New Sales Order

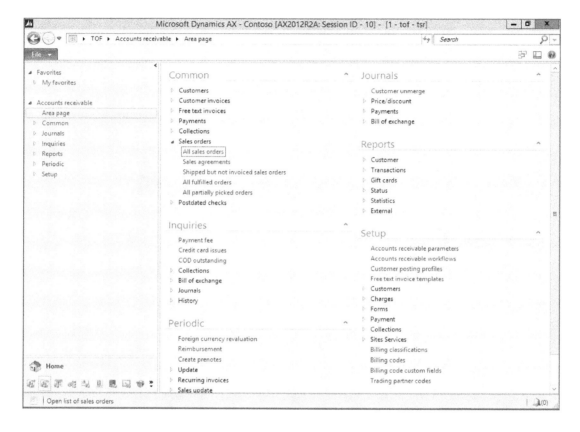

There are two different ways that you can access the Sales Orders. The first way is to click on the **All Sales Orders** menu item within the **Sales Orders** folder of the **Common** group within the **Accounts Receivable** area page.

Creating a New Sales Order

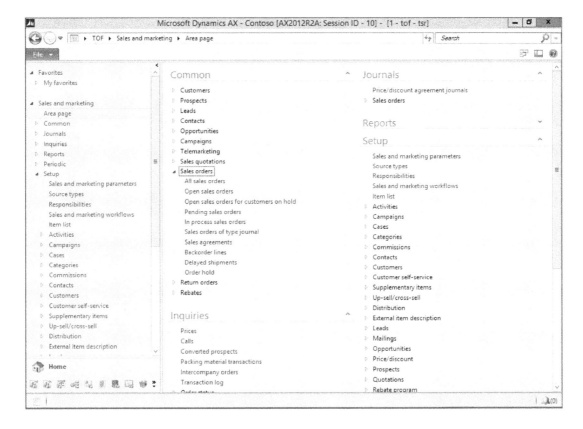

The second way is to click on the **All Sales Orders** menu item within the **Sales Orders** folder of the **Common** group within the **Sales and Marketing** area page.

Both get you to the same form.

Creating a New Sales Order

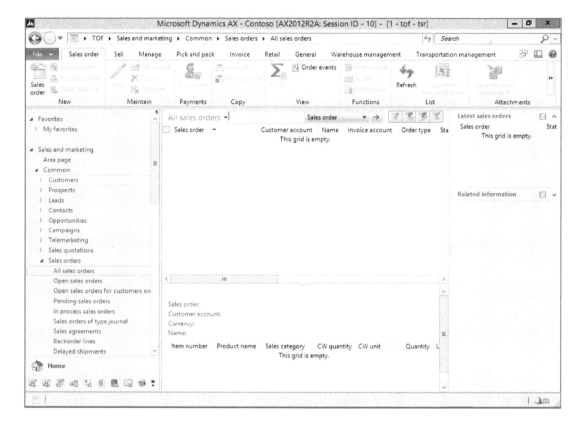

When the **All Sales Orders** list page is displayed, click on the **Sales Order** button within the **New** group of the **Sales Order** tab to start the order entry process.

Creating a New Sales Order

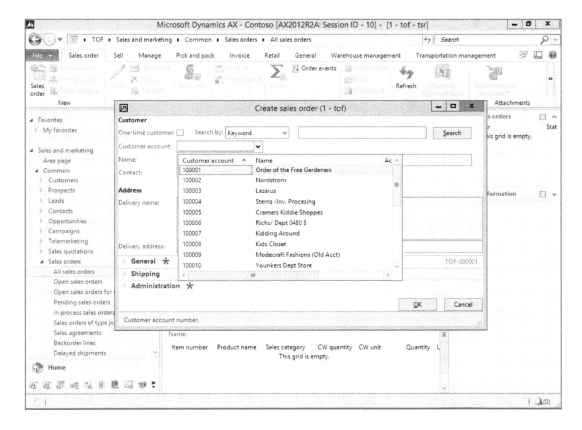

This will open up the **Create Sales Order** short form. If you know the customer's account number that you are placing the order for then you can type it into the **Customer Account** field or search for it by clicking on the **Customer Account** dropdown list.

Creating a New Sales Order

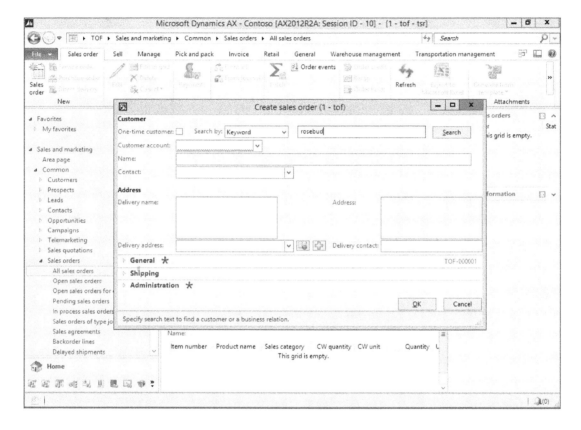

But a much easier way to find your customer is to type in a little bit of information into the **Keyword Search** field and then press enter. In this case we just type in **rosebud**.

Creating a New Sales Order

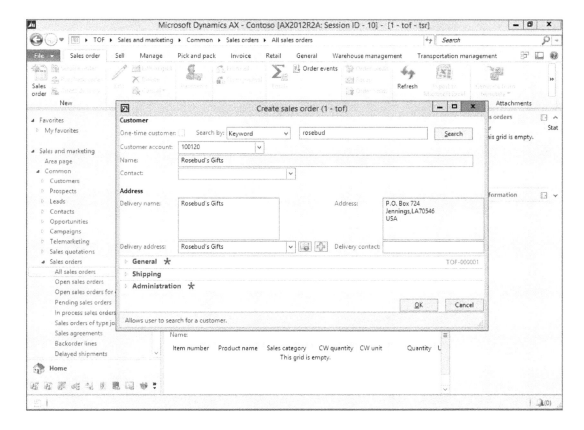

Since there is only one customer that matches **rosebud** then it is defaulted in to the short form.

Creating a New Sales Order

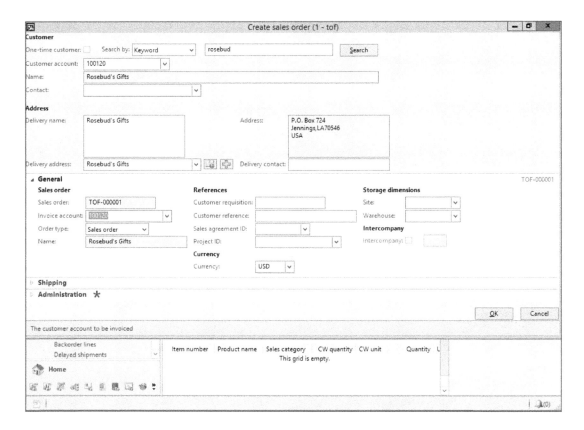

There are a number of additional fast tabs that are collapsed within the form. If you expand out the **General** fast tab then you will see some more information that you can default into the order.

Creating a New Sales Order

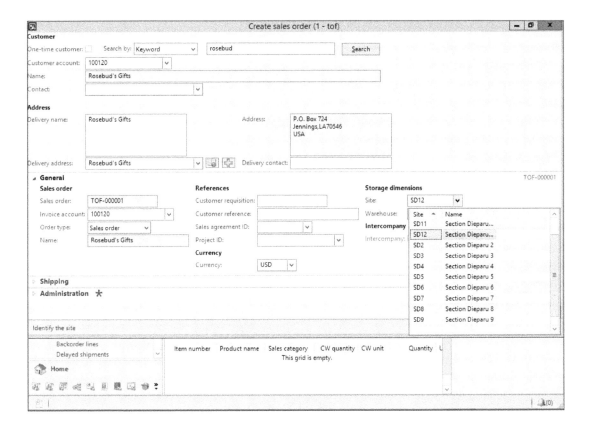

Click on the **Site** and select the **SD12** site which will be the default sourcing site for the order.

Creating a New Sales Order

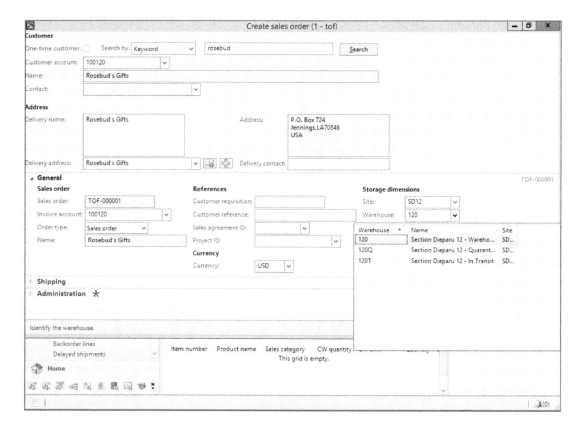

Then click on the **Warehouse** drodown and select the **120** warehouse which will be the default warehouse that we will ship this order from.

Note: You can default this information in automatically by assigning the defaults on the **Customer** record, so you won't be doing this all of the time.

Creating a New Sales Order

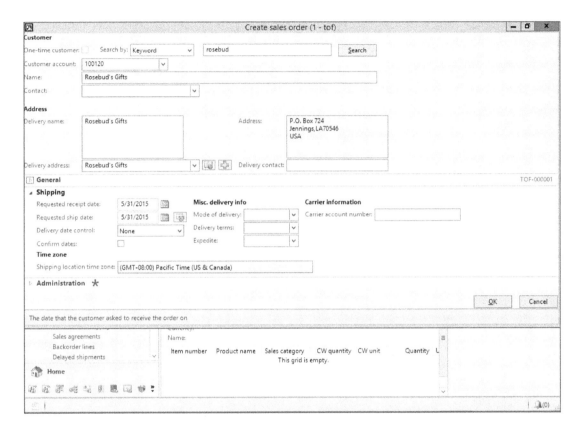

Next expand out the **Shipping** fast tab and you will see some of the shipping defaults.

Creating a New Sales Order

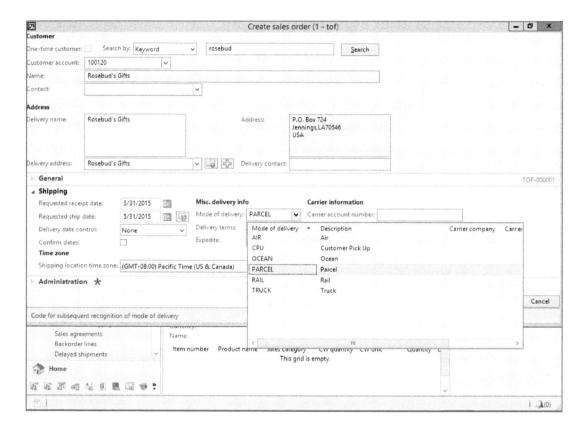

Click on the **Mode Of Delivery** dropdown and select the way that you want to ship this order. We will send it via **PARCEL** carrier.

Creating a New Sales Order

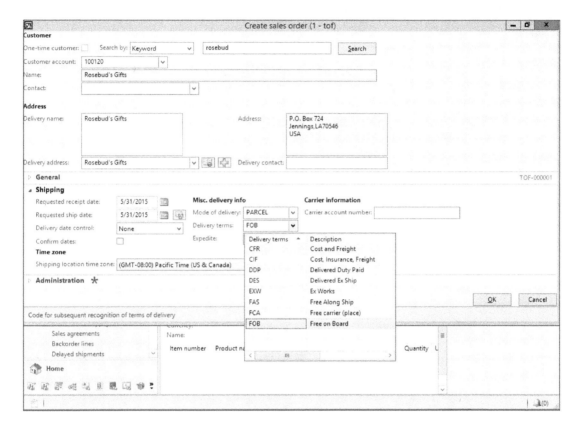

And then click on the **Delivery Terms** and select the terms that you want to include on this shipment. We will use **FOB** in this example.

Creating a New Sales Order

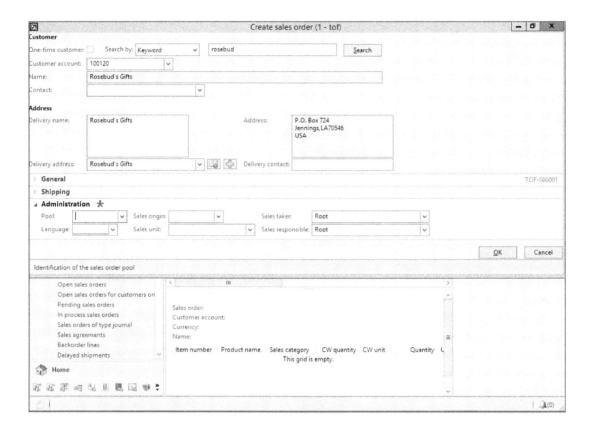

Now expand out the **Administration** fast tab.

Creating a New Sales Order

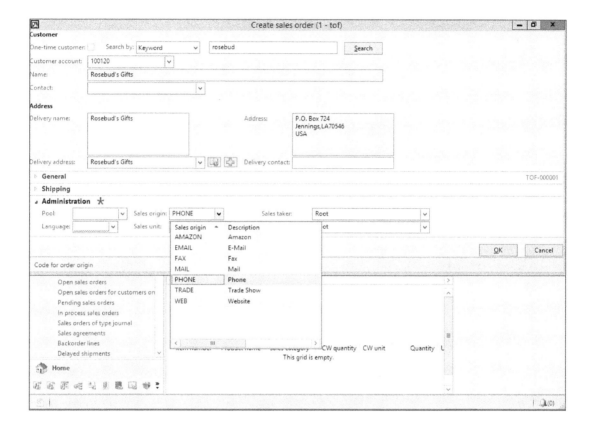

Click on the **Sales Origin** dropdown list and select the way that the order was received in. We will select **PHONE**.

Creating a New Sales Order

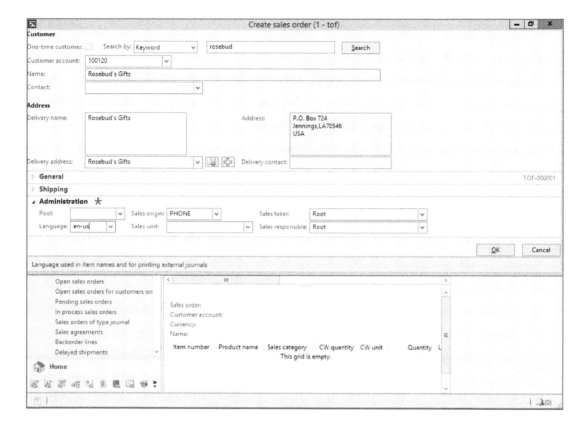

And finally, because we have not set up the defaults on the customer yet, set the **Language** to **en-us** to tell the system that we want to print out all of the documents in English.

After you have done this, click on the **OK** button to create the order.

Creating a New Sales Order

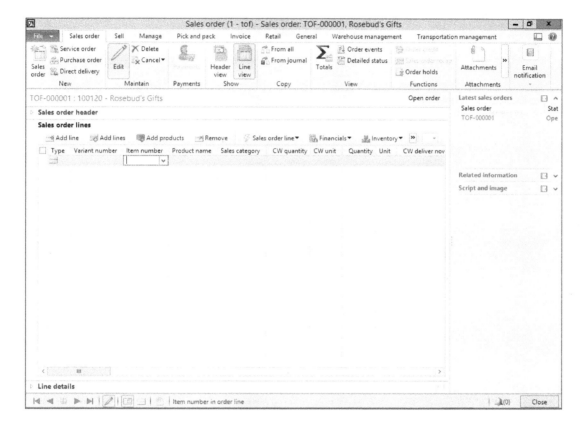

This will take you to a more traditional order entry form and you will see the order lines that you can start entering.

Creating a New Sales Order

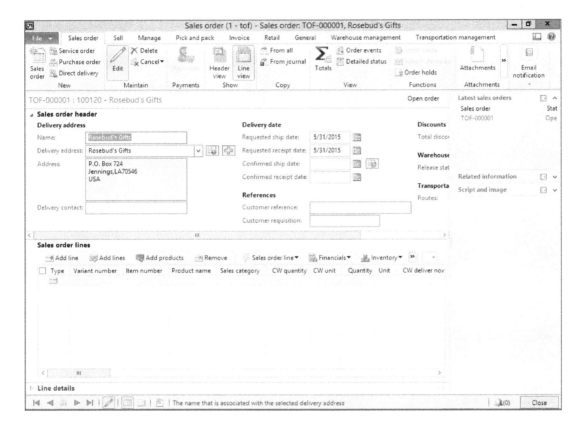

If you expand out the **Sales Order Header** fast tab you will see that you can update the main header information if you like.

Creating a New Sales Order

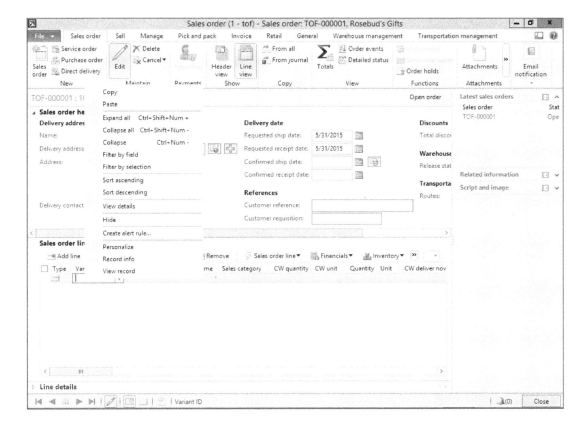

There are a number of fields that are showing on the lines that we don't really need right now, so we will quickly tidy up the form a little. Start by right-mouse-clicking on the **Variant Number** field and selecting the **Hide** option from the pop-up menu.

Creating a New Sales Order

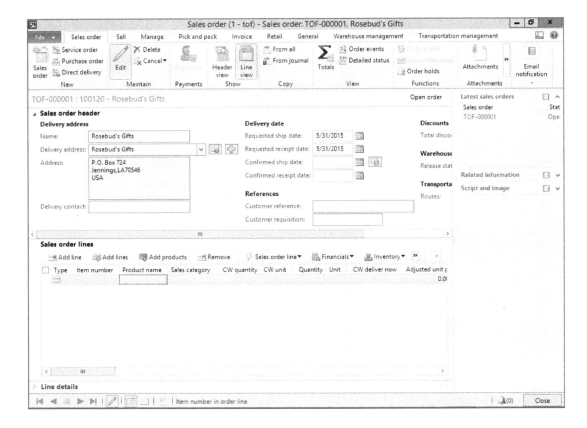

That will hide the form.

Do the same for the **Sales Category**, **CW Quantity**, **CW Unit**, and **CW Deliver Now** fields and any others that you don't want to see right now.

Creating a New Sales Order

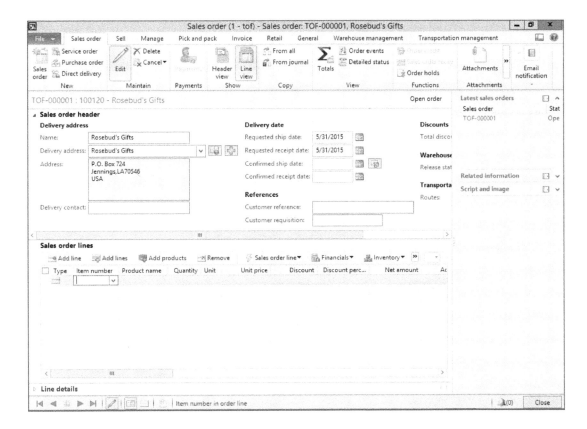

That should give you a cleaner form.

Creating a New Sales Order

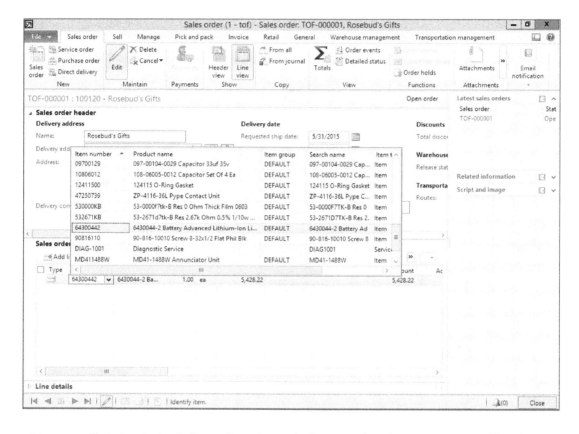

Now we will start entering in lines. If you know the item number that you want to add to the sales order then you can type it in (**64300442**) or find it by clicking on the **Item Number** dropdown list and searching for it there.

Creating a New Sales Order

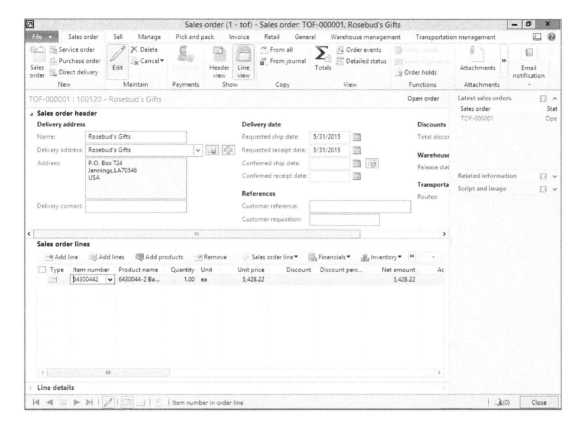

After you have selected the product then the **Product Name**, and **Price** will default in for you directly from the **Released Product** details.

Creating a New Sales Order

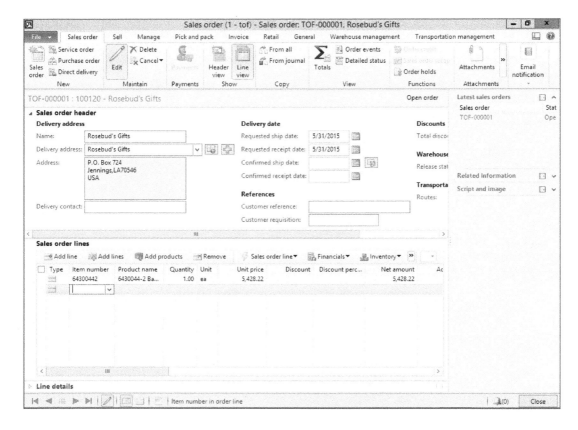

If you want to add another item, just click on the **Add Line** button in the lines menu bar and a new line will be created for you.

Creating a New Sales Order

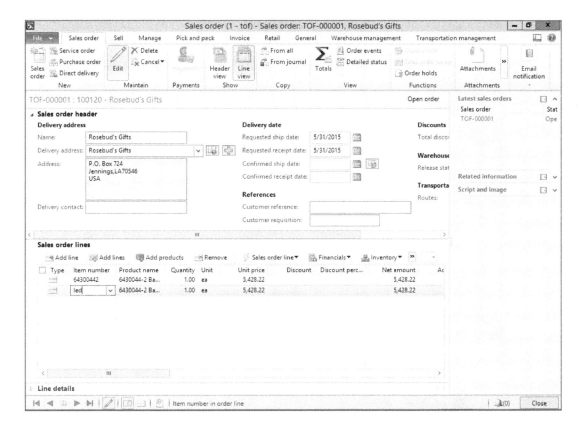

If you don't know the **Item Number** you can type in part of the product name in stead. In this case we just type in **led**.

Creating a New Sales Order

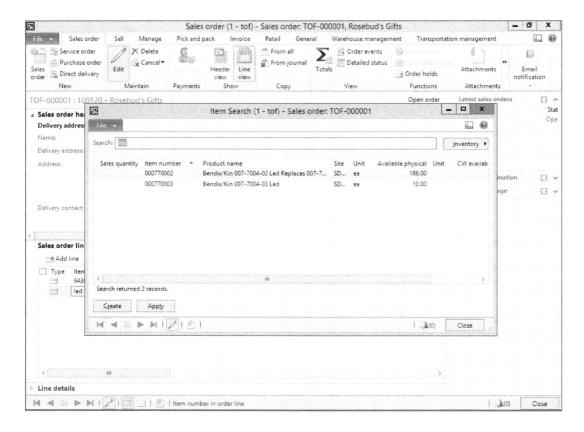

This will open up the product search results that we configured earlier on showing us the two products that match our search.

daxc

Creating a New Sales Order

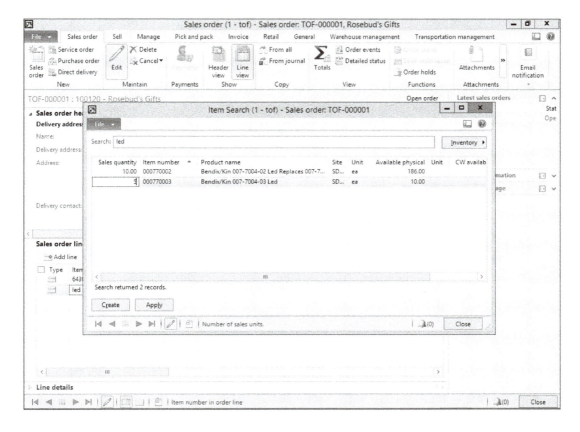

You can type in **Sales Quantities** for any of the lines that you want to order and then just click on the **Create** button to add them to the order.

Creating a New Sales Order

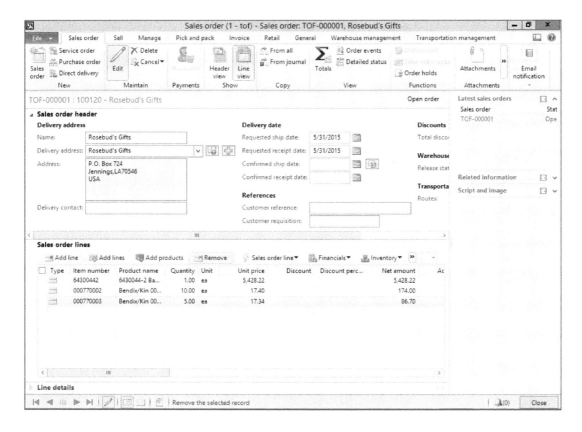

Now we have more order lines. How easy is that!

Confirming Sales Orders

Once you have entered in your order you can make it a live order simply by confirming it.

Confirming Sales Orders

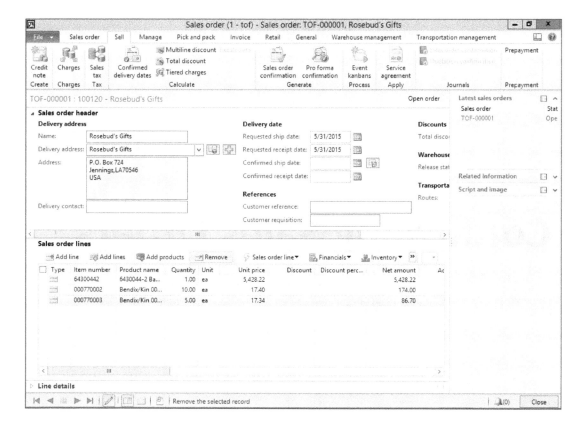

To do this, click on the **Sales Order Confirmation** button within the **Generate** group of the **Sell** ribbon bar.

Confirming Sales Orders

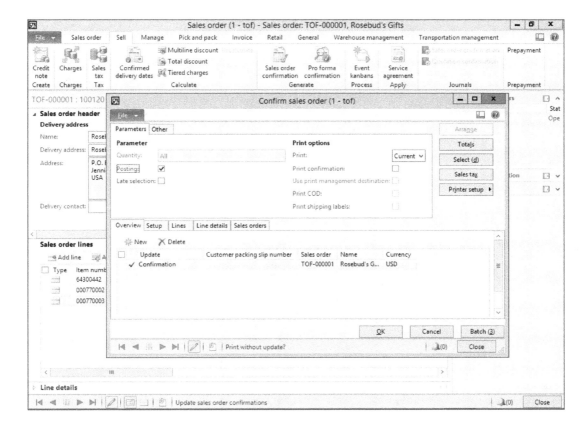

This will open up the **Confirm Sales Order** dialog box.

Confirming Sales Orders

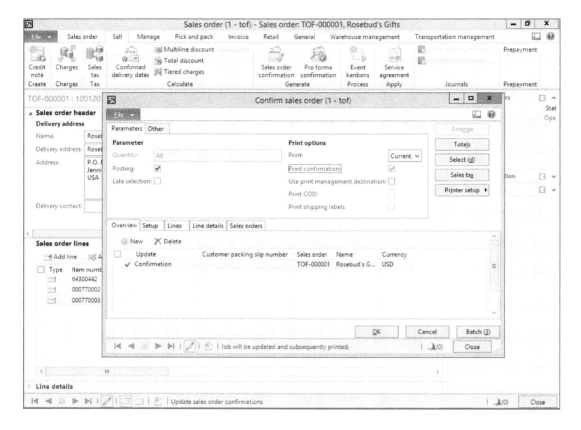

If you want to see a printed copy of the **Order Confirmation** then check the **Print Confirmation** checkbox.

Confirming Sales Orders

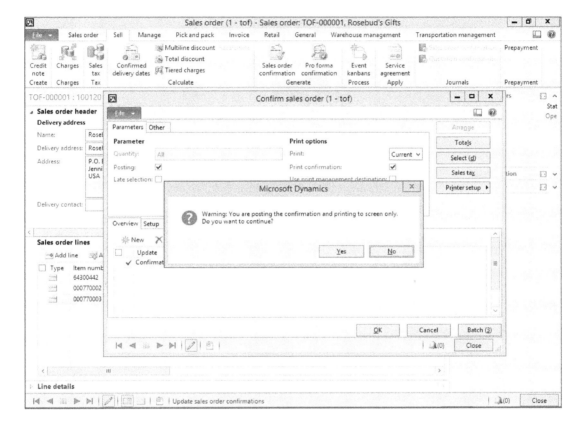

Then click on the **OK** button.

You will probably get a message saying that the order confirmation is printing to the screen, and that's OK, so click on the **Yes** button.

Confirming Sales Orders

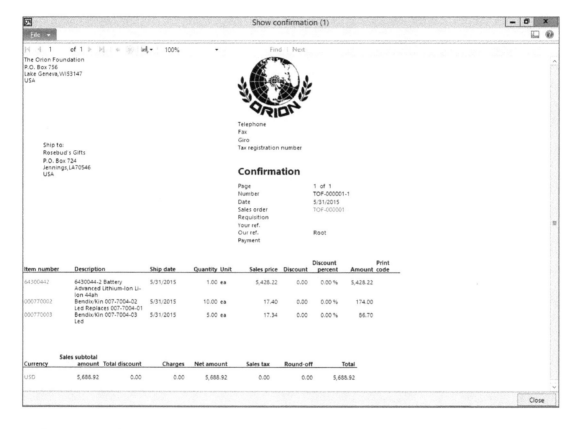

After a couple of seconds, you will see the **Order Confirmation**.

After you have finished admiring it in all of it's glory, click on the **Close** button.

Printing The Sales Order Picking Ticket

Now that the order is confirmed, it has been released to the warehouse for picking. So the next step is to print out the **Picking Ticket**.

Printing The Sales Order Picking Ticket

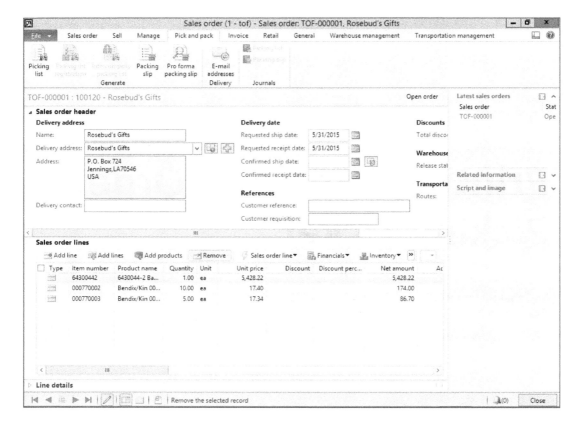

To do this, click on the **Picking List** button within the **Generate** group of the **Pick and Pack** ribbon bar.

Printing The Sales Order Picking Ticket

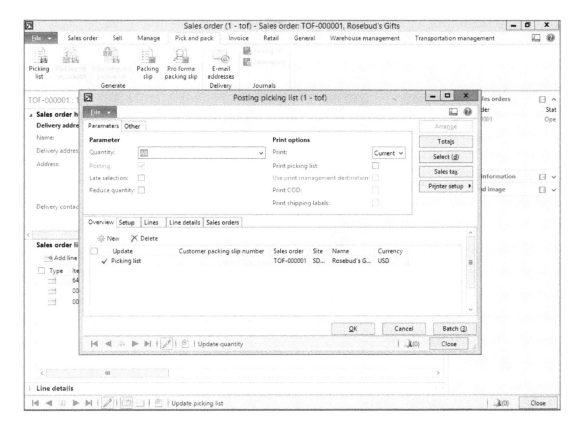

This will open up the **Print Picking Ticket** dialog box.

Printing The Sales Order Picking Ticket

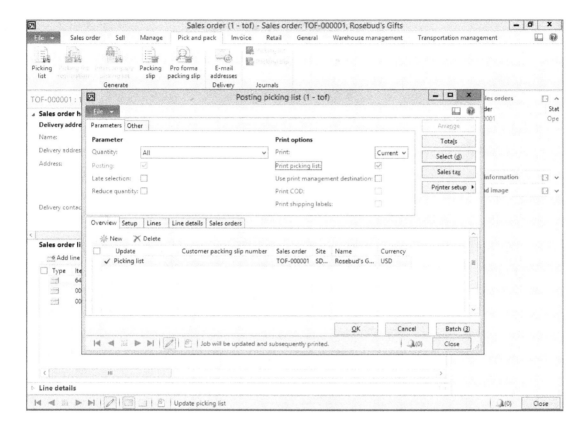

If you want to see a printed copy of the **Picking List** then check the **Print Picking List** checkbox.

Printing The Sales Order Picking Ticket

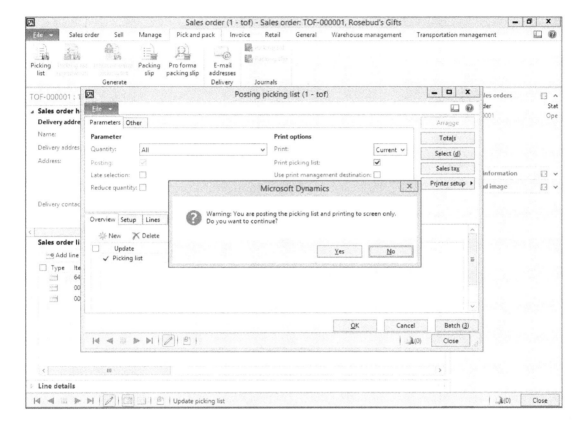

Then click on the **OK** button.

You will probably get a message saying that the order confirmation is printing to the screen, and that's OK, so click on the **Yes** button.

Printing The Sales Order Picking Ticket

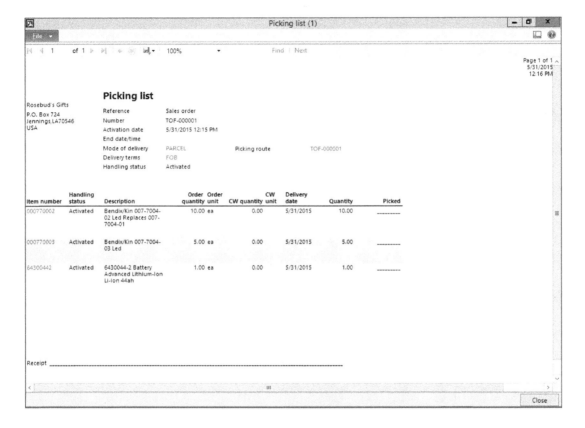

After a couple of seconds, you will see the **Picking List**.

Just click on the **Close** button to exit from the form.

Registering The Picking List

Once the Picking Ticket has been created we need to register the items to make sure that we are picking the right inventory.

Registering The Picking List

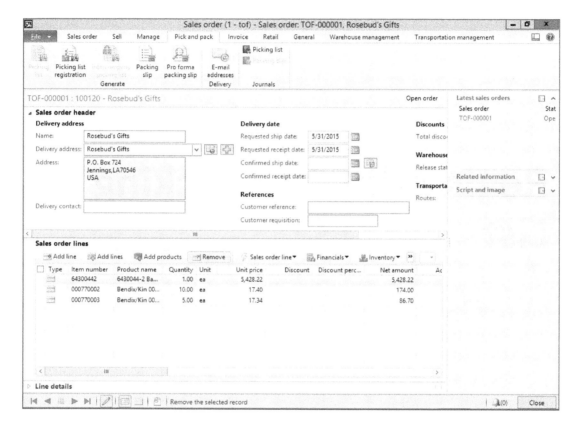

To do this, click on the **Picking List Registration** button within the **Generate** group of the **Pick and Pack** ribbon bar.

Registering The Picking List

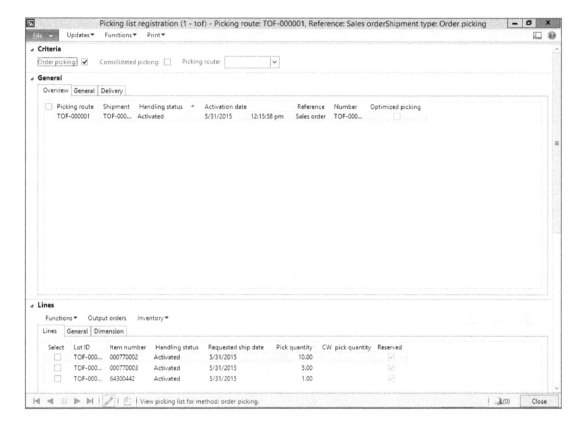

This will open up the **Picking List Registration** form.

Registering The Picking List

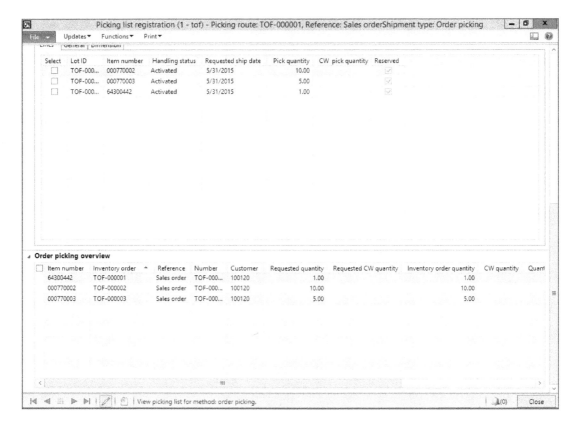

If you scroll down to the bottom of the form you will see that all of the line items are listed for the Pick List.

Registering The Picking List

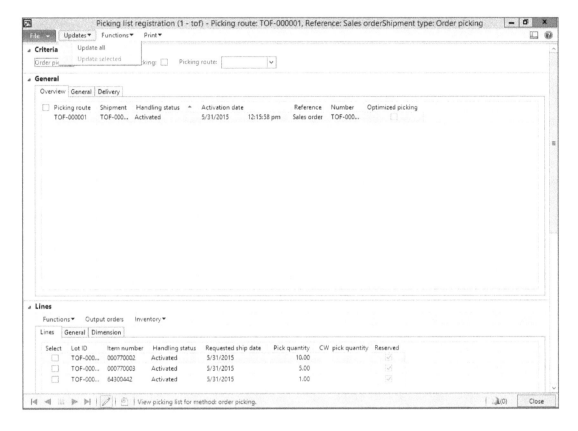

All you need to do is click on the **Update** button in the menu bar and select the **Update All** menu item.

Registering The Picking List

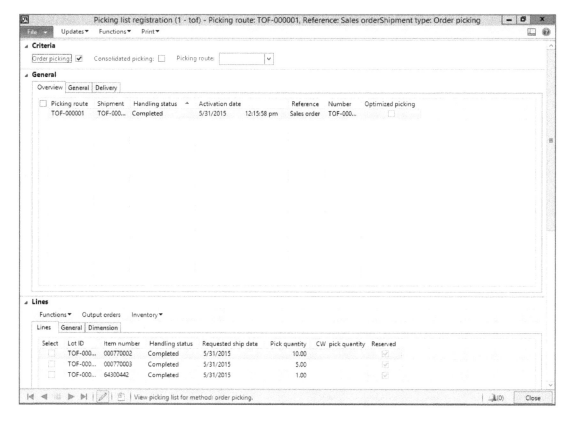

This will change the **Handling Status** on all of the lines from **Active** to **Completes** meaning the picking has been performed.

When you have don't this, just click on the **Close** button to exit from the form.

Printing The Packing Slip

The last step in the Pick and Pack process is to print out the **Packing Slip** to indicate that the product is packed and out the warehouse door.

Printing The Packing Slip

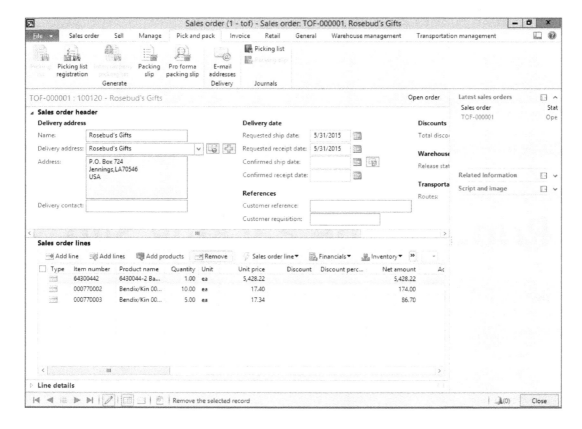

To do this, click on the **Packing Slip** button within the **Generate** group of the **Pick and Pack** ribbon bar.

Printing The Packing Slip

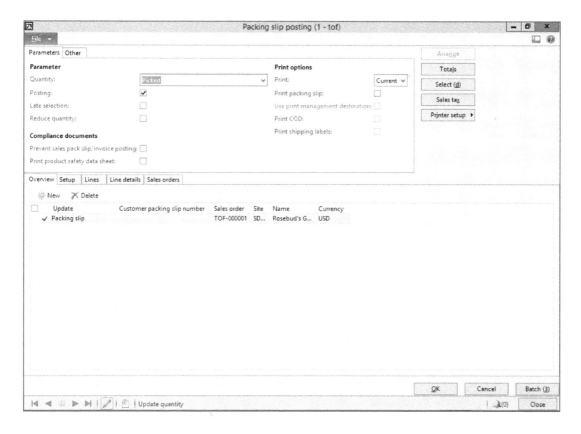

This will open up the **Packing Slip Posting** dialog box.

Printing The Packing Slip

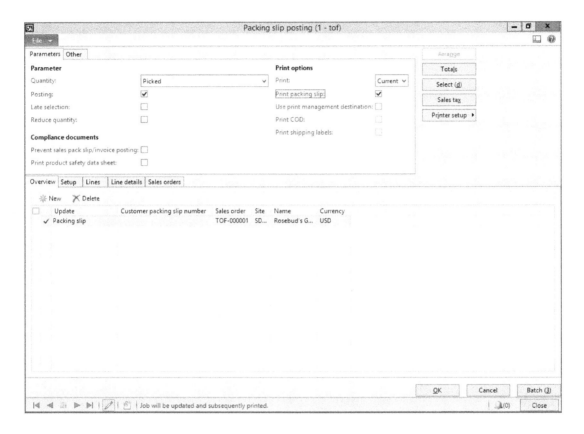

If you want to see a printed copy of the **Packing Slip** then check the **Print Packing Slip** checkbox.

Printing The Packing Slip

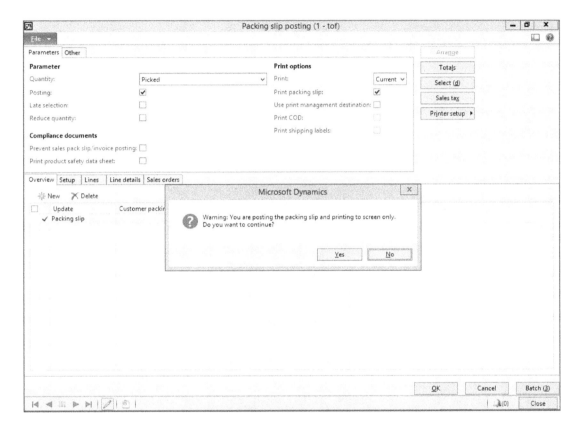

Then click on the **OK** button.

You will probably get a message saying that the order confirmation is printing to the screen, and that's OK, so click on the **Yes** button.

Printing The Packing Slip

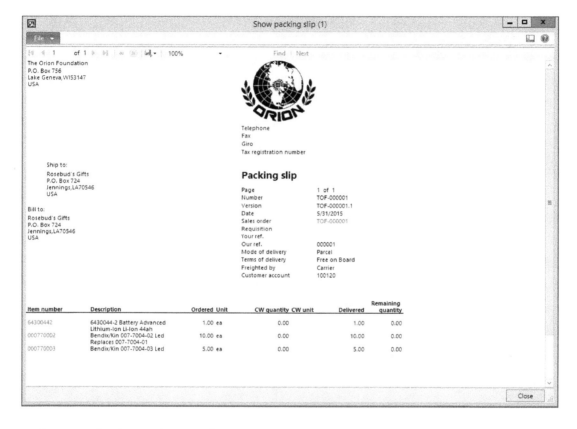

After a couple of seconds, you will see the **Packing Slip**.

Just click on the **Close** button to exit from the form.

Invoicing The Sales Order

Now all that is left for you to do is to Invoice the Sales Order.

Invoicing The Sales Order

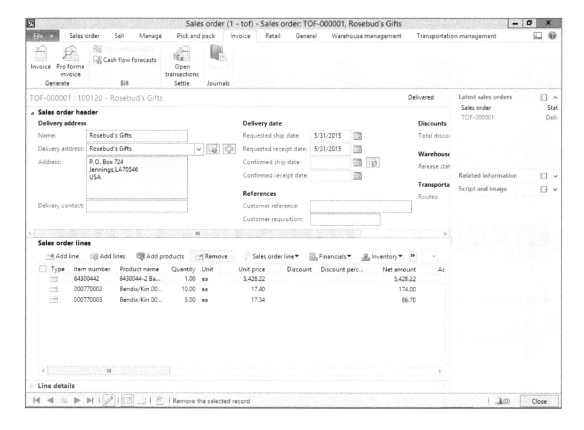

To do this, click on the **Invoice** button within the **Generate** group of the **Invoice** ribbon bar.

Invoicing The Sales Order

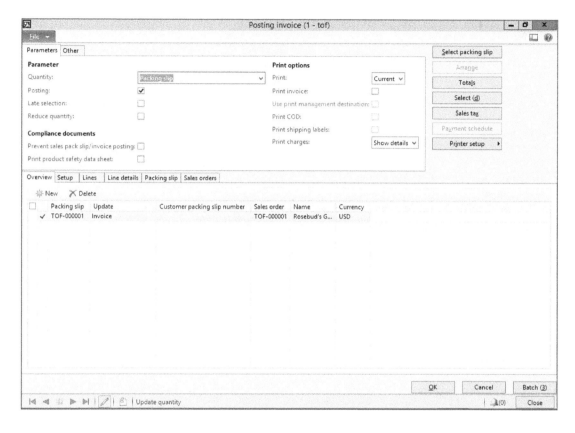

This will open up the **Posting Invoice** dialog box.

Invoicing The Sales Order

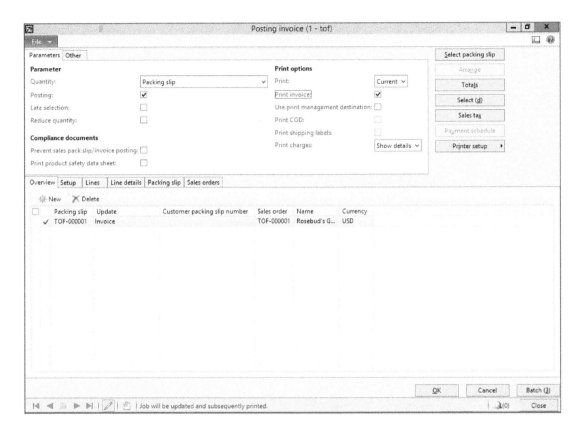

If you want to see a printed copy of the **Invoice** then check the **Print Invoice** checkbox.

Invoicing The Sales Order

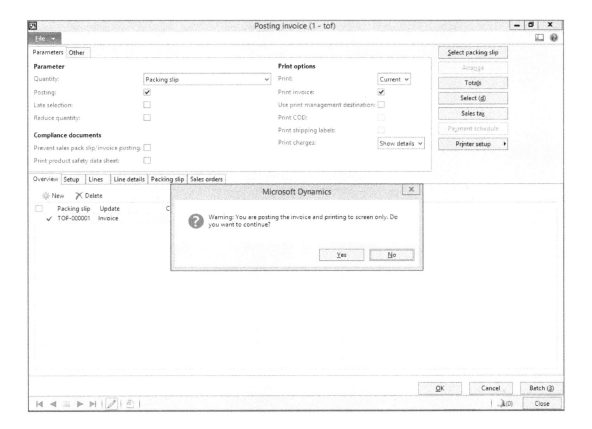

Then click on the **OK** button.

You will probably get a message saying that the order confirmation is printing to the screen, and that's OK, so click on the **Yes** button.

Invoicing The Sales Order

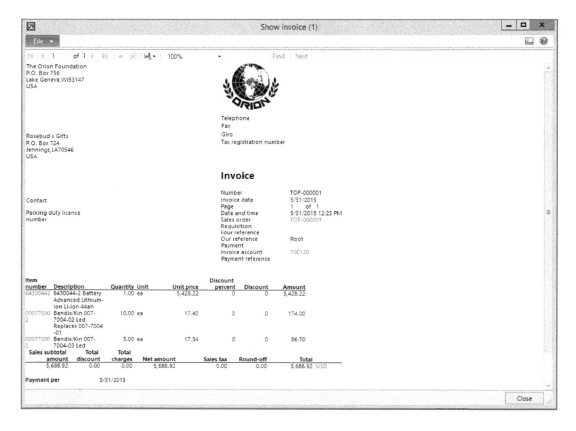

After a couple of seconds, you will see the **Invoice**. How easy is that?

Just click on the **Close** button to exit from the form.

Viewing The Sales Invoice In Accounts Receivable

Once you have created the invoice through the sales process then it becomes available for the Receivables group to process.

Viewing The Sales Invoice In Accounts Receivable

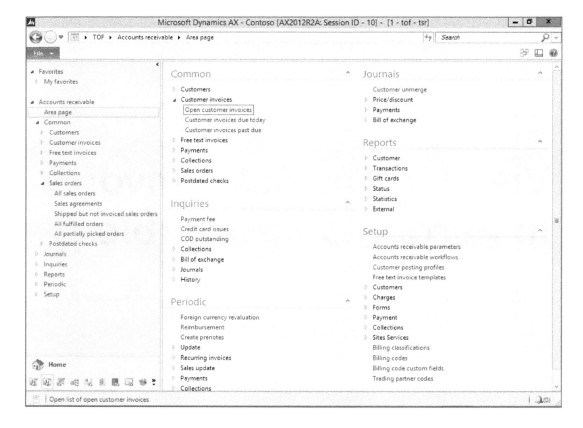

To view the invoice just click on the **Open Customer Invoices** menu item within the **Customer Invoices** folder of the **Common** group within the **Accounts Receivable** area page.

Viewing The Sales Invoice In Accounts Receivable

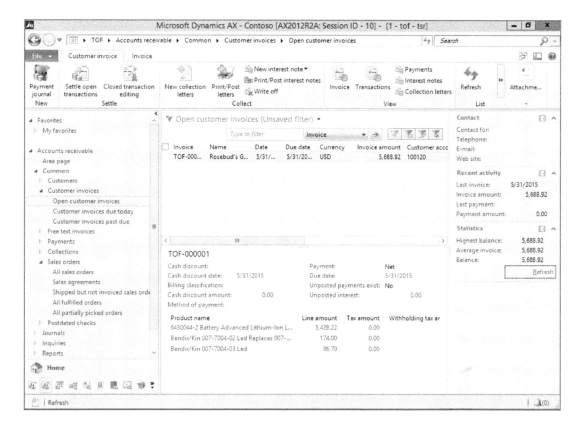

When the **Open Customer Invoices** list page is displayed you will see that your invoice is waiting there for you.

CONFIGURING SALES PRICING

Now that we have the Order to Invoice process configured we can start refining our pricing and start creating price lists that are specific to products, and customers, and also enable features like margin tracking and price detail inquiries within Dynamics AX.

Viewing Price Details On Sales Orders

To start off though we will take a quick look at how you can view all of the pricing information that is being recorded against our sales orders.

Viewing Price Details On Sales Orders

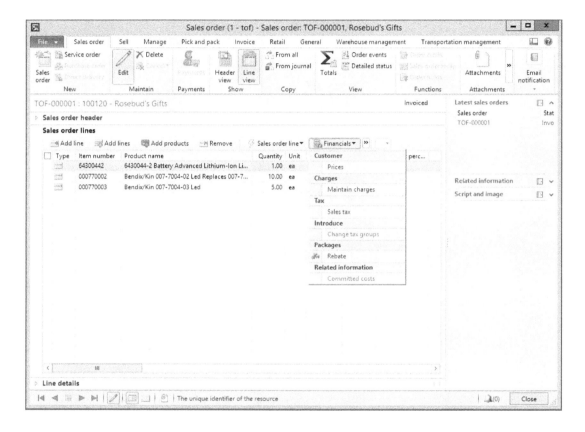

To do this, open up your sales order and then click on the **Financial** button within the **Sales Order Lines** menu bar and select the **Prices** menu item.

Viewing Price Details On Sales Orders

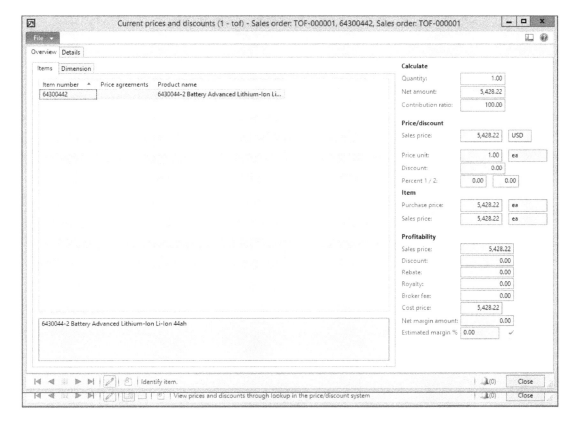

This will open up a **Current Prices and Discounts** form that will show you all of the product information and also a breakdown of all the price details for that line. This is a great way to validate that the prices on your sales order lines are correct.

When you have finished here just click on the **Close** button to exit from the form.

Enabling The Advanced Price Details Inquiry On Orders

There is another version of the **Price Details** form that is available for you in addition to the basic inquiry which will give you a lot more detail on the prices, although this is an optional view and you need to enable the feature.

Enabling The Advanced Price Details Inquiry On Orders

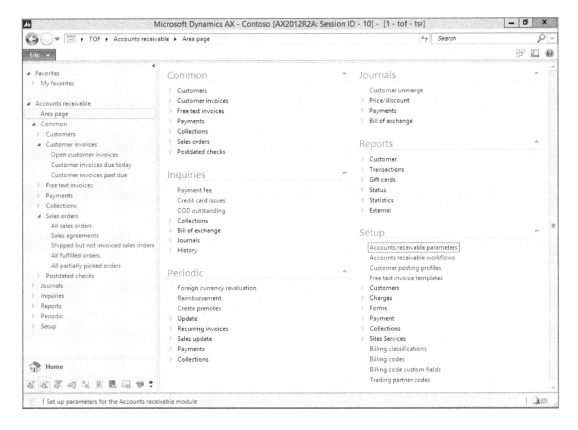

To do this click on the **Accounts Receivable Parameters** menu item within the **Setup** group of the **Accounts Receivable** area page.

Enabling The Advanced Price Details Inquiry On Orders

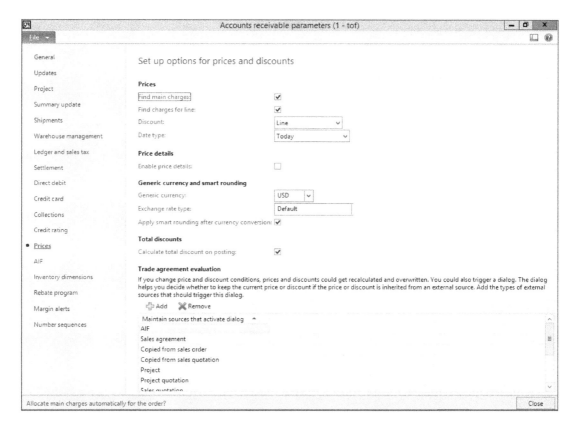

When the **Accounts Receivable Parameters** form is displayed, click on the **Prices** tab to view all of the **Pricing and Discount** options.

Enabling The Advanced Price Details Inquiry On Orders

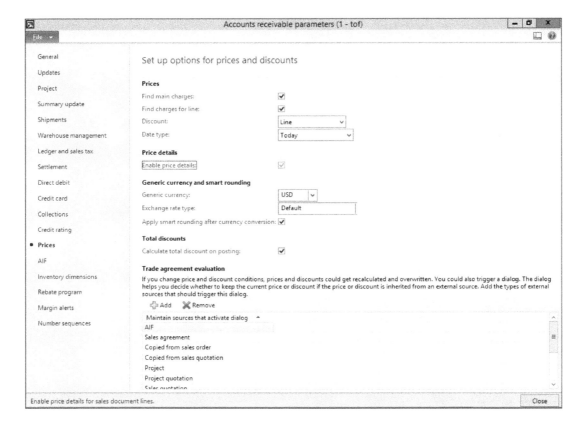

All you need to do is click on the **Enable Price Details** checkbox and then click on the **Close** button to exit from the form.

Viewing The Advanced Price Details On Sales Orders

Now we can see a little bit meatier version of the price details inquiry.

Viewing The Advanced Price Details On Sales Orders

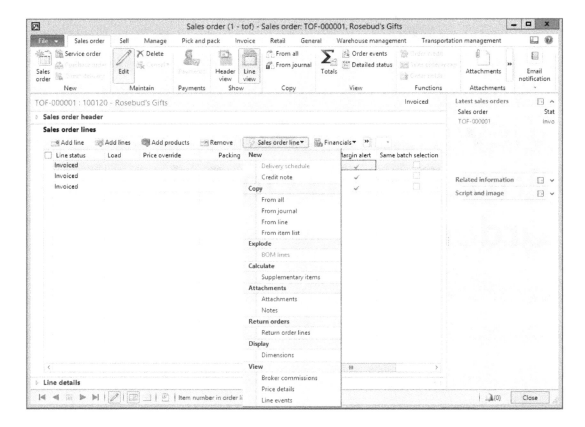

To do this, open up your sales order and then click on the **Sales Order Line** button in the **Sales Order Lines** menu bar and then select the **Price Details** menu item within the **View** group.

Viewing The Advanced Price Details On Sales Orders

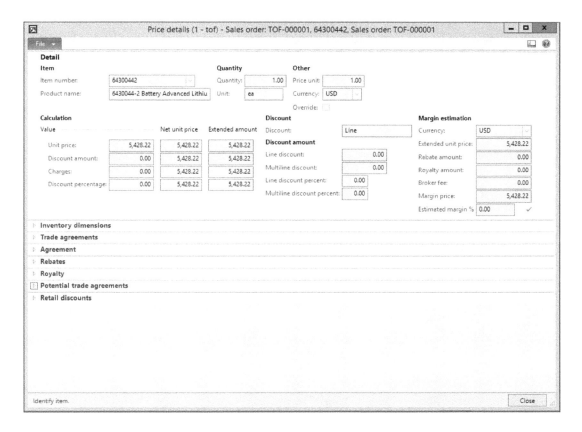

When the **Price Details** form is displayed you will see some of the information that you saw on the basic form plus a little more.

Note: As we start building more prices and discount structures this is a great inquiry to see them all in action.

Enabling Margin Alerts On Sales Orders

One other feature that you may want to take advantage of is the **Margin Alerts** which will allow you to see how much money you are making on each sales order line and also alert you if you are not making enough on a line by line basis/

Enabling Margin Alerts On Sales Orders

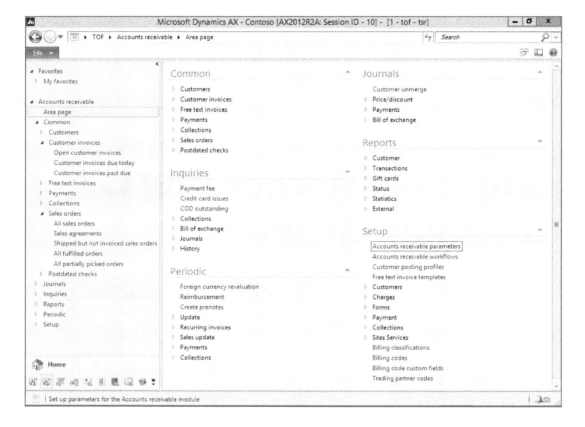

To do this click on the **Accounts Receivable Parameters** menu item within the **Setup** group of the **Accounts Receivable** area page.

Enabling Margin Alerts On Sales Orders

When the **Accounts Receivable Parameters** form is displayed, switch to the **Marking Alerts** tab and you will see all of the Margin setup options.

Enabling Margin Alerts On Sales Orders

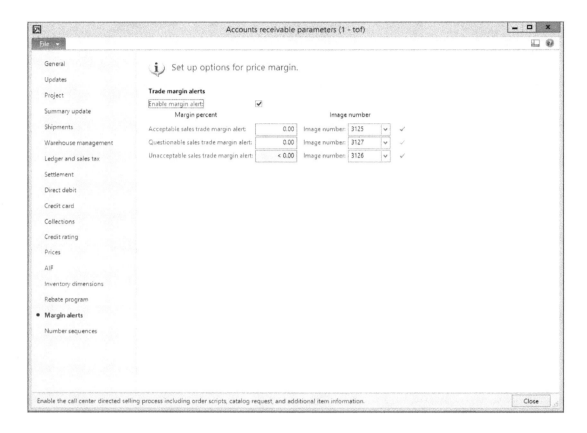

To start using the margin alerts just click on the **Enable Margin Alert** checkbox.

Enabling Margin Alerts On Sales Orders

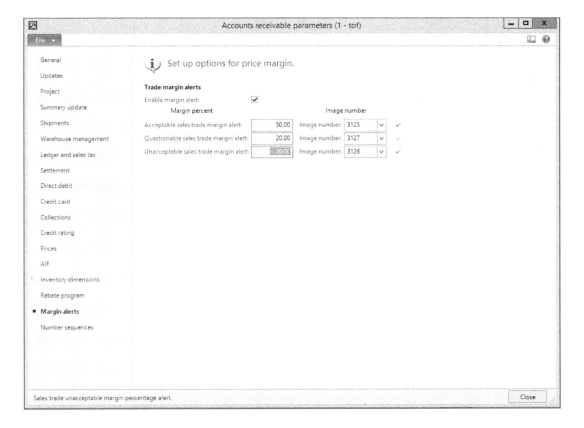

Then set the **Acceptable Sales Trade Margin Alert** field to be the lowest acceptable sales margin that you want to target for. In this example **50**% seems like a good target.

And then set the **Questionable Sales Trade Margin Alert** field to be the lowest sales margin that you want will accept be before it's unacceptable. In this example **20**% seems good.

After you have done that just click on the **Close** button to exit from the form.

Viewing Sales Margin Alerts On Sales Orders

Now that you have the **Sales Margin Alerts** configured you can start viewing them on the sales order.

Viewing Sales Margin Alerts On Sales Orders

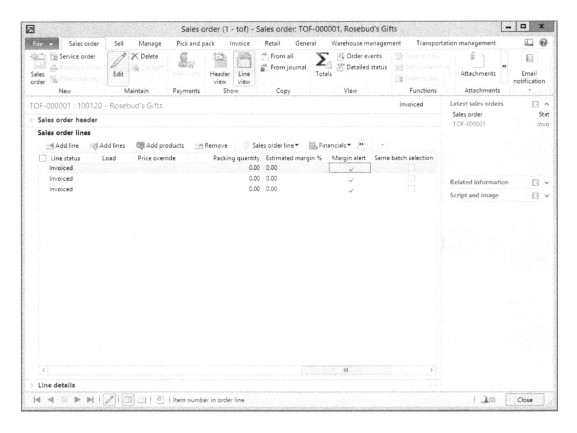

To do this just open up the Sales Order and scroll over to the right a little within the lines and you will see that there are two new fields showing the **Estimated Margin %** and the **Margin Alerts**. Because our price is the same as the cost right now we are not making any margin at all. Good to know.

Activating Trade Agreements For Use On Sales Orders

Now that we have seen how we can view and track all of the price information on the sales order, it is time to start refining our prices by adding pricing lists and agreements with customers. Before we can do this though we need to tell the system what types of pricing structures we are going to allow people to set up.

Activating Trade Agreements For Use On Sales Orders

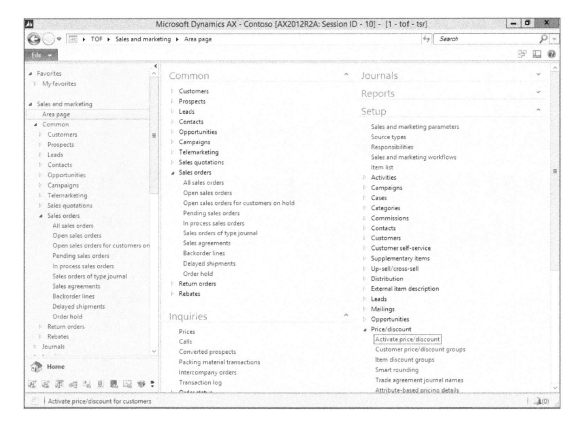

To do this, click on the **Activate Price/Discount** menu item within the **Price/Discount** folder of the **Setup** group within the **Sales and Marketing** area page.

Activating Trade Agreements For Use On Sales Orders

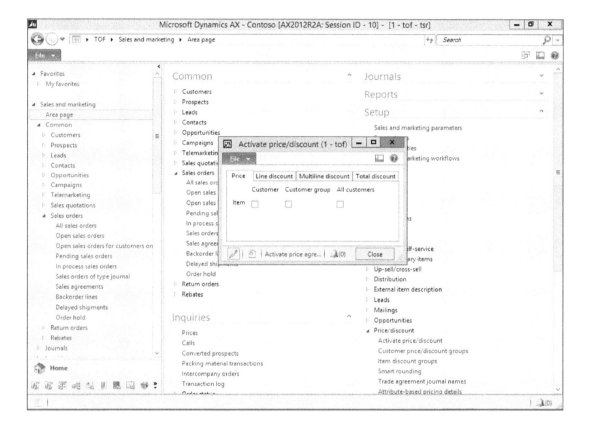

This will open up the **Activate Price/Discount** maintenance form.

Activating Trade Agreements For Use On Sales Orders

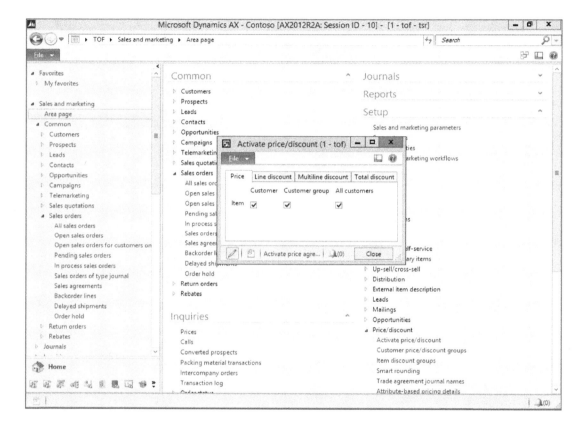

The first tab that is shown in the form is the **Price** tab which shows you all of the different pricing combinations that are available. On the left of the matrix you will see all of the different **Item** options that are available (in this case just one) and then along the top you will see all of the different **Customer** combinations that are available (which include just pricing for a customer, a group of customers, or all customers).

Check all of the boxes to enable item prices for one, some or all customers.

Activating Trade Agreements For Use On Sales Orders

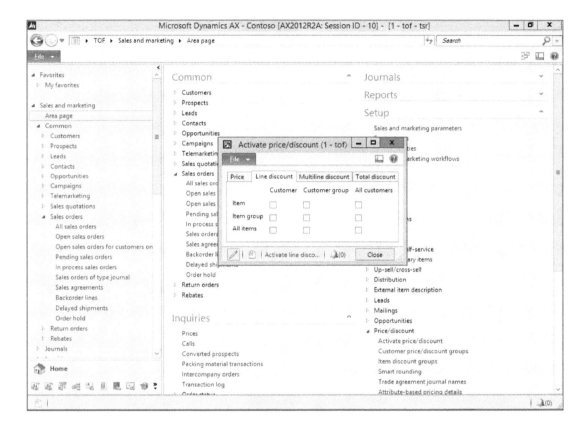

Even though in this section we are talking about pricing, we might as well configure the valid discounting options here as well. So switch to the **Line Discounts** tab. You will notice on this tab there are more combinations that you can enable because the **Item** options have been expanded out to allow you to have discounts by one item, a group of items and also all items.

Activating Trade Agreements For Use On Sales Orders

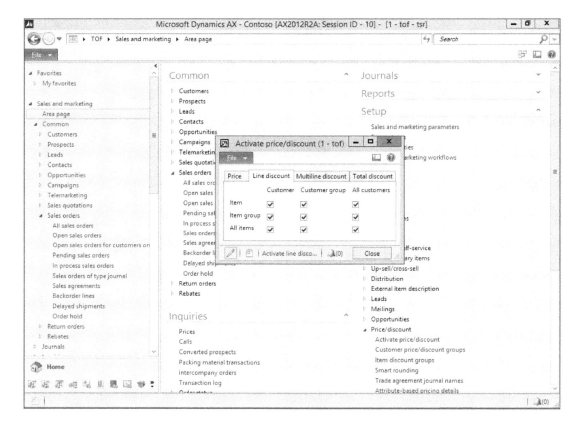

If you wanted you could check only the discount combinations that you want to allow the users to use, or in this case we will just check them all to give us the best discounting options later on.

Activating Trade Agreements For Use On Sales Orders

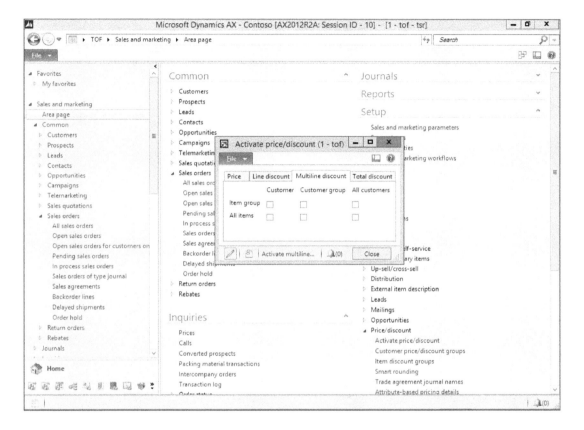

Now switch to the **Multiline Discounts** tab. Here you will notice that there is no **Item** combinations that you can enable which makes sense because this is used for grouping multiple lines together fir grouped discounts.

Activating Trade Agreements For Use On Sales Orders

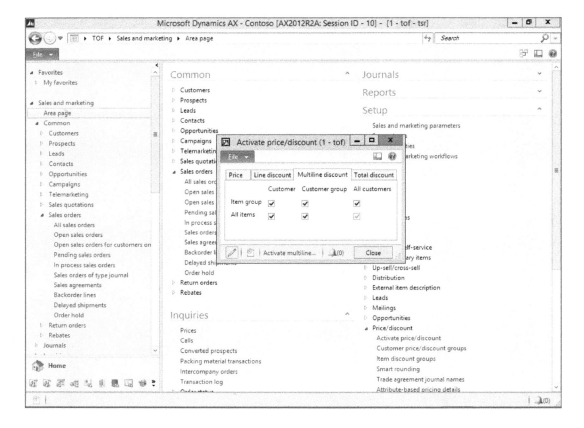

If you wanted you could check only the discount combinations that you want to allow the users to use, or in this case we will just check them all to give us the best discounting options later on.

Activating Trade Agreements For Use On Sales Orders

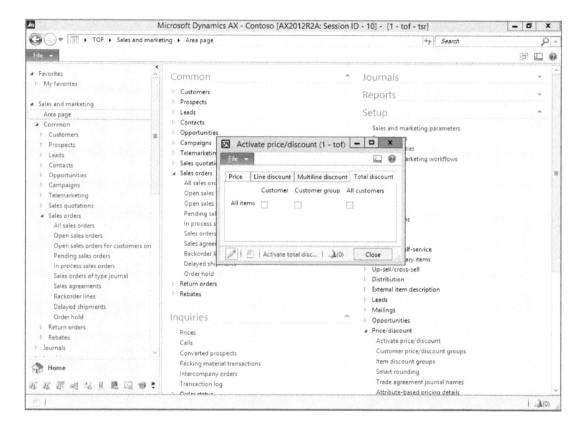

Finally switch to the **Total Discounts** tab. Here you will notice that there is only an **All Items** combination that you can enable because this discount type is applied at the header level.

Activating Trade Agreements For Use On Sales Orders

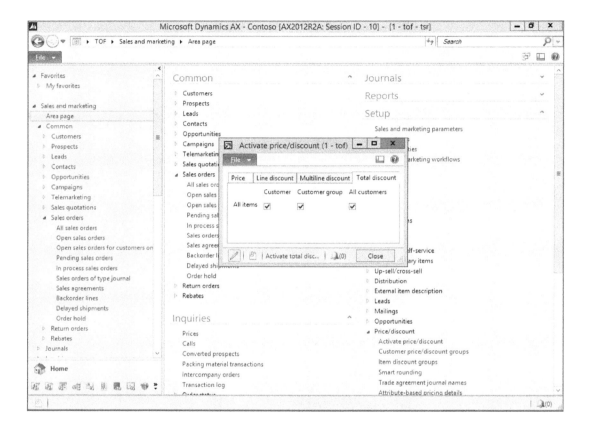

Check all of the boxes to enable total item discounts for one, some or all customers.

After you have done that click on the **Close** button to exit from the form.

Specifying The Pricing Storage Dimensions

Another tweak that you may want to make around the pricing is to specify the **Storage Dimensions** that you want to use when you are creating your prices. Within Dynamics AX you have the ability to have different prices by dimension if you really want. What that means is that you could have different sales prices by site, by warehouse, and even by location if you like. Or you can set the prices so that they do not use the **Storage Dimensions** if you like... which is what we will do to make the setup a little simpler.

Specifying The Pricing Storage Dimensions

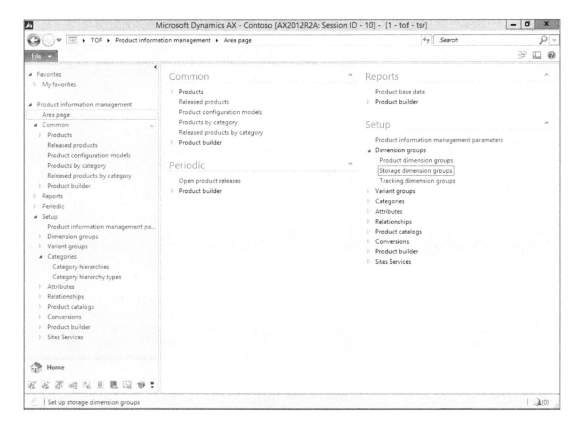

To configure this, click on the **Storage Dimension Groups** menu item within the **Dimension Groups** folder of the **Setup** group within the **Product Information Management** area page.

Specifying The Pricing Storage Dimensions

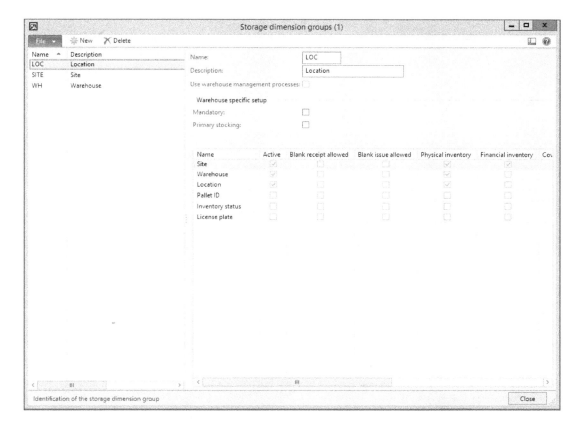

When the **Storage Dimension Groups** maintenance form is displayed select the dimension group that you want to configure – in this case the **LOC** (Location) **dimension.**

Specifying The Pricing Storage Dimensions

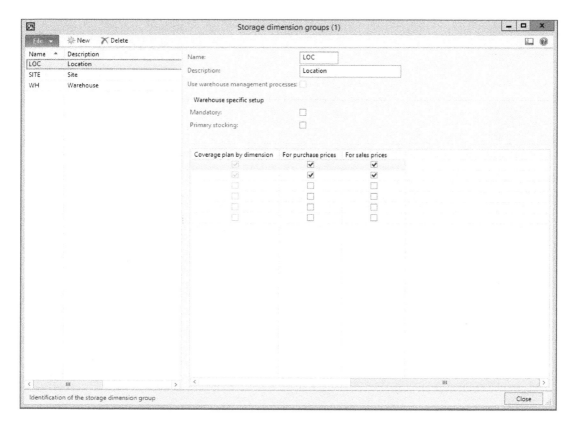

Scroll over to the right within the storage dimension options and you will see two columns that relate to pricing. The **For Purchase Prices** column allows you to specify if the dimensions are used within Procurement and the **For Sales Prices** column allows you to turn on or off the dimensions within the **Sales** area.

Specifying The Pricing Storage Dimensions

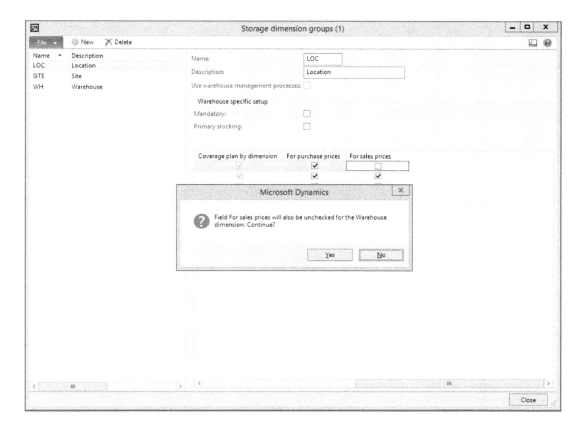

Uncheck the **For Sales Prices** for the **Site** dimension and when the warning dialog box is displayed just click on the **Yes** button to continue.

Specifying The Pricing Storage Dimensions

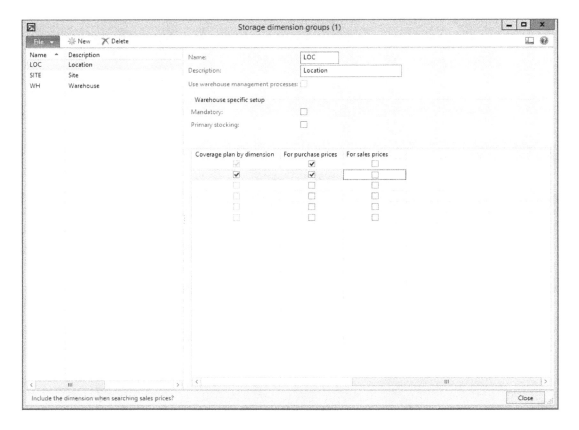

Then uncheck the **For Sales Prices** for the **Warehouse** dimension to remove all active dimensions for pricing.

You can update the other Storage Dimensions is you want as well, and when you are done just click on the **Close** button to exit from the form.

Creating Trade Agreement Types To Track Different Pricing Structures

All of the price lists (or Trade Agreements) that we will set up are going to be associated with a **Trade Agreement Type**. So the next step that we need to do is to create a Trade Agreement Type that we can use to track our sales price lists.

Creating Trade Agreement Types To Track Different Pricing Structures

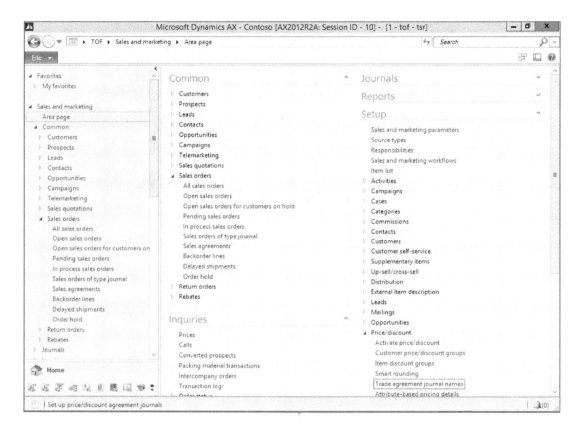

To do this click on the **Trade Agreement Journal Names** menu item within the **Price/Discount** folder of the **Setup** group within the **Sales and Marketing** area page.

Creating Trade Agreement Types To Track Different Pricing Structures

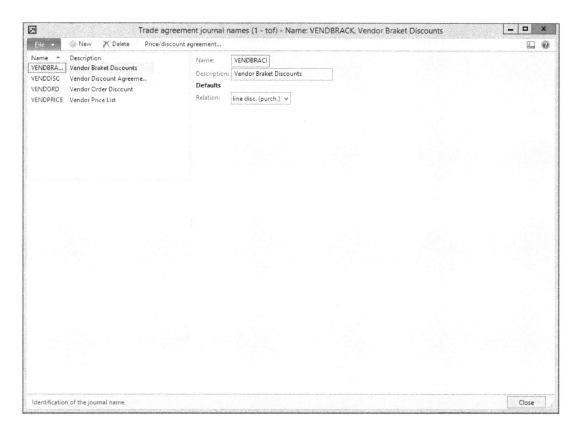

When the **Trade Agreement Journal Names** maintenance form is displayed you will notice that it already has a number of different Journal Names although they are all related to Purchasing. That is because the **Trade Agreements** are shared between the Sales and Procurement areas giving you one single place to maintain all of your pricing and discounting structures.

Creating Trade Agreement Types To Track Different Pricing Structures

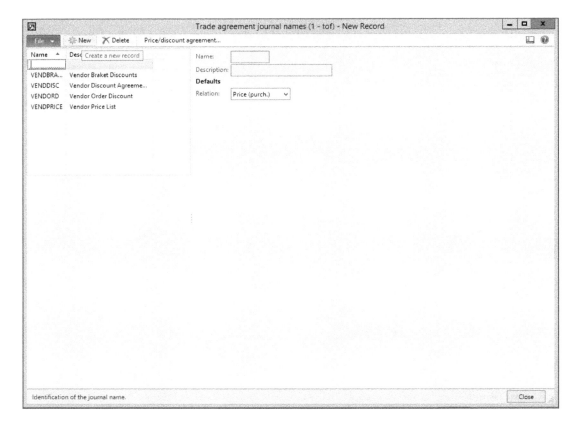

Now click on the **New** button in the menu bar to create a new record.

Creating Trade Agreement Types To Track Different Pricing Structures

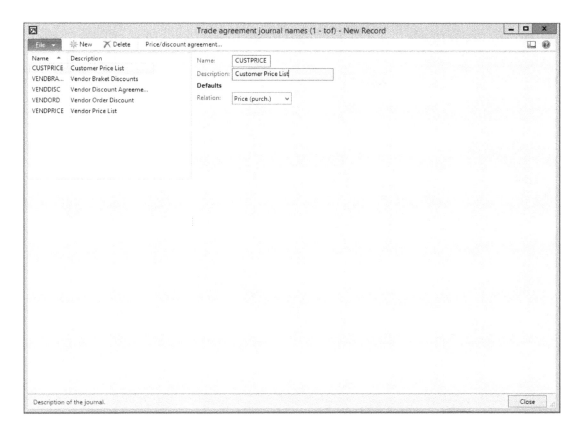

Set the **Name** to be **CUSTPRICE** and then set the **Description** to **Customer Price List**.

Creating Trade Agreement Types To Track Different Pricing Structures

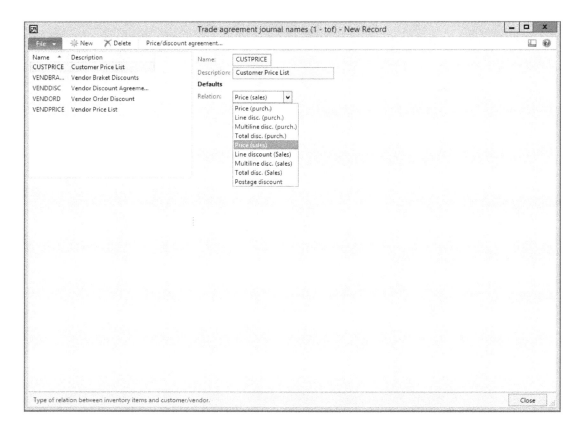

Then click on the **Relation** dropdown list and select the **Price (Sales)** option to indicate that this Trade Agreement journal will track sales prices by default.

You can add other types of price lists if you like and when you are done just click on the **Close** button to exit from the form.

Creating A Base Price List With A Trade Agreement

Now that we have our Journal Names configured we can start creating our price lists.

Creating A Base Price List With A Trade Agreement

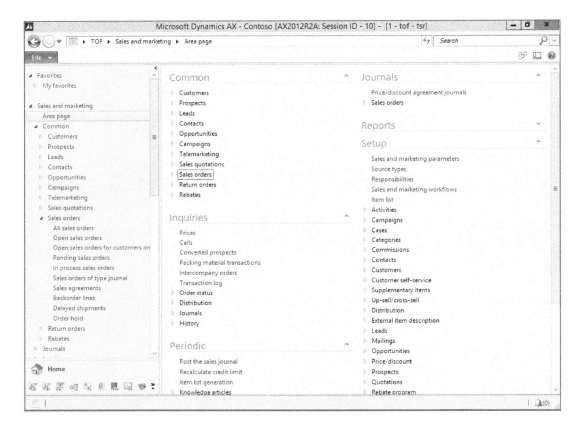

To do this click on the **Price/Discount Agreement Journals** menu item within the **Journals** group of the **Sales and Marketing** area page.

Creating A Base Price List With A Trade Agreement

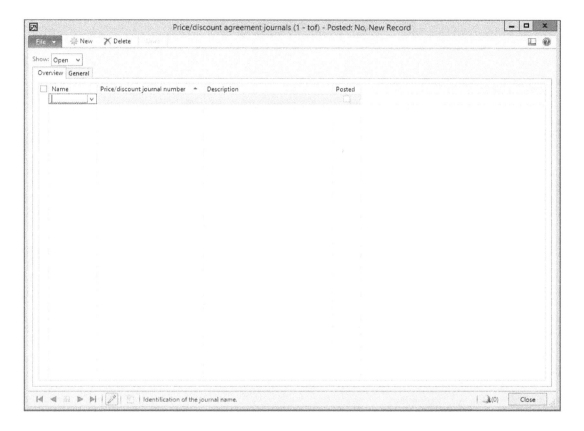

When the **Price/Discount Agreement Journals** maintenance form is displayed, click on the **New** button in the menu bar to create a new record.

Creating A Base Price List With A Trade Agreement

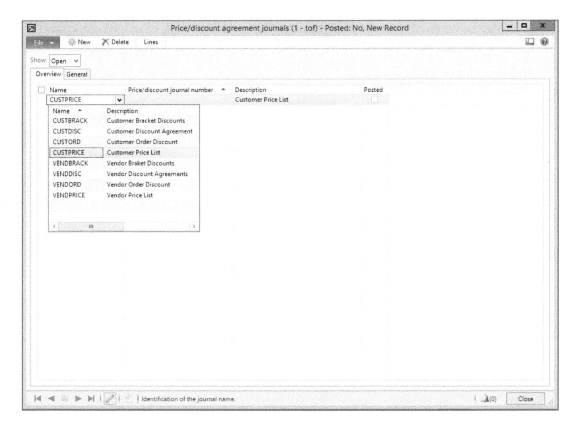

Then click on the **Name** dropdown list to select the **Trade Agreement Journal Name** that you want to use for the price list, and select the **CUSTPRICE** option.

Creating A Base Price List With A Trade Agreement

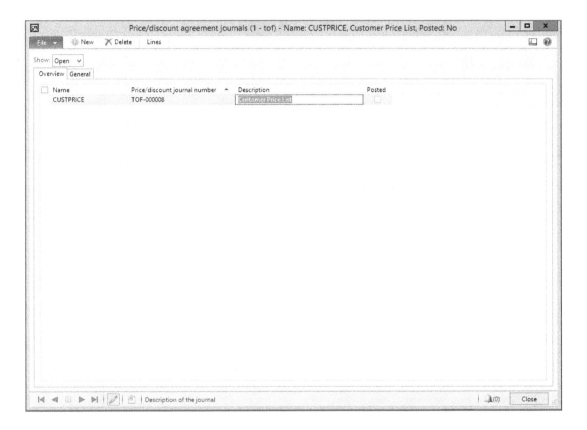

Next tab over to the **Description** field. You will notice that this defaults in from the Journal Name.

Creating A Base Price List With A Trade Agreement

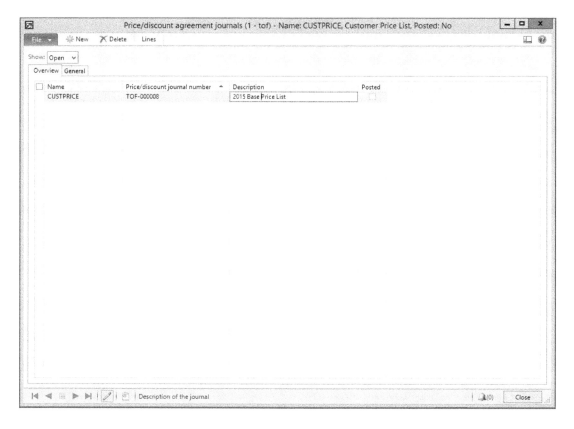

You can update the **Description** to be something that is a little more specific to this price list like **2015 Base Price List**.

After you have done that, click on the **Lines** button to start setting up the price list lines.

Creating A Base Price List With A Trade Agreement

That will open up the **Journal Lines, Price Discount Agreement** list page where we can start setting up our price list.

Creating A Base Price List With A Trade Agreement

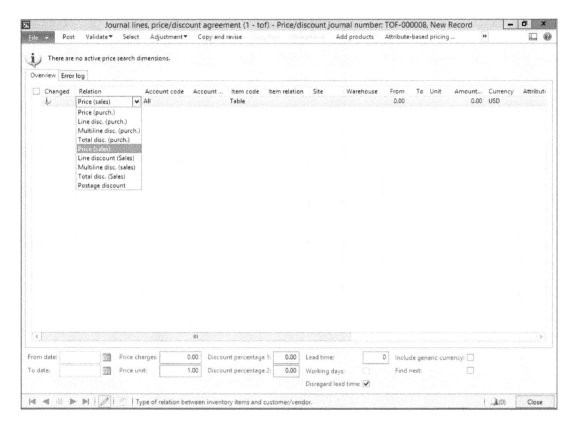

Note: Even though this Journal Agreement type is a **Price (Sales)** type by default, if you want you can click on the **Relation** dropdown list and change it to a different pricing or discounting relation – although for now let's just leave it as **Price (sales)**

Creating A Base Price List With A Trade Agreement

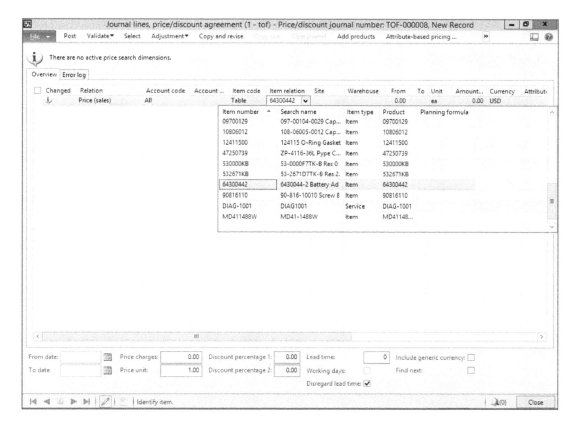

Now click on the **Item Relation** dropdown list and select the item that you want to set up the sales price for. In our data we select the **64300442** item.

Creating A Base Price List With A Trade Agreement

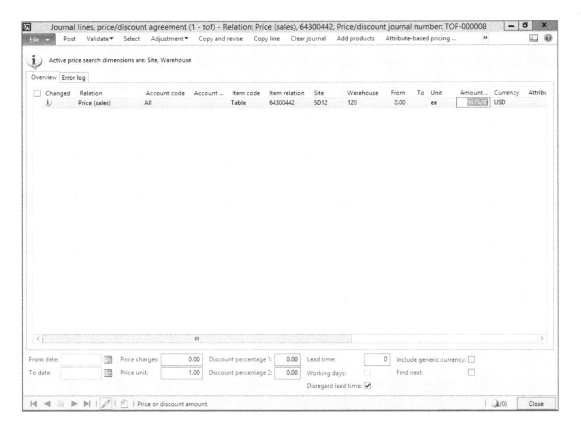

And then within the **Amount** field set the sales price that you want to apply to the product - $5975.00 seems fair.

Creating A Base Price List With A Trade Agreement

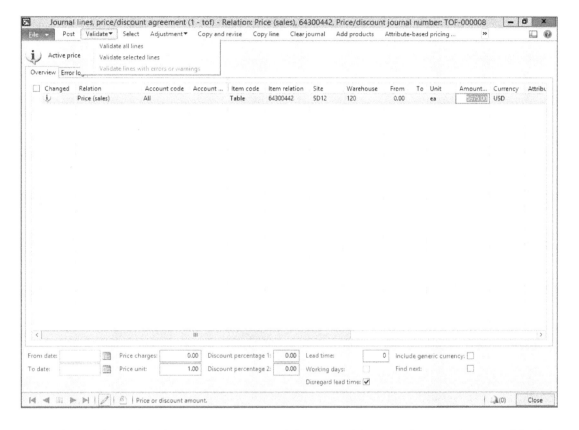

Now that we have the sales price set we can validate our pricing to make sure that everything is good. To do this click no the **Validate** button in the menu bar and select the **Validate All Lines** menu item.

Creating A Base Price List With A Trade Agreement

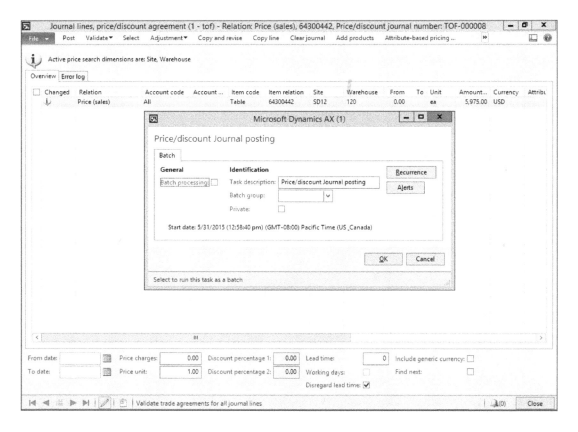

When the validation dialog box is displayed just click on the **OK** button.

Creating A Base Price List With A Trade Agreement

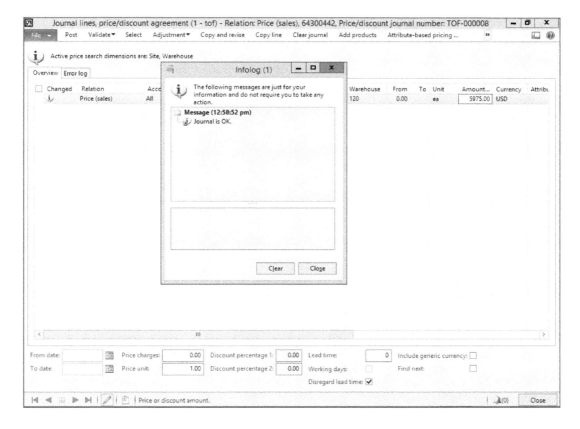

If the journal looks good then you will get an InfoLog saying that and just click on the **Close** button.

Creating A Base Price List With A Trade Agreement

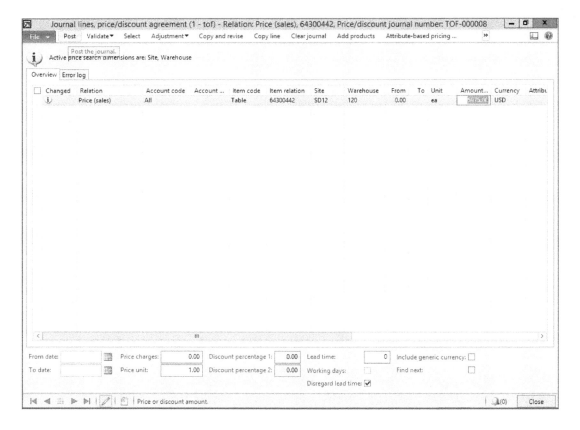

To make the pricing agreement active so that it will show up in the sales orders you need to **Post** it. To do this click on the **Post** button in the menu bar.

Creating A Base Price List With A Trade Agreement

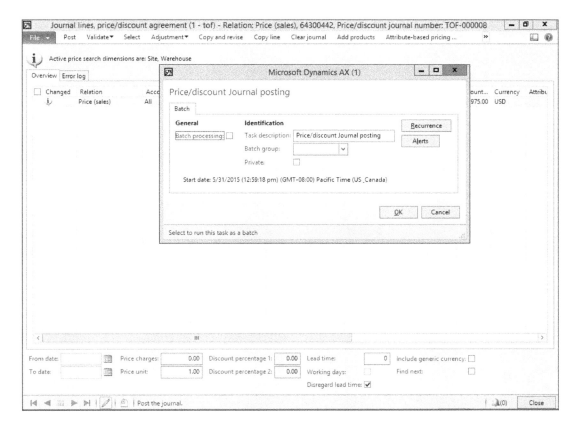

When the **Price/Discount Journal Posting** dialog box is displayed, click on the **OK** button to update the price journal.

Creating A Base Price List With A Trade Agreement

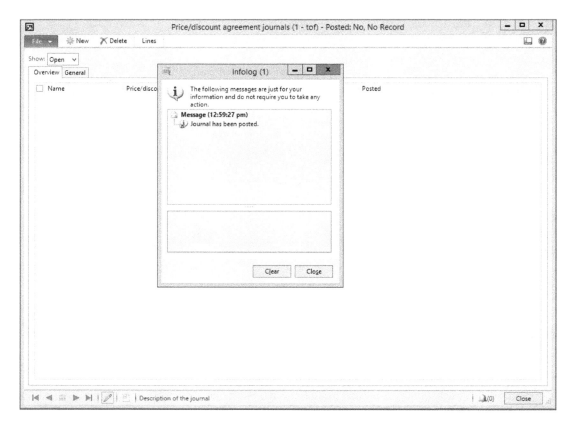

If everything looks good to AX then you will get an InfoLog telling you so.

Creating A Base Price List With A Trade Agreement

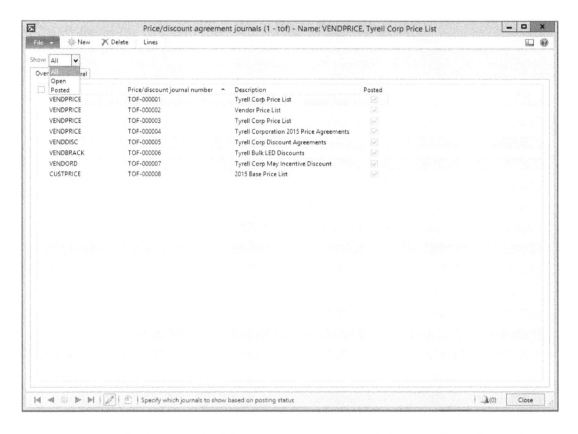

When you return back to the **Price/Discount Agreement Journals** list page, if you click on the **Show** field and select the **All** option then you will see your price list and also see that it has been posted.

Creating A Base Price List With A Trade Agreement

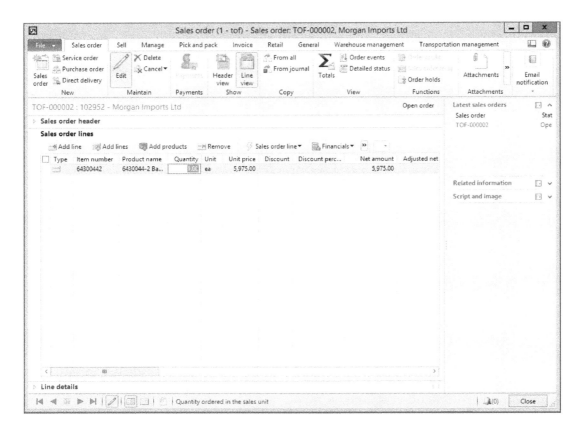

To see the price in action just enter in a new sales order for the item that you created the price list for and you will see that the new price is shown on the sales order line.

Creating A Base Price List With A Trade Agreement

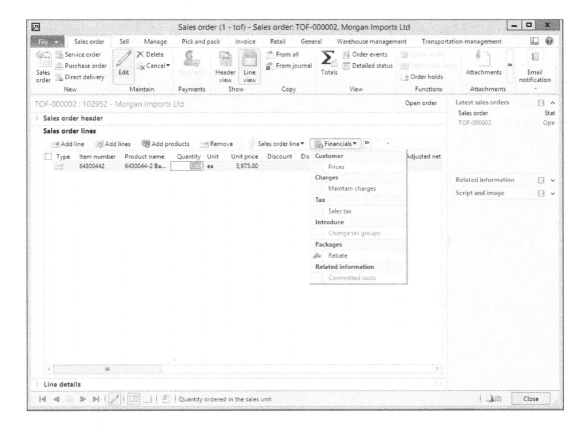

Now click on the **Financials** menu button on the Sales Order Lines menu bar and select the **Prices** menu item.

Creating A Base Price List With A Trade Agreement

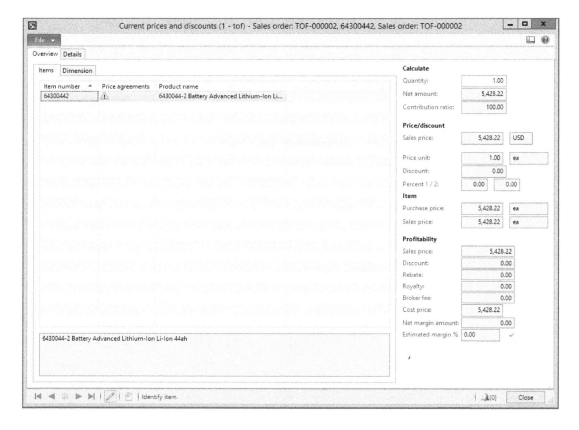

When the **Current Prices and Discounts** form is displayed you will see a alert icon on the sales order line showing that there are **Price Agreements** in place.

Creating A Base Price List With A Trade Agreement

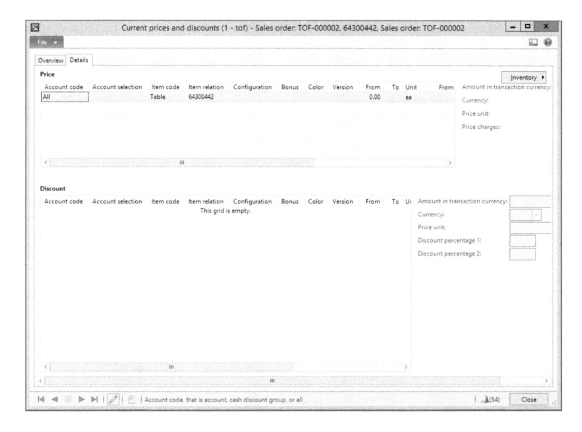

If you switch to the **Details** tab then you will see the trade agreement that has been applied to this order line.

Creating A Base Price List With A Trade Agreement

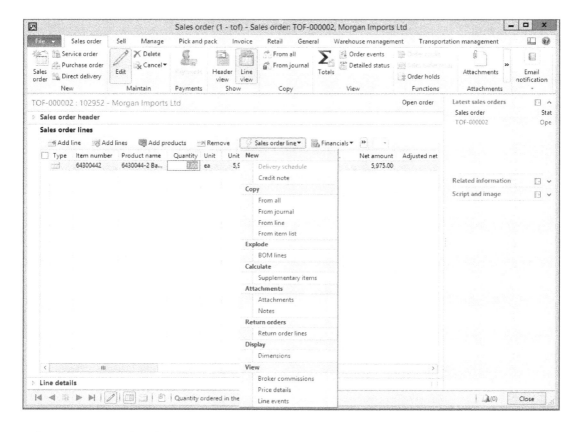

If you want more detailed price information then click on the **Sales Order Line** button in the **Sales Order Lines** menu bar and select the **Price Details** menu item.

Creating A Base Price List With A Trade Agreement

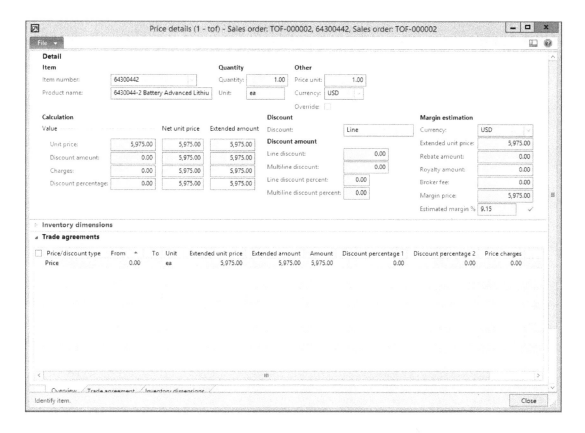

This will take you into the advanced price details form and if you expand out the **Trade Agreements** fast tab then you will see that your new trade agreement is shown there.

Creating A Base Price List With A Trade Agreement

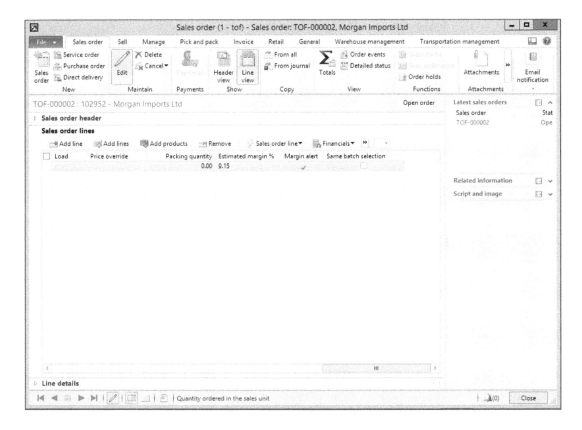

Also now if you look at the **Margin Alerts** on the sales order line, although we are not making a lot of margin on this sale, we are making a little bit of money.

How cool is that!

Viewing Sales Prices Associated With A Product

Viewing the price lists through the Trade Agreements is not the only way that you can track your prices. If you want to see what price lists are associated with an individual product then you can save a little bit of time and view them directly from the Released Product.

Viewing Sales Prices Associated With A Product

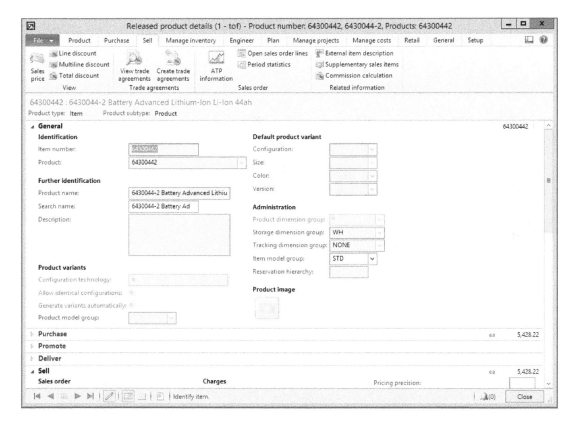

To do this just open up your **Released Product Details** and then click on the **View Trade Agreements** button within the **Trade Agreements** group of the **Sell** ribbon bar.

Viewing Sales Prices Associated With A Product

When the **View Trade Agreements** form is displayed you will see all of the current trade agreements that you have associated with the product.

Updating An Existing Trade Agreement

One of the tricks that is useful to know when it comes to the Trade Agreements is that you can make revisions to them directly from the **View Trade Agreements** form. This is a quick and easy way to change your prices without having to do a lot of navigation within the system.

Updating An Existing Trade Agreement

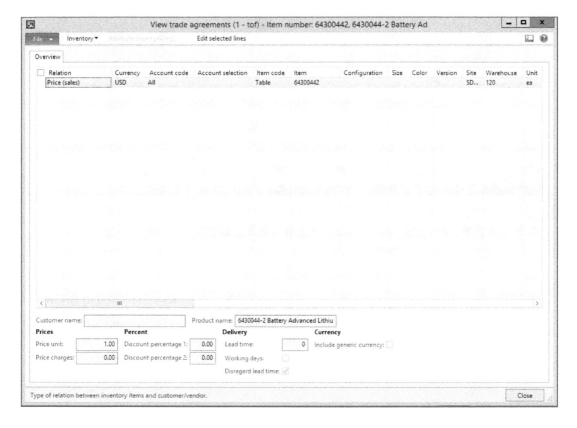

All you need to do to do this is select the lines within the current **Trade** Agreement that you are looking at and then click on the **Edit Selected Lines** button in the menu bar.

Updating An Existing Trade Agreement

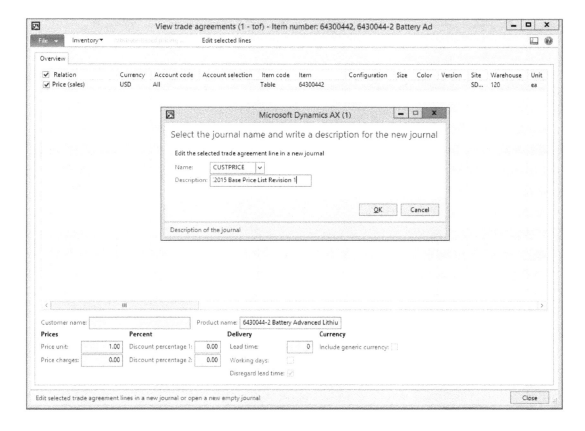

This will ask you for a **Trade Agreement Name** for the price adjustment and also for a **Description**.

Note: One thing to understand about the pricing within Dynamics AX is that you are not really updating a price list, you are making adjustments to them through Pricing Journals. So what this is really doing is asking for the type and name of the adjustment journal that you are creating.

After you have done this, click on the **OK** button.

Updating An Existing Trade Agreement

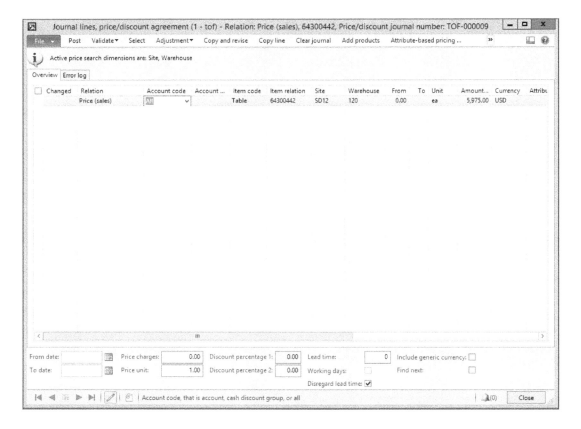

This will take you into the **Journal Lines** form that you with the Trade Agreement line already loaded in for you.

Updating An Existing Trade Agreement

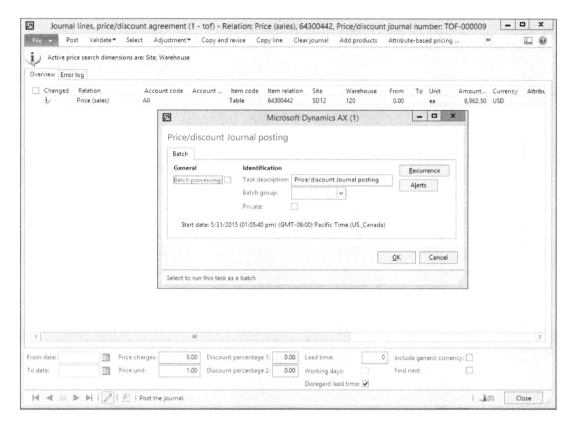

All you need to do is change the journal line (for example – update the **Amount** field) and then click on the **Post** button in the menu bar.

When the **Journal Posting** confirmation dialog box is displayed, click on the **OK** button.

Updating An Existing Trade Agreement

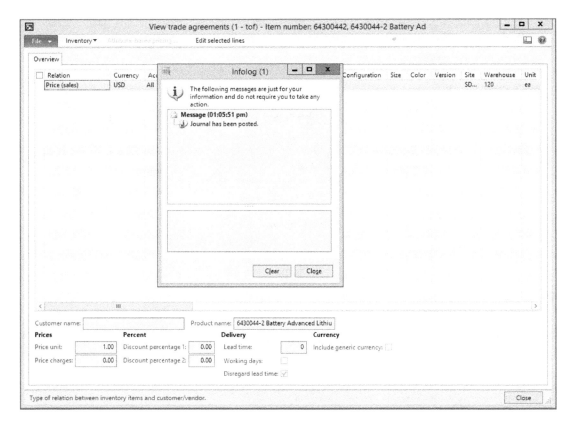

If everything goes well you will get an InfoLog message saying so and you can then click on the **Close** button to finish the process.

Updating An Existing Trade Agreement

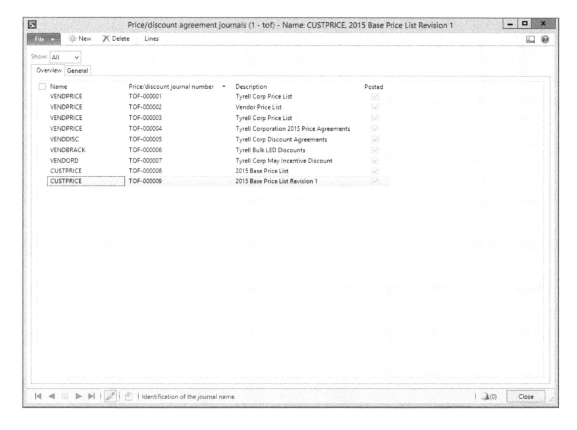

If you return to the **Price/Discount Agreement Journals** form then you will notice that there is now a new Journal entry that has been posted that contains the updates that you just made.

Updating Price Lists Through Excel

If you are just updating more than just a couple of Price Journal lines, then you might want to take advantage of the feature within Dynamics AX that allows you to update all of your prices through Excel. This is a very useful feature and also saves so much time when you are making mass updates.

Updating Price Lists Through Excel

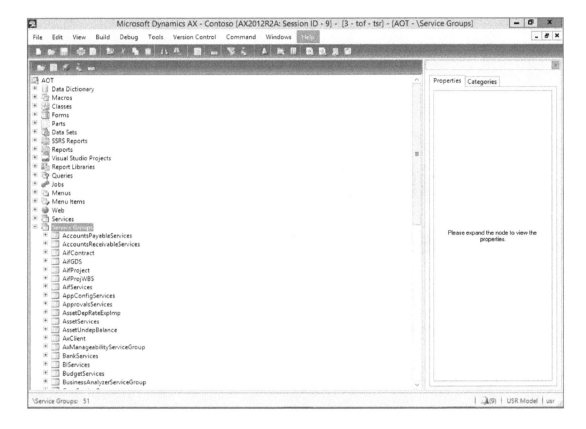

Before we can do this though we need to set up one thing and that is to deploy the service that will allow the prices to be updated from Excel. This may seem technical, but it's not really. To do this, open up the AOT development environment (just press **CTRL+D**) and expand out the **Service Groups** folder.

Updating Price Lists Through Excel

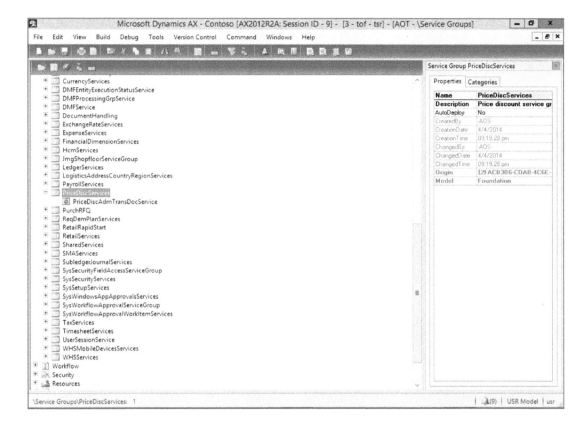

Then scroll down and find the **PriceDiscService**.

Updating Price Lists Through Excel

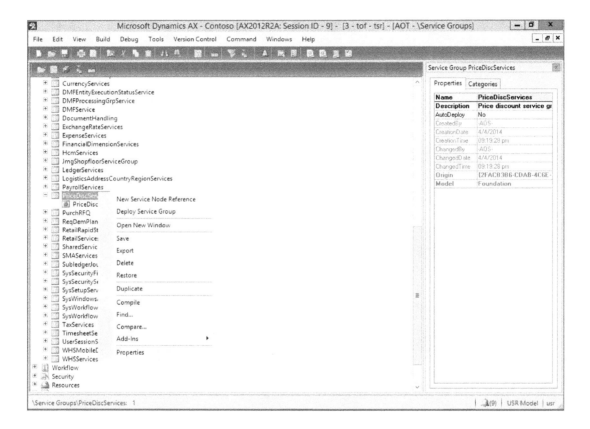

Right-mouse-click on the **PriceDiscService** and select the **Deploy Service Group** menu item.

Updating Price Lists Through Excel

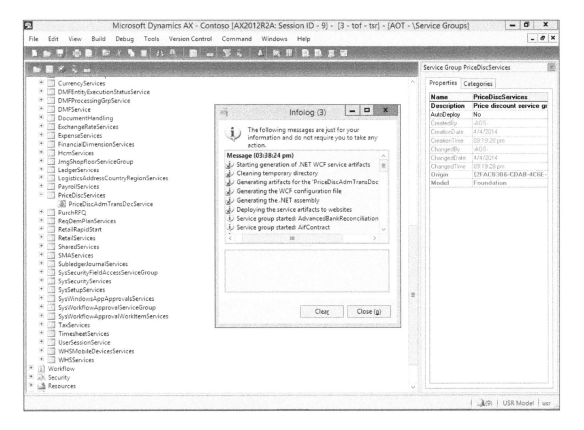

The system will run for a little bit, then you should get an InfoLog saying that the service was deployed. Click on the **Close** button to dismiss the message an then close out of **AOT** (press **ALT+F4**).

Updating Price Lists Through Excel

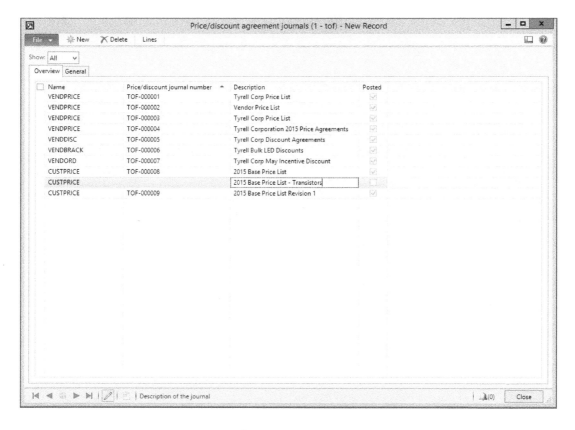

To see this in action, open up the **Price/Discount Agreement Journals** list page, click on the **New** button in the menu bar to create a new record, and then set the **Name** to **CUSTPRICE** and the **Description** to **2015 Base Price List – Transistors**.

Then click on the **Lines** button in the menu bar.

Updating Price Lists Through Excel

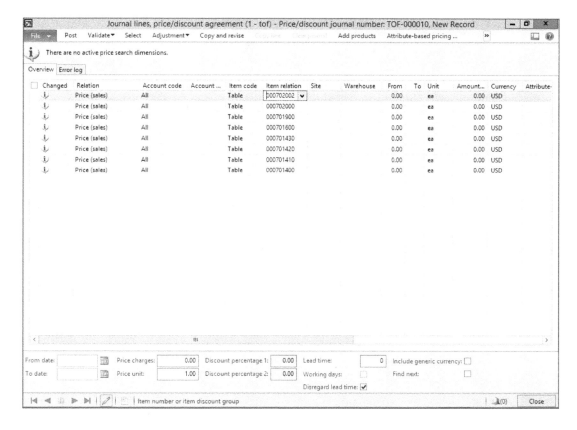

When the **Journal Lines** are displayed, add in a few products to the price list. Don't worry about updating the **Amount** just yet – we will do that in just a bit.

Updating Price Lists Through Excel

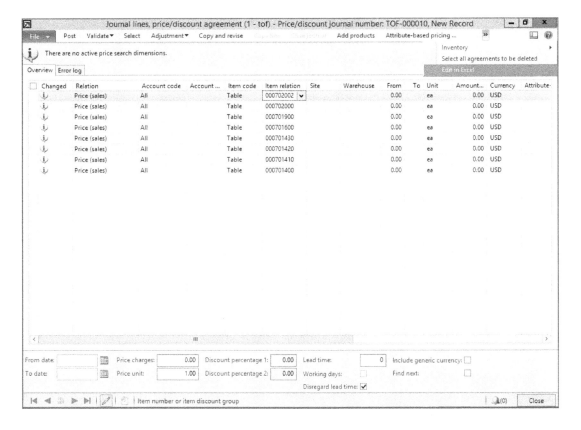

After you have all of the lines in the journal, click on the **Edit In Excel** button in the menu bar.

Updating Price Lists Through Excel

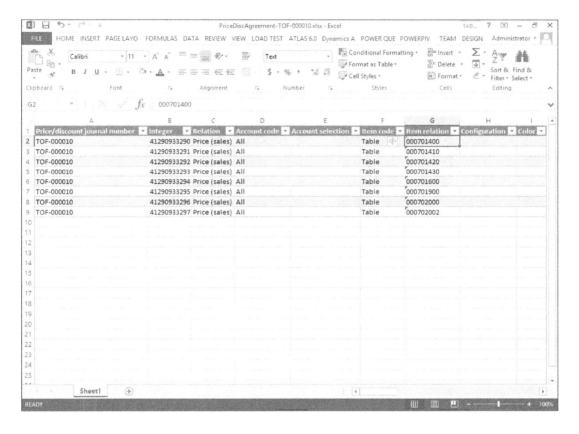

This will open up Excel and create a worksheet for you that shows you all of the lines that were in your journal.

Updating Price Lists Through Excel

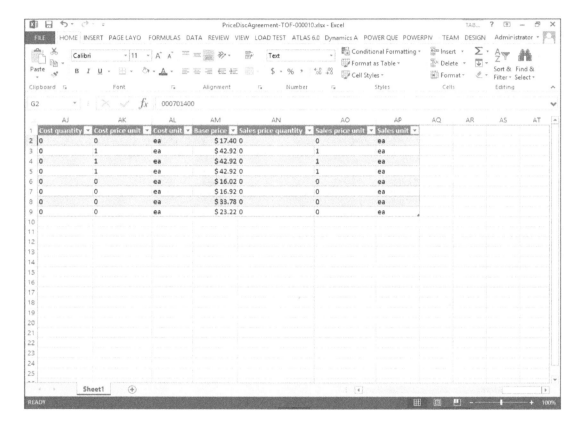

One useful feature is that there is a little more information that is carried over within the worksheet. If you scroll all the way to the right of the form then you will be able to see that the **Base Price** is there.

Updating Price Lists Through Excel

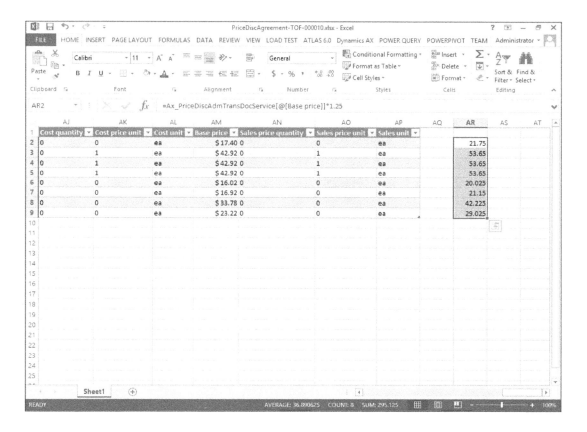

If you just want to create a sales price that is a simple markup of the base price then you can just create a formula within Excel – because that is what Excel is good at.

Updating Price Lists Through Excel

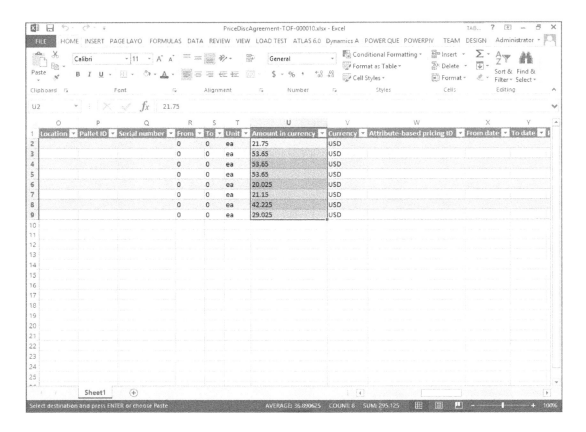

Then you can just cut and paste the calculated price over into the **Amount In Currency** column of the worksheet.

Updating Price Lists Through Excel

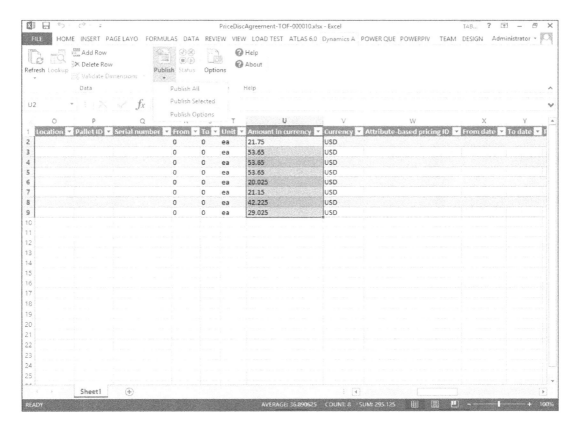

Now all you need to do is click on the **Publish** button within the **Update** group of the **Dynamics AX** ribbon bar and then select the **Publish All** menu item.

Updating Price Lists Through Excel

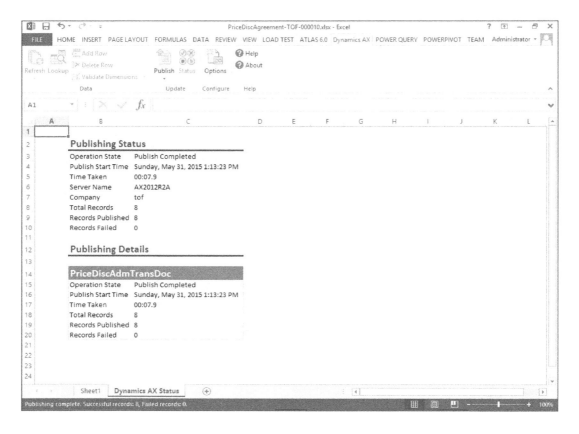

Excel will then update the prices and if you click on the **Dynamics AX Status** tab then you will see that it has updated all of the lines for you.

Updating Price Lists Through Excel

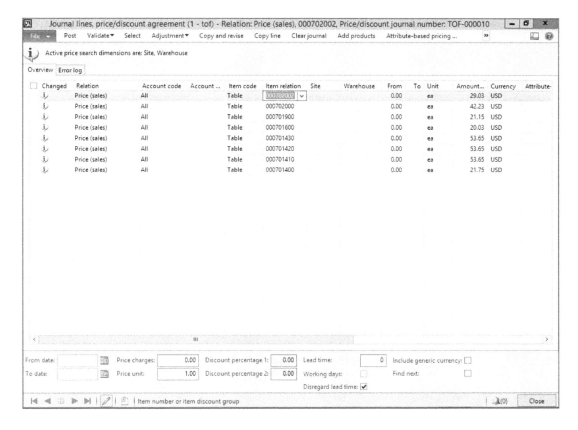

If you don't believe Excel then switch back to the **Journal Lines** and refresh the contents (Press **F5**) and you will see that all of the lines have an **Amount**.

Updating Price Lists Through Excel

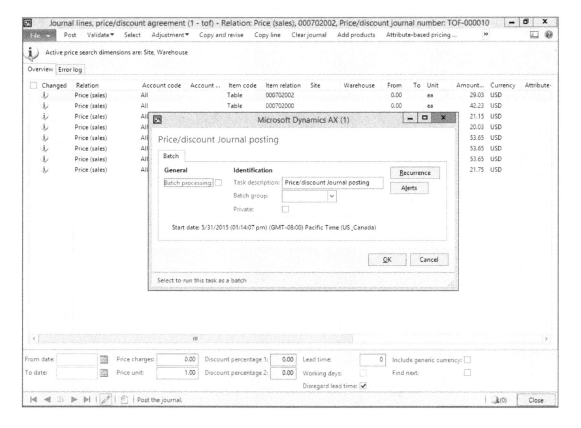

All that is left to do is to click on the **Post** button in the menu bar, and click on the **OK** button when the **Posting** dialog box is displayed.

Updating Price Lists Through Excel

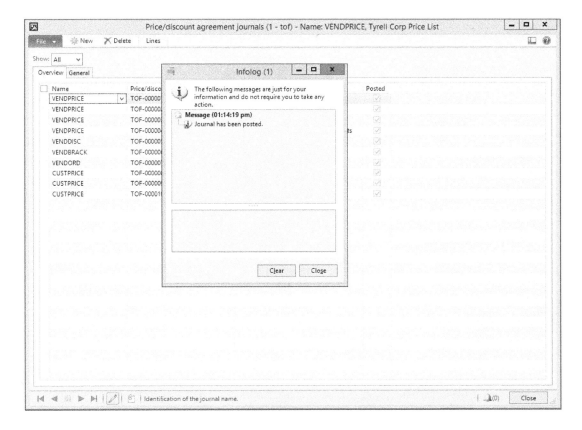

If everything is OK then you will get an InfoLog that says the journal has been posted and you are done.

How easy is that?

Viewing Pricing Agreements For Customers

Just like within the **Products** you can also view all of the associated trade agreements and prices through the **Customers** maintenance form. This is a great way to see what customers should be paying for products and also to see what incentives they are getting.

Viewing Pricing Agreements For Customers

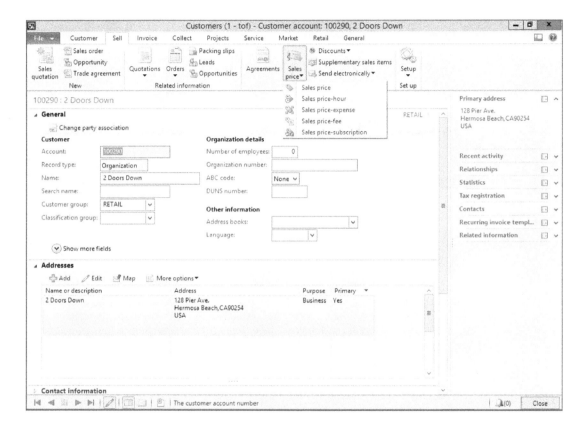

To do this, open up any of the **Customers** details and then click on the **Sales Prices** button within the **Pricing** group of the **Sell** ribbon bar and then select the **Sales Prices** menu item.

Viewing Pricing Agreements For Customers

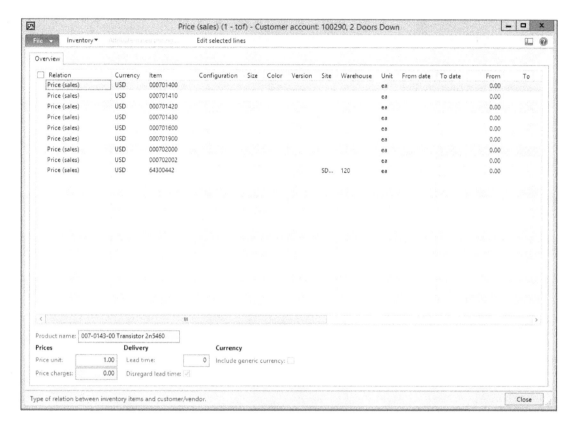

This will open up a **Price** list that only shows the **Prices (Sales)** journals that apply to the customer.

Viewing Pricing Agreements For Customers

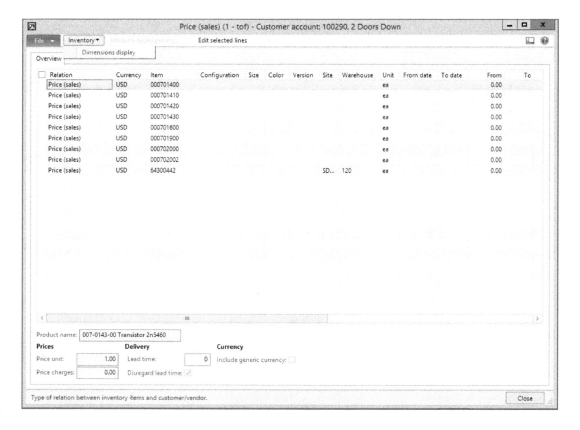

One thing that you may notice is that all of the inventory dimensions are being shown on this inquiry. Something that you may want to do is click on the **Inventory** button in the menu bar and select the **Dimension Display** menu item.

Viewing Pricing Agreements For Customers

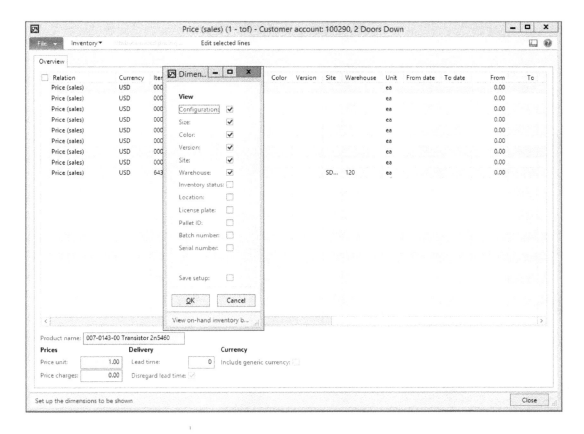

This will open up the **Dimension** Manager dialog box.

Viewing Pricing Agreements For Customers

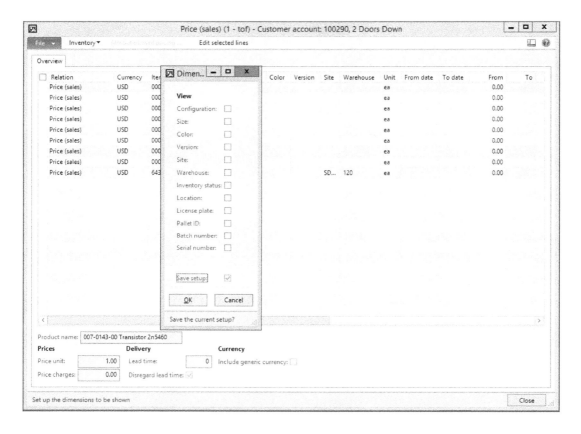

Just uncheck all of the dimensions, check the **Save Setup** checkbox and then click on the **OK** button.

Viewing Pricing Agreements For Customers

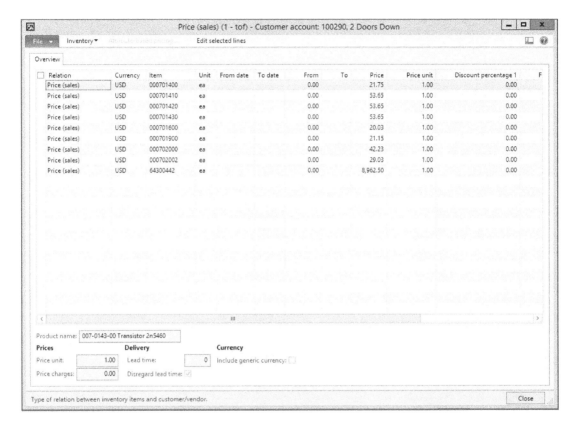

Now it's a little easier to see all of the prices that are associated with the customer.

When you are done just click on the **Close** button to exit out of the form.

Creating Customer Specific Price Lists

Up until now we have just been creating price lists for products which all of the customers would be eligible for. But that is not all that you are able to do. Another type of price list that you may want to create is one that is just for an individual customer.

Creating Customer Specific Price Lists

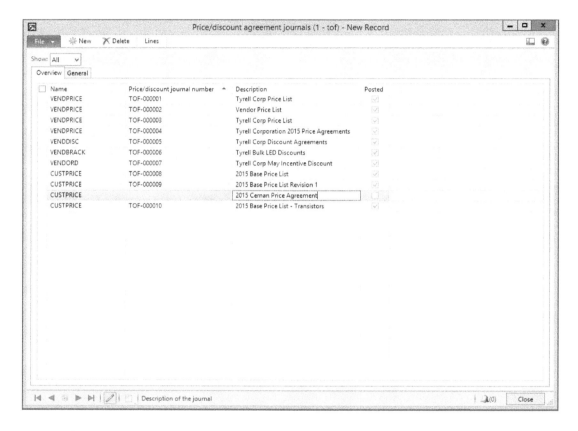

To do this open up the **Price/Discount Agreement Journals** maintenance form. Then click on the **New** button, set the **Name** to **CUSTPRICE** and then set the **Description** to **2015 Cernan Price Agreement**.

When you have done that click on the **Lines** button in the menu bar.

Creating Customer Specific Price Lists

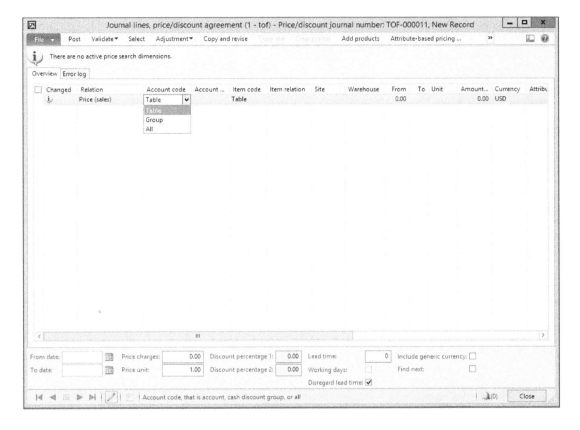

When the **Journal Lines** are displayed, click on the **Account Type** dropdown list and select the **Table** option to specify that this price line will be associated with a single customer.

Creating Customer Specific Price Lists

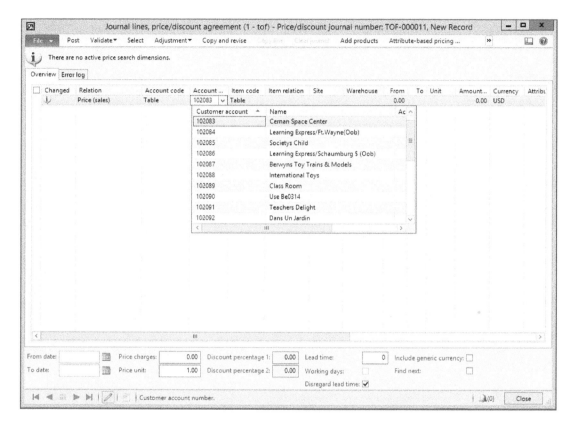

This will allow you then to click on the **Account Relation** dropdown list and select a customer that you want to apply this price list to.

Creating Customer Specific Price Lists

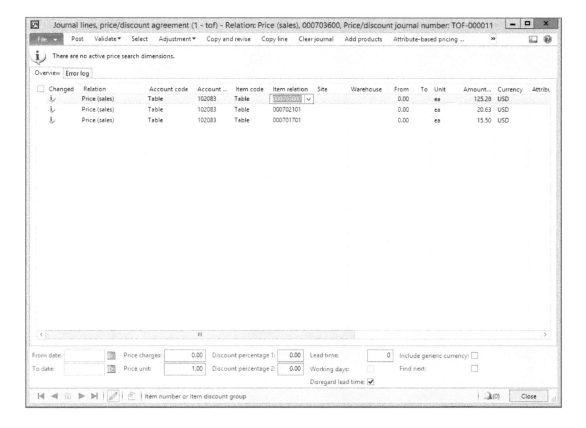

Then select the **Product** from the **Item Relation** dropdown list and specify the **Amount**.

Repeat the process for any other products that you want the customer to get special pricing on.

Creating Customer Specific Price Lists

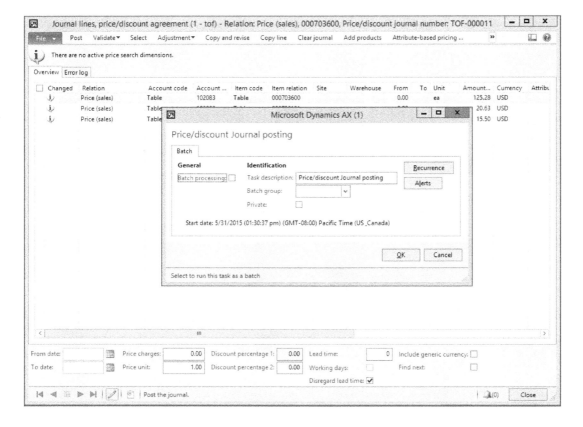

When you are done, click on the **Post** button in the menu bar and then click on the **OK** button on the **Porting Confirmation** dialog box

Creating Customer Specific Price Lists

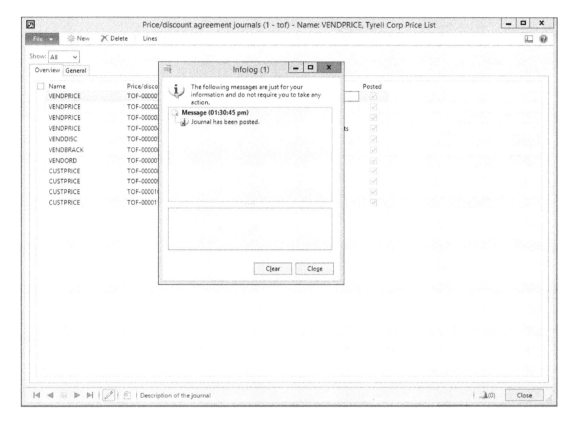

If everything is OK then you will get an InfoLog box telling you that and you can then click **Close** to finish the process.

Creating Customer Specific Price Lists

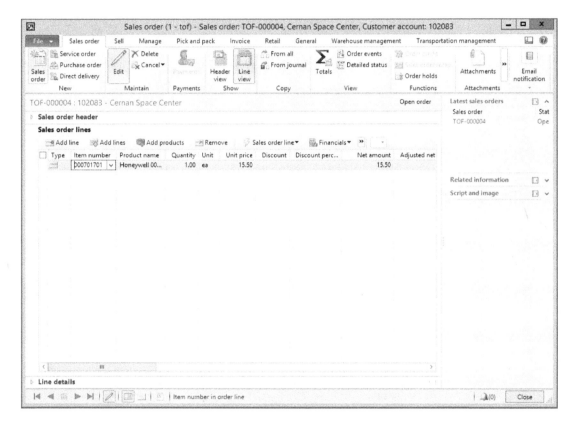

To test this out, just create a **Sales Order** for that customer and also for the items that you had within the agreement and you should see that the customer specific pricing comes through.

Creating Customer Specific Price Lists

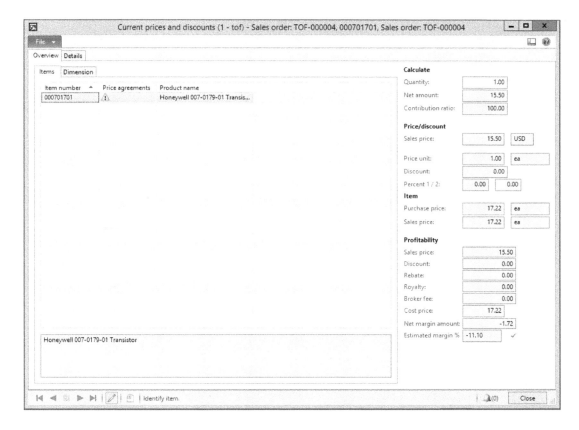

If you also look at the **Price Details** inquiry then you will see the sales price, and also the original sales price as reference.

After you are done just click on the **Close** button to exit from the form.

Creating Customer Pricing Groups

Creating individual customer price lists is OK, but if you have more than a handful of customers then setting up the individual pricing could get a little tedious. If you have common pricing that applies to multiple customers then there is a better option and that is to set up **Customer Pricing Groups** and then create price lists for the groups. The first step is to create **Customer Pricing Groups**.

Creating Customer Pricing Groups

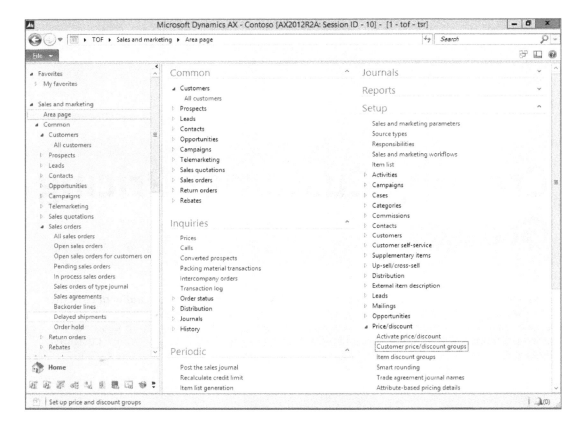

To do this click on the **Customer Price/Discount Groups** menu item within the **Price/Discount** folder of the **Setup** group within the **Sales and Marketing** area page.

Creating Customer Pricing Groups

When the **Customer Price/Discount Groups** maintenance form is displayed, click on the **New** button in the menu bar to create a new record.

Creating Customer Pricing Groups

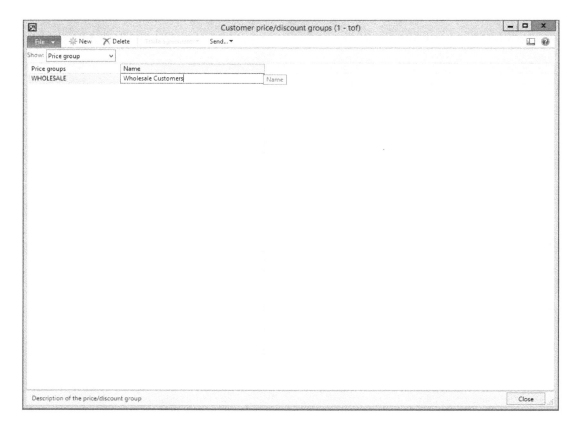

Then set the **Price Groups** code to **WHOLESALE** and the **Name** to **Wholesale Customers**.

Creating Customer Pricing Groups

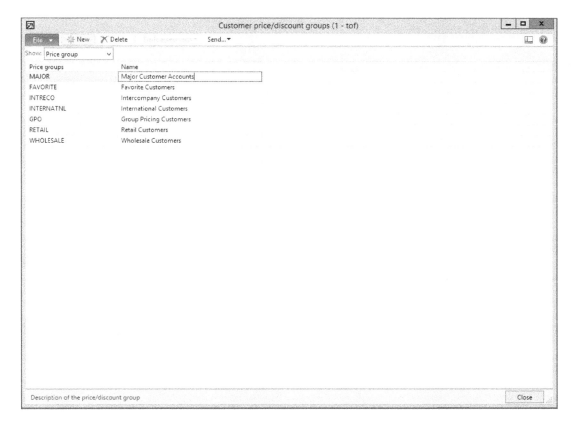

Repeat the process by adding in any other groups that you may want to use for your pricing. Here are a few examples.

RETAIL   **Retail**
GPO   **Group Pricing Customers**
INTERNATNL   **International Customers**
INTERCO   **Intercompany Customers**
FAVORITE   **Favorite Customers**
MAJOR   **Major Customer Accounts**

When you are done, just click on the **Close** button to exit from the form.

Configuring Customer Account Details

Once you have your **Price Groups** configured you then need to associate them with your **Customers** to add them to the group.

Configuring Customer Account Details

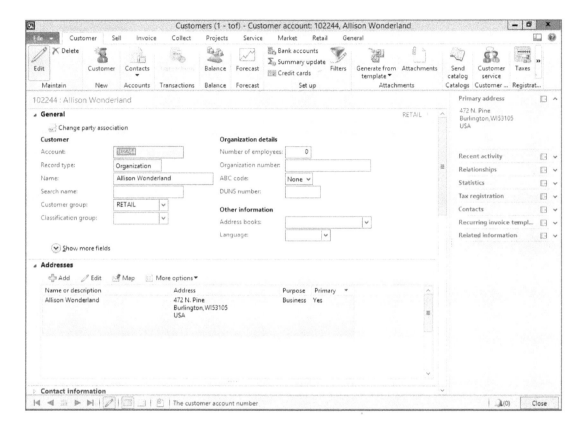

To do this open up your **Customer Details** form for the **Customer** that you want to add to the group.

Configuring Customer Account Details

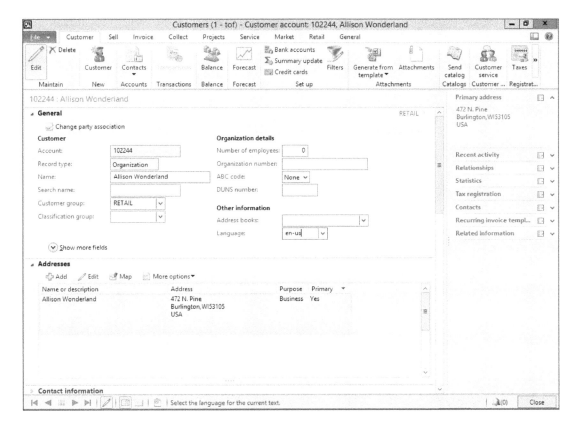

While we are here we will take advantage of this and set up some of the default codes for the customer so that we don't have to update them every time we create a sales order. Start off by setting the **Language** to **en-us** on the **General** fast tab.

Configuring Customer Account Details

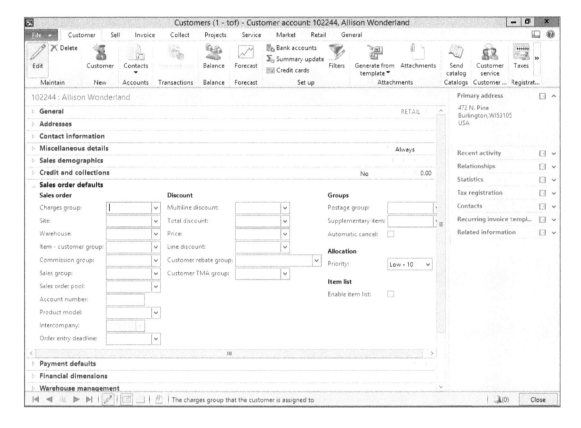

Next switch to the **Sales Order Defaults** fast tab and you will see that there are a lot of other sales codes that we can configure for the customer.

Configuring Customer Account Details

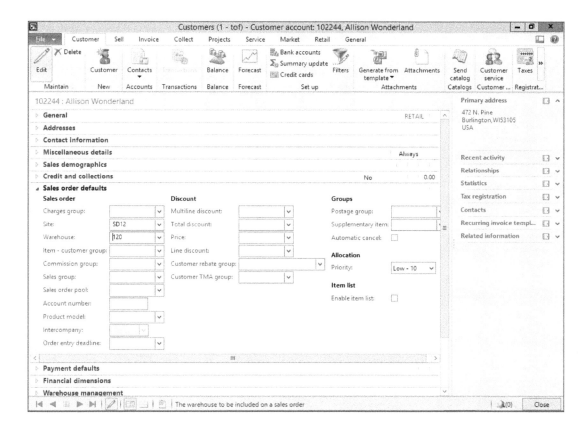

Set the **Site** to **SD12** and the **Warehouse** to **120**.

Configuring Customer Account Details

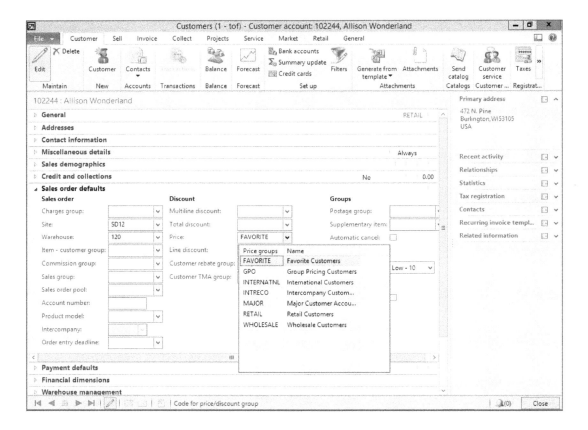

Then click on the **Price** dropdown list and select the **FAVORITE** price group.

Configuring Customer Account Details

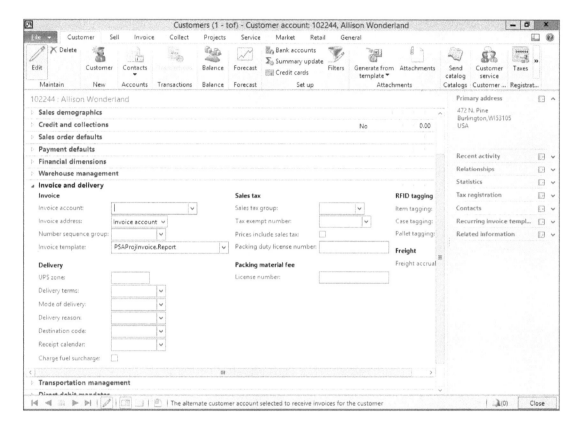

Finally, switch to the **Invoice And Delivery** fast tab.

Configuring Customer Account Details

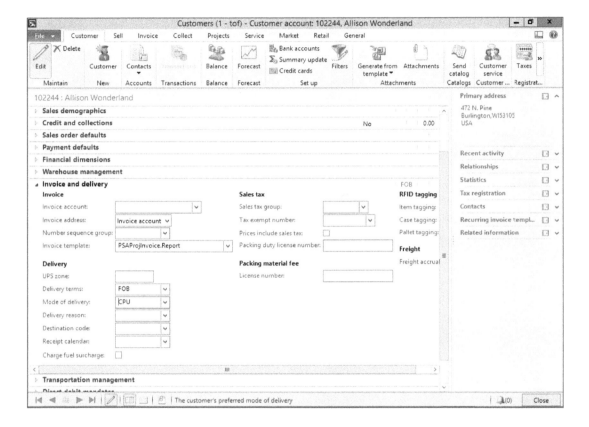

On this tab set the **Delivery Terms** to **FBO** and the **Mode of Delivery** to **CPU**.

When you are done, just click on the **Close** button to exit from the form.

Creating Price Lists For Customer Groups

Now we are all set and we can start creating our Customer Group Price Lists.

Creating Price Lists For Customer Groups

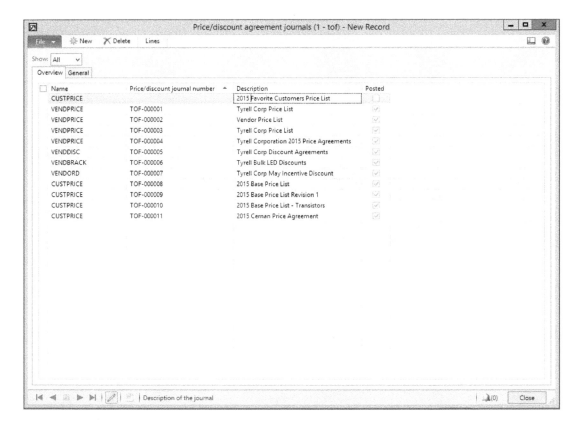

To do this, open up the **Price/Discount Agreement Journals** list page, click on the **New** button to create a new record, set the **Name** to **CUSTPRICE**, the **Description** to **2015 Favorite Customers Price List** and then click on the **Lines** button in the menu bar.

Creating Price Lists For Customer Groups

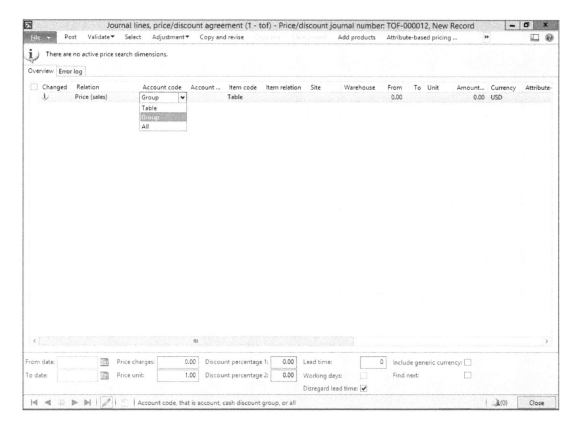

When the **Journal Lines** maintenance form is displayed, click on the **Account Code** dropdown list and select the **Group** option.

Creating Price Lists For Customer Groups

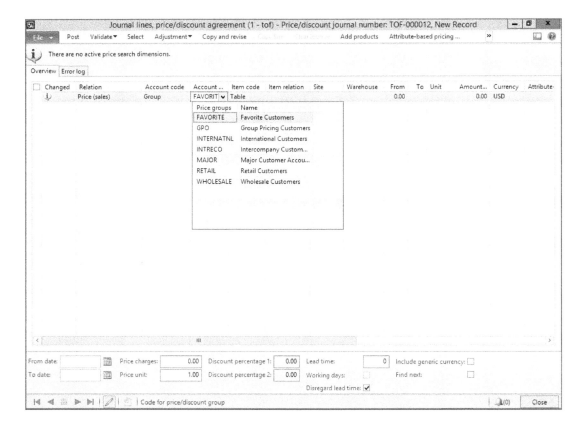

This will allow you to click on the **Account Relation** dropdown list and select the **FAVORITE** price group that you just created.

Creating Price Lists For Customer Groups

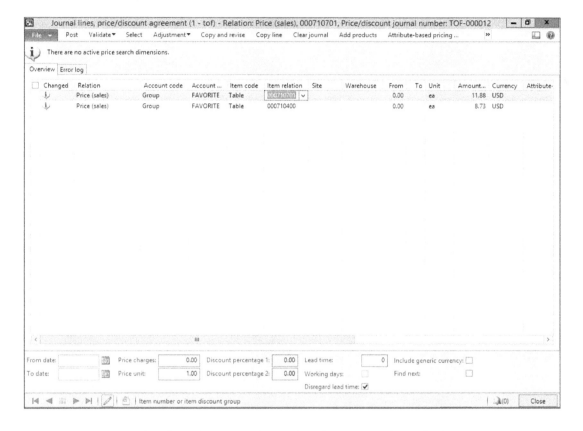

Then select the **Product** from the **Item Relation** dropdown list and specify the **Amount**.

Repeat the process for any other products that you want the customer group to get special pricing on.

Creating Price Lists For Customer Groups

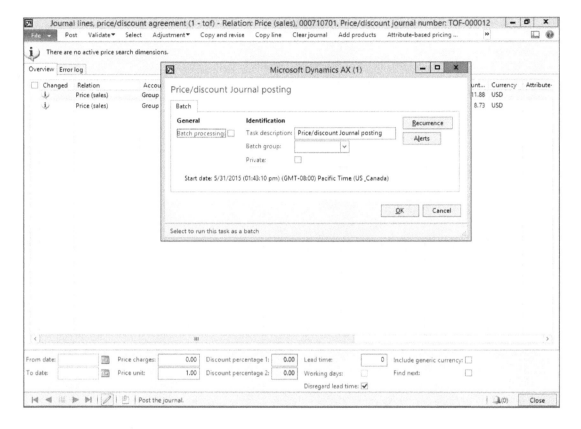

When you are done just click on the **Post** button in the menu bar and then click on the **OK** button when the **Posting Confirmation** dialog box is displayed.

Creating Price Lists For Customer Groups

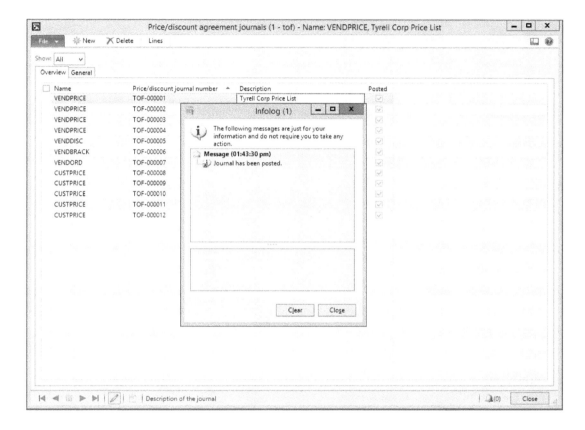

If everything is OK then you will get an InfoLog box telling you that and you can then click **Close** to finish the process.

Creating Price Lists For Customer Groups

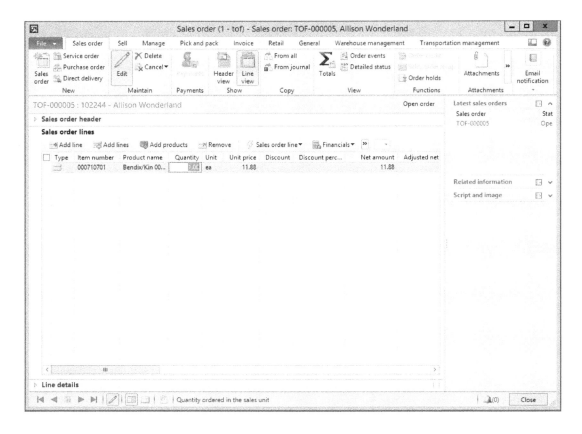

To test this out, just create a **Sales Order** for the customer that has the **FAVORITE** pricing group and also for the items that you had within the agreement and you should see that the customer group pricing comes through.

Creating Price Lists For Customer Groups

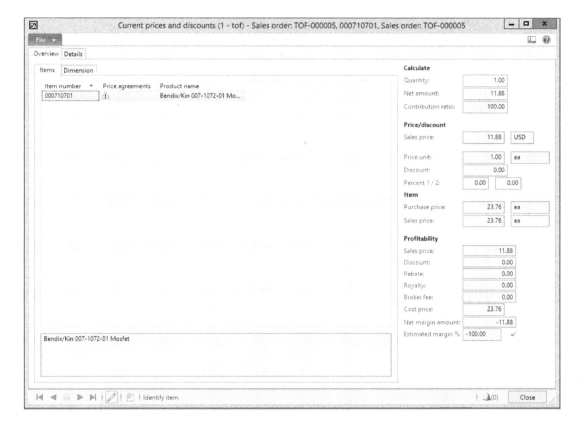

If you also look at the **Price Details** inquiry then you will see the sales price, and also the original sales price as reference.

After you are done just click on the **Close** button to exit from the form.

Configuring Smart Rounding

There is a clever little feature within Dynamics AX that you may want to take advantage of called **Smart Rounding**. What this allows you to do is create rounding rules for you sales prices that round to the nearest value. For example – you can set up rules that will round to the nearest 95 cents if you want. This allows you to create price lists based on maybe a margin calculation and then round them so that they look tidy. Before you apply smart rounding to your pricelists though you need to set up the rules.

Configuring Smart Rounding

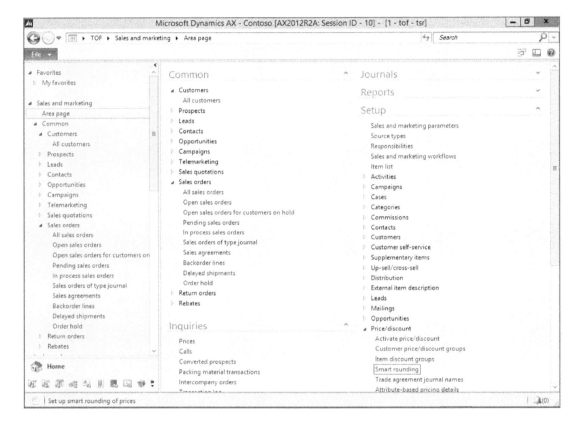

To do this click on the **Smart Rounding** menu button within the **Price/Discount** folder of the **Setup** group within the **Sales and Marketing** area page.

Configuring Smart Rounding

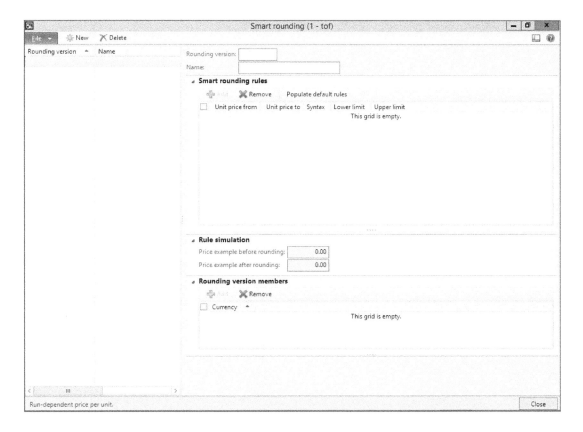

When the **Smart Rounding** maintenance form is displayed, click on the **New** button in the menu bar to create a new record.

Configuring Smart Rounding

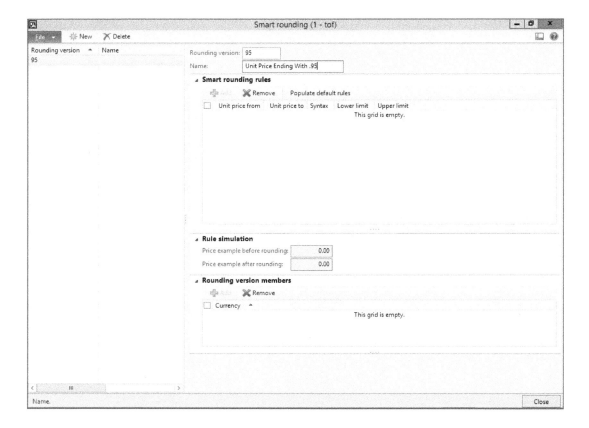

Set the **Rounding Version** code to **95** and the **Name** to **Unit Price Ending with 95**.

Configuring Smart Rounding

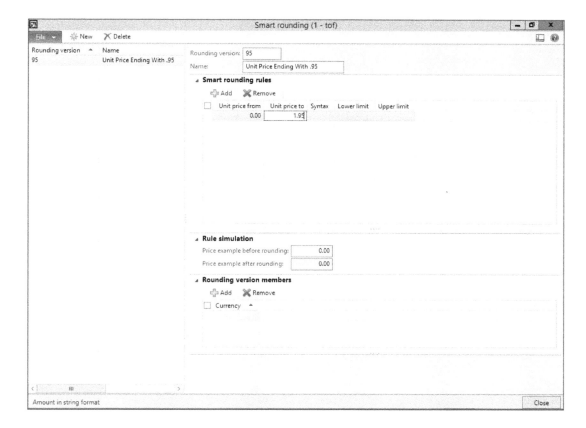

Now click on the **Add** button in the **Smart Rounding Rules** tab to create a rounding rule.

Set the **Unit Price From** value to **0.00** and the **Unit Price To** to **1.95**.

Configuring Smart Rounding

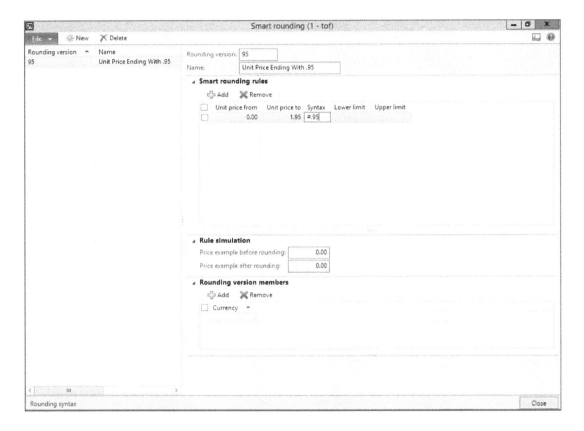

Then set the **System** to **#.95** which tells the system to round to the .95 cents.

Configuring Smart Rounding

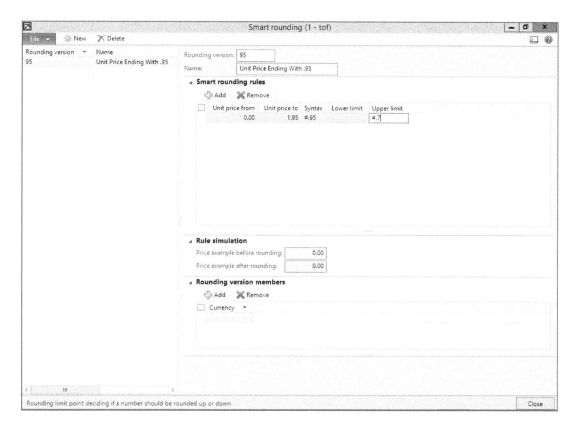

Then set the **Upper Limit** to **#.70** which tells the system to only round up if the number is greater than this amount.

Configuring Smart Rounding

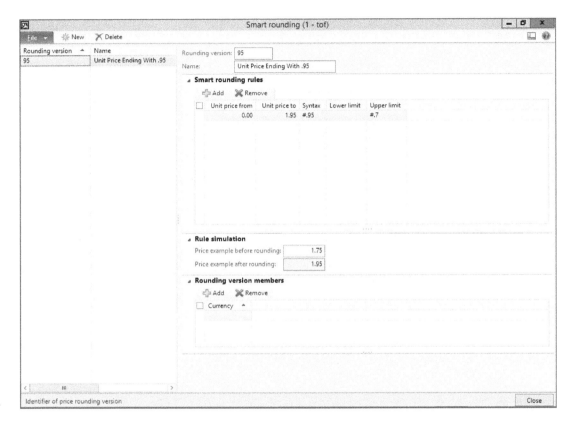

You can test your rule by typing in a value into the **Price Example Before Rounding** field. You will then be able to see the results in the **Price Example After Rounding** field.

Configuring Smart Rounding

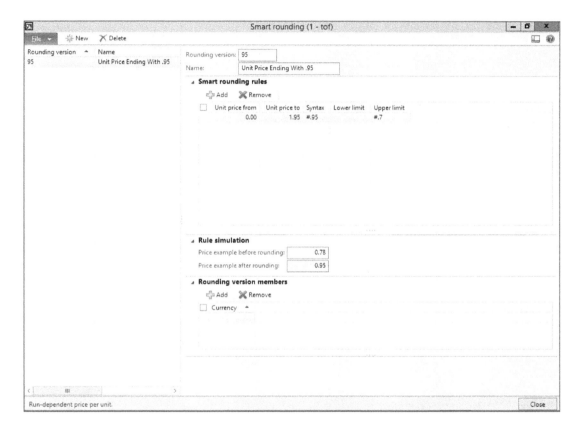

Type in **0.70** just to verify that everything is working.

Configuring Smart Rounding

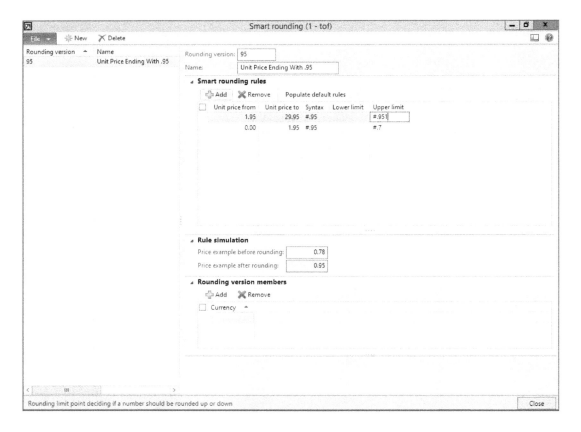

Now click on the **Add** button again to create another rule. This time set the **Unit Price From** to **1.95**, the **Unit Price To** to **29.95**, the **System** to **#.95** and the **Upper Limit** to **#.951** so that it is just above the first rounding rule.

Configuring Smart Rounding

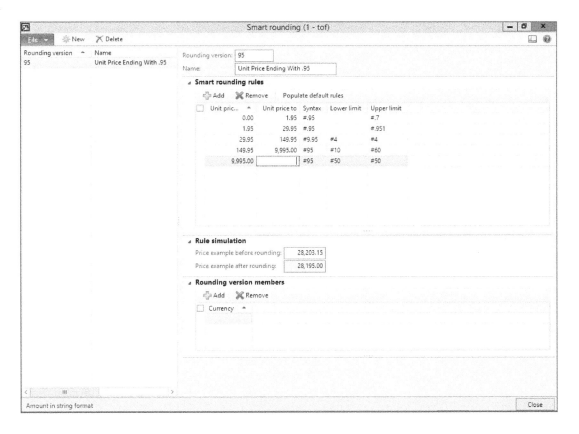

You can continue adding your rules and keep in mind that you don't have to round to the nearest 95 cents, you can round to higher denominations as well.

Price From	Price To	System	Lower Limit	Upper Limit
29.95	149.95	#9.95	#4	#4
149.95	9,995.00	#95	#10	#60
9,995.00		#95	#50	#50

When you are done just click on the **Close** button to exit from the form.

Applying Smart Rounding To Sales Prices

Now that you have your **Smart Rounding** rules configured you can start using them on your price lists to tidy up your pricing.

Applying Smart Rounding To Sales Prices

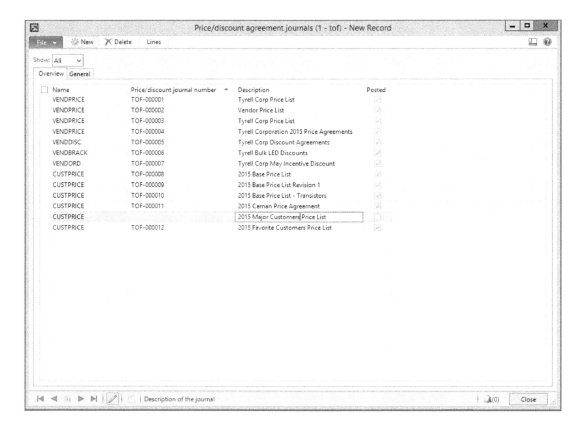

To do this return to the **Price/Discount Agreement Journals**, click on the **Add** button to create a new record, set the **Name** to **CUSTPRICE**, the **Description** to **2015 Major Customers Price List** and then click on the **Lines** button in the menu bar.

Applying Smart Rounding To Sales Prices

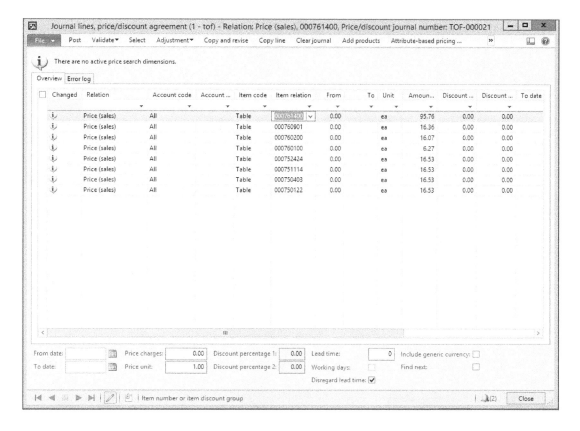

When the **Journal Lines** are displayed, add in all of the pricing lines for the products that you want to have within the price list.

Applying Smart Rounding To Sales Prices

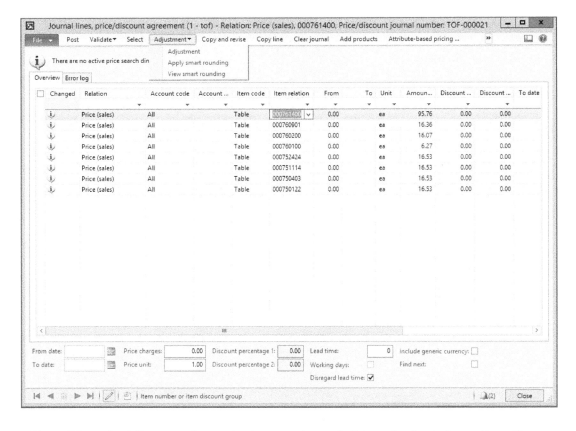

Then click on the **Adjustment** button in the menu bar and click on the **Apply Smart Rounding** menu item.

Applying Smart Rounding To Sales Prices

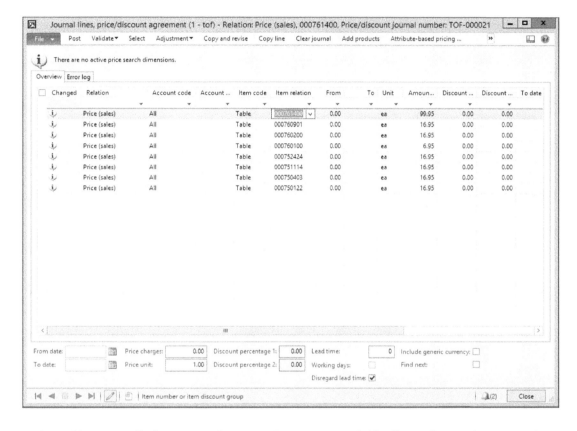

Almost like magic all of your irregular pricing is now neat and tidy all rounding to the nearest 95 cents.

How cool is that!

Configuring Tiered Pricing Agreements

Up until now we have been creating simple price lists that the customers will receive regardless of how much that they buy, but you are not limited to just that option. You can further refine your pricing by adding filters and selections based on quantity and even have prices based on effective dates.

Configuring Tiered Pricing Agreements

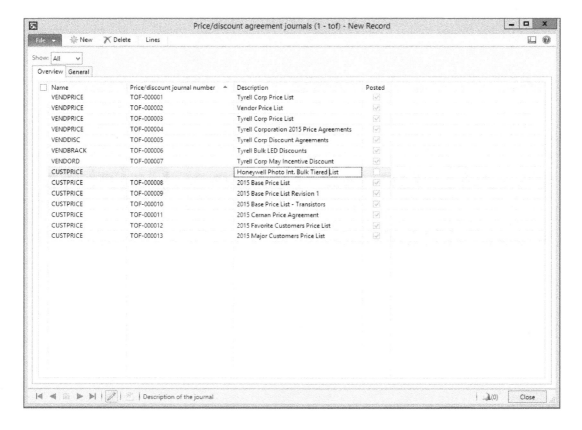

To do this, open up the **Price/Discount Agreement Journals** list page, click on the **New** button to create a new record, set the **Name** to **CUSTPRICE**, the **Description** to **Honeywell Photo Int. Bulk Tiered List** and then click on the **Lines** button in the menu bar.

daxc

Configuring Tiered Pricing Agreements

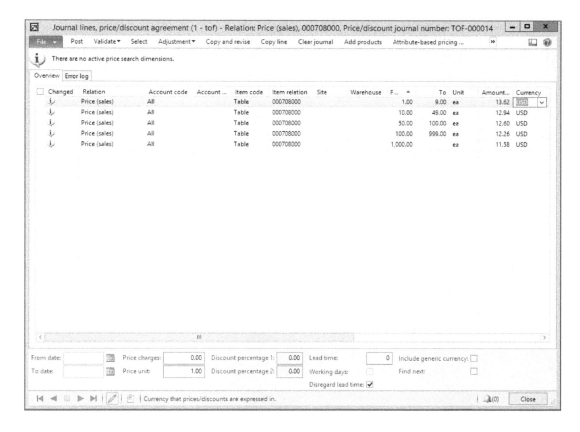

When the **Journal Lines** maintenance form is displayed, create multiple journal lines for the same product, but this time set the **From Quantity** and **To Quantity** so that you have pricing tiers that do not overlap and also have different **Amounts** for the price.

Configuring Tiered Pricing Agreements

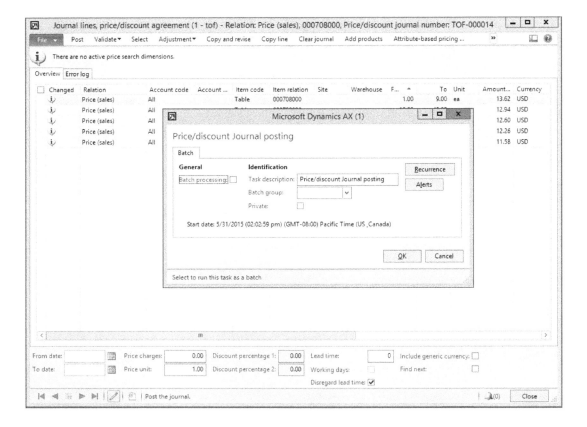

When you are done, click on the **Post** button in the menu bar to post the Trade Agreement and when the **Posting Confirmation** dialog box is displayed, click on the **OK** button.

Configuring Tiered Pricing Agreements

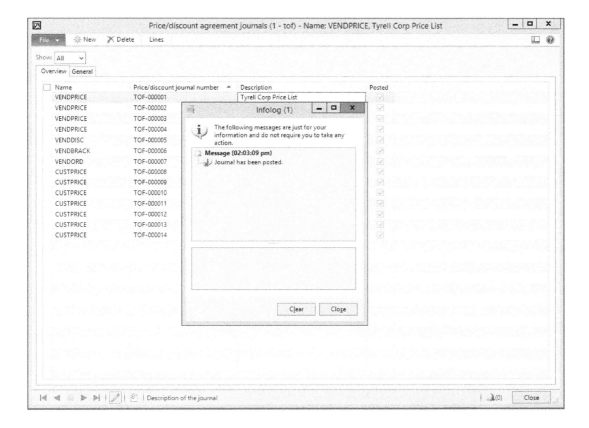

If everything works out then you will get an InfoLog that tells you that and you can click on the **Close** button to exit from the form.

Configuring Tiered Pricing Agreements

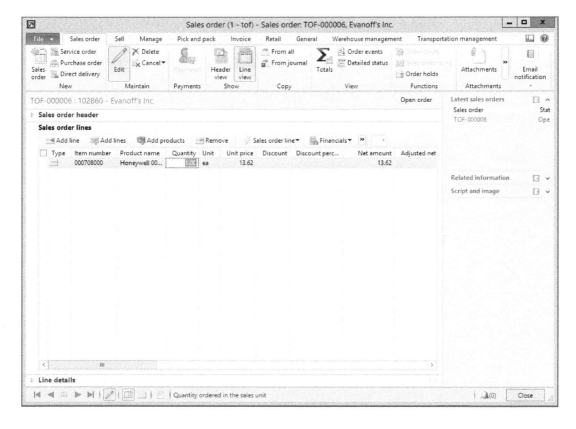

To test this out, create a new sales order for the product that you just created the price list for, and set the **Quantity** to **1**. You will see the first tiers price show up.

Configuring Tiered Pricing Agreements

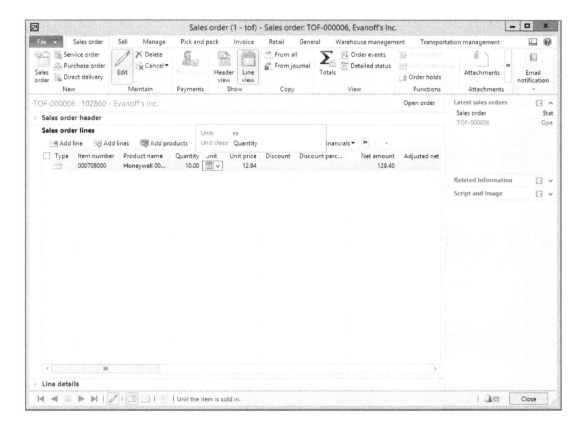

If you increase the **Quantity** to **10** then the new **Price** will be displayed.

Configuring Tiered Pricing Agreements

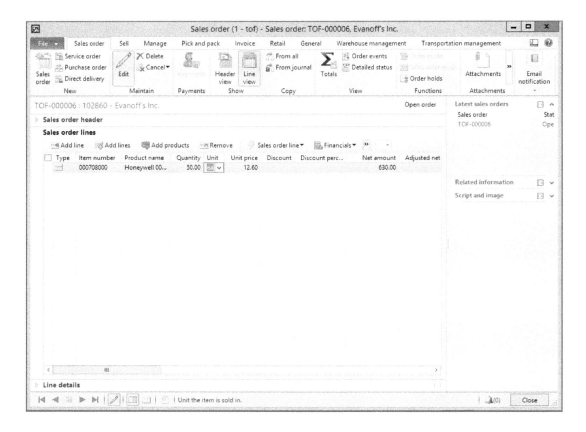

If you update it again to **50** then a new price will automatically be displayed.

How easy is that!

CONFIGURING SALES ORDER DISCOUNTS

Once you have the Sales Prices configured, the next area that you will probably want to look at are the Discounting capabilities within Dynamics AX. There are a few different types of discounts that you may want to take advantage of within the system, including **Line Discounts**, **Multiline Discounts** and also **Total Order Discounts**. With all of these different discounting options you will probably be able to handle almost any discounting structure that you can think of.

Creating Trade Agreement Types To Track Different Discounting Structures

Before we start setting up the discounts we first need to set up a few additional **Trade Agreement Types** that we will use to differentiate the different discounting structures.

Creating Trade Agreement Types To Track Different Discounting Structures

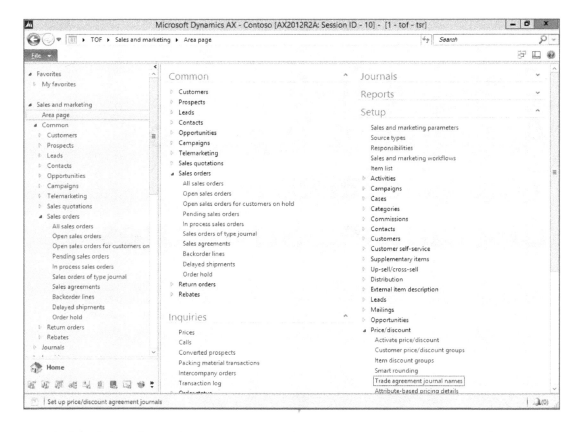

To do this, click on the **Trade Agreement Journal Names** menu item within the **Price/Discount** folder of the **Setup** group within the **Sales and Marketing** area page.

Creating Trade Agreement Types To Track Different Discounting Structures

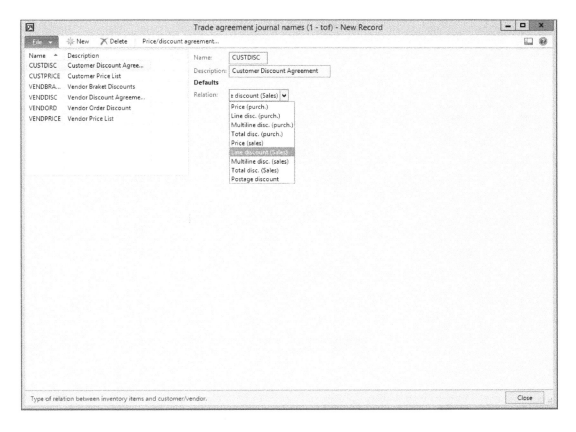

When the **Trade Agreement Journal Names** maintenance form is displayed, click on the **New** button in the menu bar to create a new record. Then set the **Name** to **CUSTDISC** and the **Description** to **Customer Discount Agreement**.

Then click on the **Relation** dropdown list and select the **Line Discount (Sales)** option.

Creating Trade Agreement Types To Track Different Discounting Structures

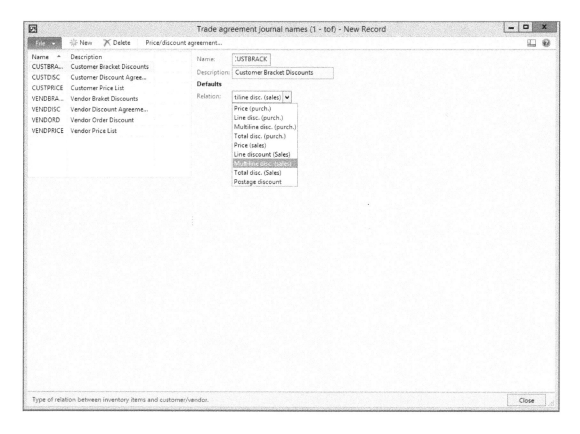

Click on the **New** button in the menu bar to create another new record. Then set the **Name** to **CUSTBRACK** and the **Description** to **Customer Bracket Discounts**.

Then click on the **Relation** dropdown list and select the **Multiline Disc (Sales)** option.

Creating Trade Agreement Types To Track Different Discounting Structures

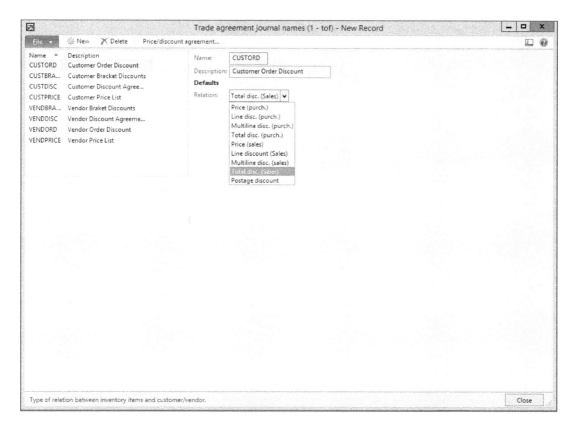

Click on the **New** button in the menu bar to create one last record. Then set the **Name** to **CUSTORD** and the **Description** to **Customer Order Discounts**.

Then click on the **Relation** dropdown list and select the **Total Disc (Sales)** option.

Creating Trade Agreement Types To Track Different Discounting Structures

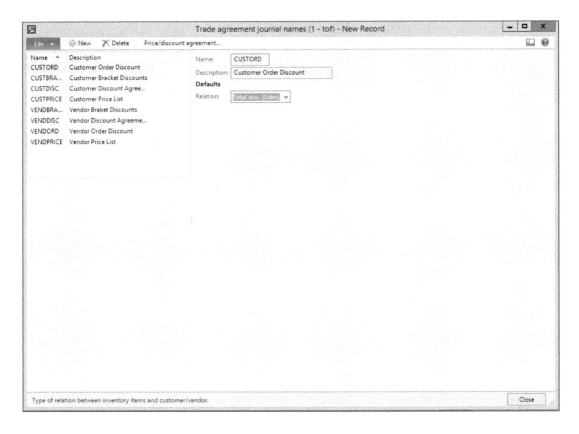

You can continue to add additional discount types if you like and when you are done just click on the **Close** button to exit from the form.

Configuring Customer Line Discount Agreements

Now we can start creating some discounts. The first one that we will create will be a simple customer discount agreement where the customer receives a flat discount on all of their order lines.

Configuring Customer Line Discount Agreements

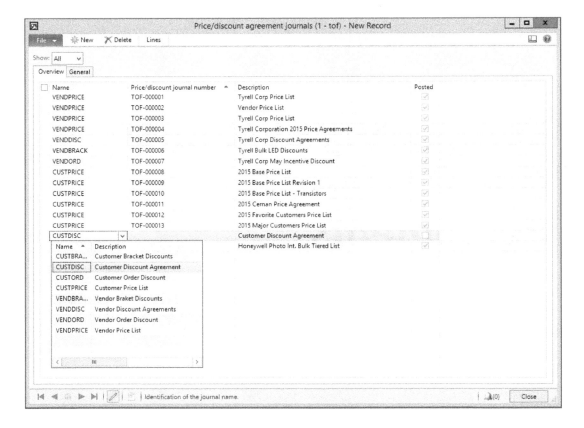

To do this, open up the **Price/Discount Agreement Journals** list page, click on the **New** button in the menu bar and then click on the **Name** field and select the **CUSTDISC** agreement type from the dropdown list.

Configuring Customer Line Discount Agreements

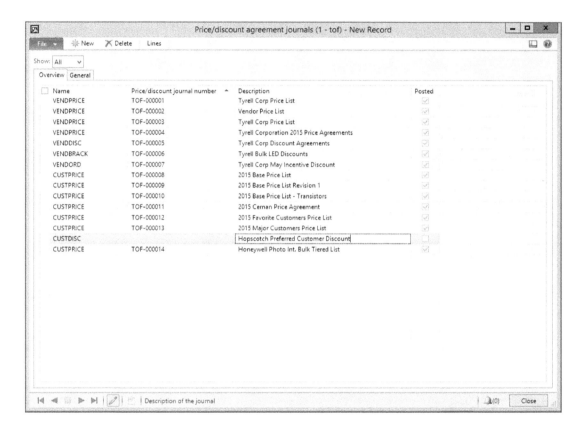

Then change the **Description** to something a little more descriptive like **Hopscotch Preferred Customer Discount**.

After you have done that, click on the **Lines** button in the menu bar.

Configuring Customer Line Discount Agreements

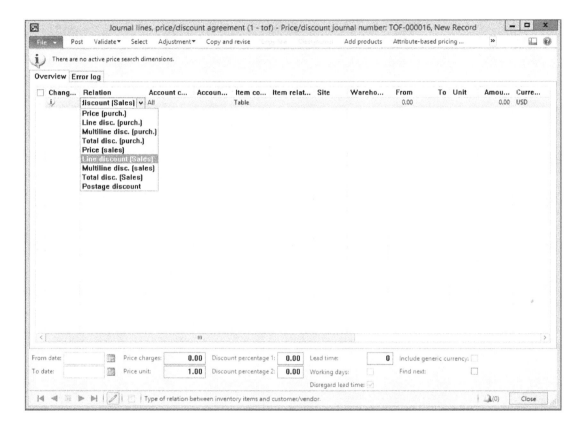

When the **Journal Lines** maintenance form is displayed, the **Relation** will automatically default in to be the **Line Discount (Sales)** option. You can change this if you want but for now just leave it as it is.

Configuring Customer Line Discount Agreements

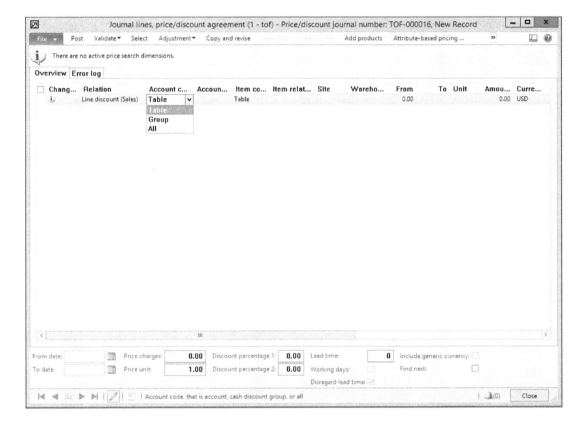

Then click on the **Account Code** dropdown list and select the **Table** option because this discount will only apply to one customer.

Configuring Customer Line Discount Agreements

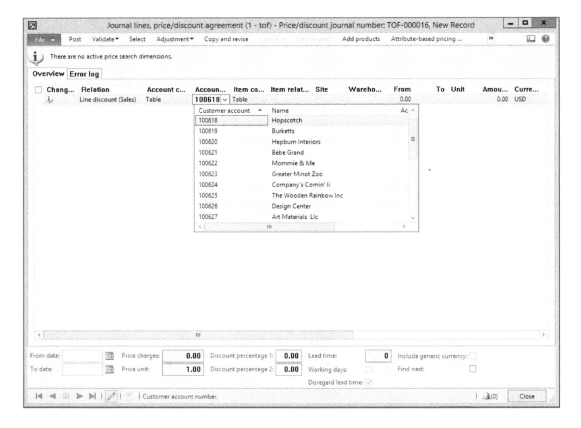

Then click on the **Account Relation** dropdown box and you will be able to choose the customer that you want to apply this discount to – in our case we choose **100618**.

Configuring Customer Line Discount Agreements

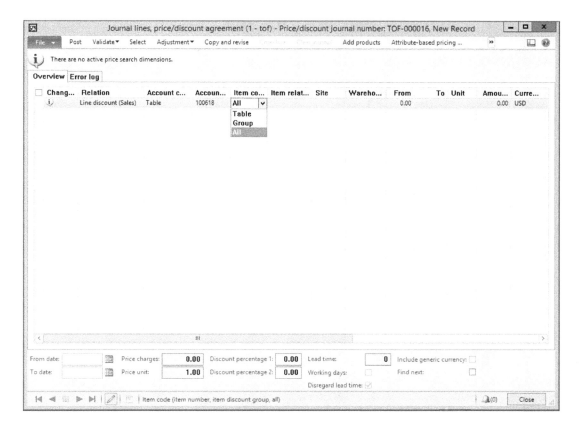

Click on the **Item Code** dropdown list and select the **All** option which will indicate that this discount will apply to all products that this customer purchases.

Configuring Customer Line Discount Agreements

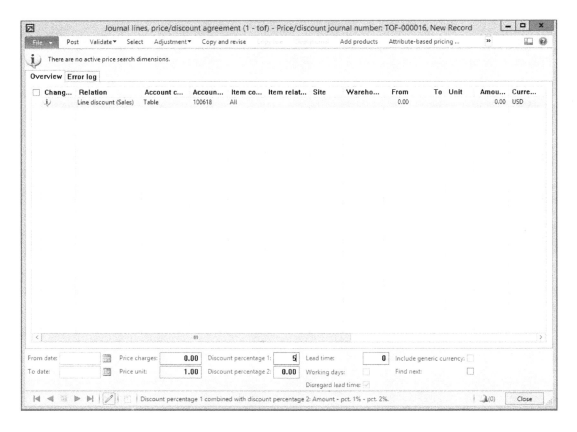

Now that you have the selection relations configured, look down in the footer of the form and you will see that there are fields called **Discount Percentage 1** and **Discount Percentage 2**. Set the **Discount Percentage 1** field to **5** to set the discount to 5%.

Configuring Customer Line Discount Agreements

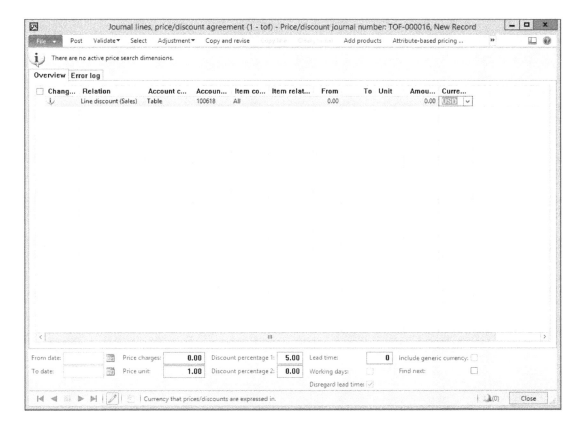

Before we move on, lets tidy up the form a little to make it a little easier to use. Start off by hiding the **Site** and **Warehouse** fields.

Configuring Customer Line Discount Agreements

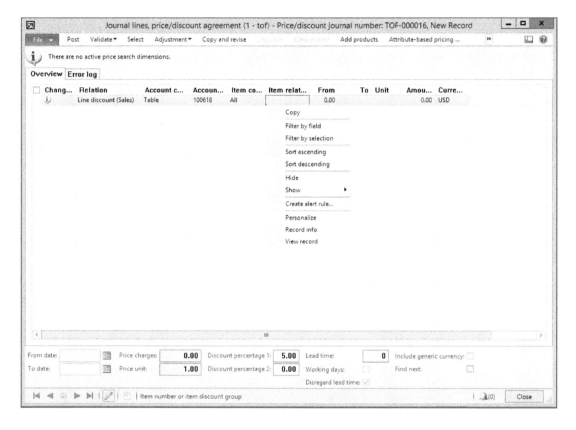

Also, updating the Discounts in the footer may seem a little odd, so let's add them to the table. To do this, right-mouse-click on the grids table and select the **Personalize** menu item.

Configuring Customer Line Discount Agreements

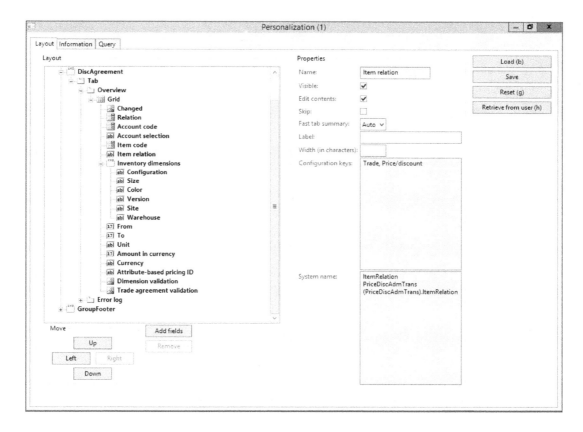

When the **Personalization** form is displayed, you will see all of the different fields within the grid. Click on the **Add Fields** button.

Configuring Customer Line Discount Agreements

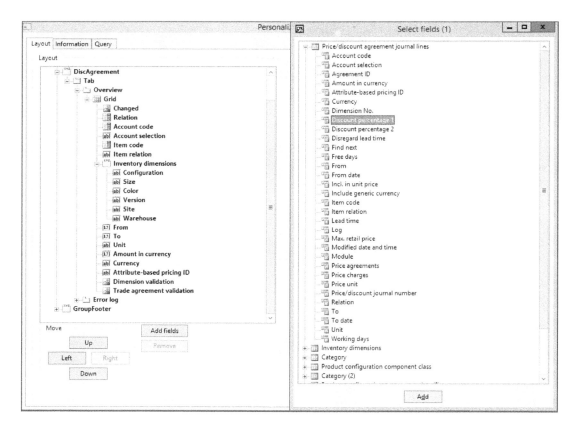

This will open up a field browser with all of the available fields that you can add to the form. Select the **Discount Percentage 1** field and then click on the **Add** button.

Configuring Customer Line Discount Agreements

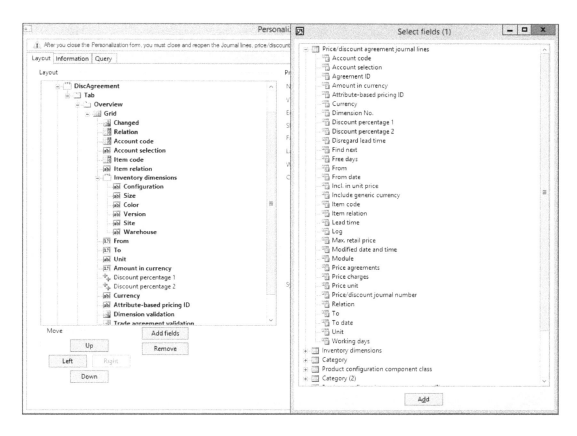

Then click on the **Discount Percentage 2** field and click on the **Add** button again to add it to the grid. You will notice that both of these fields are showing up in the grid details now.

Configuring Customer Line Discount Agreements

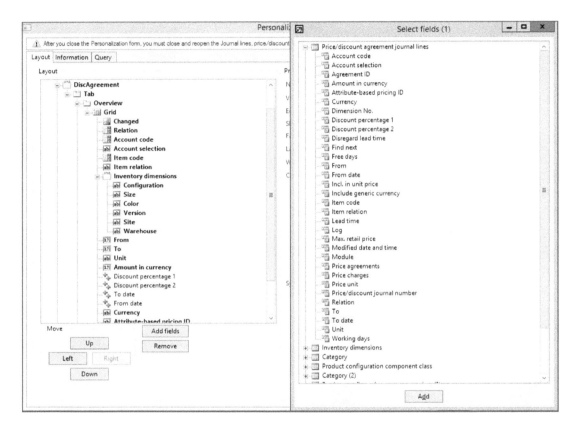

To finish the process off, add the **To Date** field and also the **From Date** so that we can use them later on.

Configuring Customer Line Discount Agreements

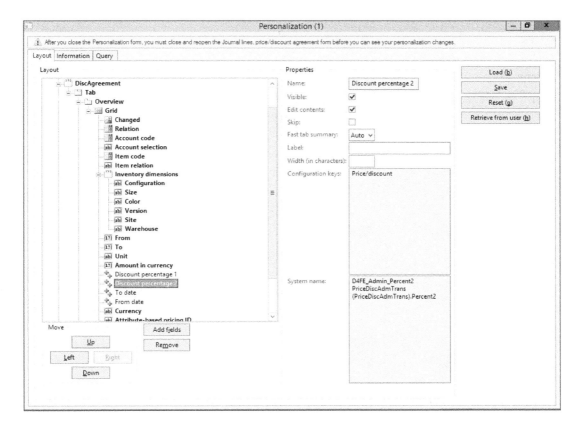

When you have done that, close out of the **Field Explorer** and then close down the **Personalization** form.

Configuring Customer Line Discount Agreements

Now you will see the two discount fields are in the grid and also the to and from dates. That makes things a little better.

Configuring Customer Line Discount Agreements

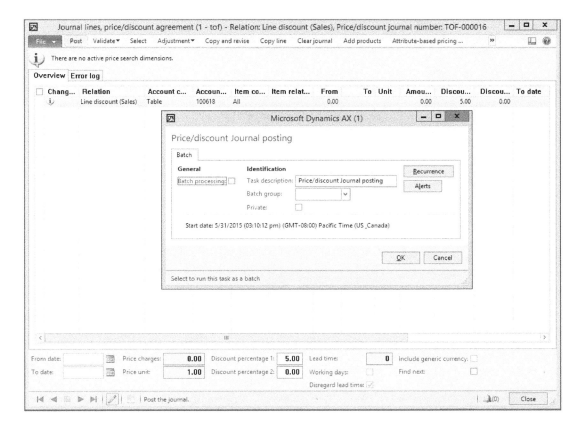

Now just click on the **Post** button in the menu bar, and when the **Posting Confirmation** dialog box is displayed, click on the **OK** button.

Configuring Customer Line Discount Agreements

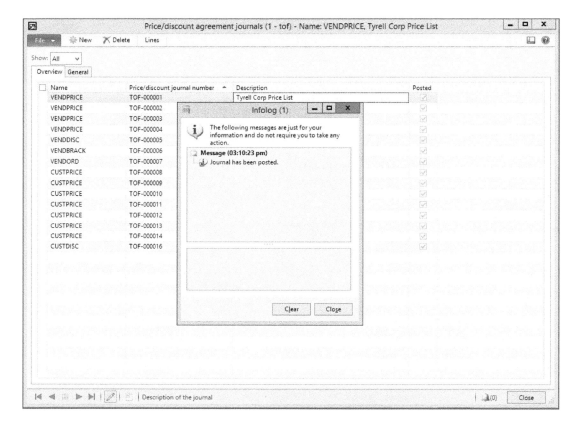

If everything works out you will get a message saying that the Journal was posted and you can click on the **Close** button to exit from the form.

Configuring Customer Line Discount Agreements

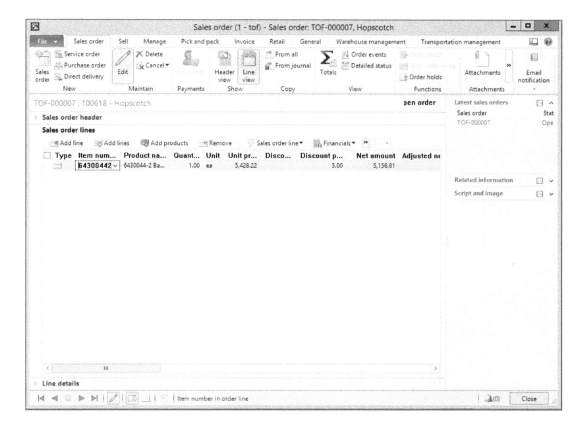

To test the disco0unt, just enter in an order for the customer and you will notice that every line that you enter for them will have a discount automatically applied to them.

That was easy.

Creating Tiered Volume Based Line Discounts

You can get even more clever with your discounts by creating quantity based tiered discounts.

Creating Tiered Volume Based Line Discounts

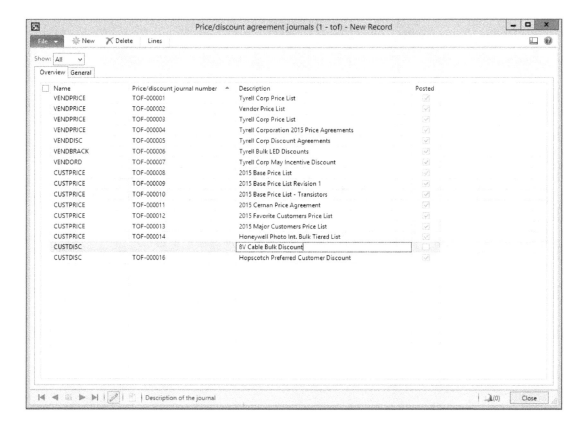

To do this, open up the **Price/Discount Agreement Journals** list page, click on the **New** button in the menu bar to create a new record, set the **Name** to be **CUSTDISC** and the **Description** to **BV Cable Bulk Discount**. Then click on the **Line** button in the menu bar.

Creating Tiered Volume Based Line Discounts

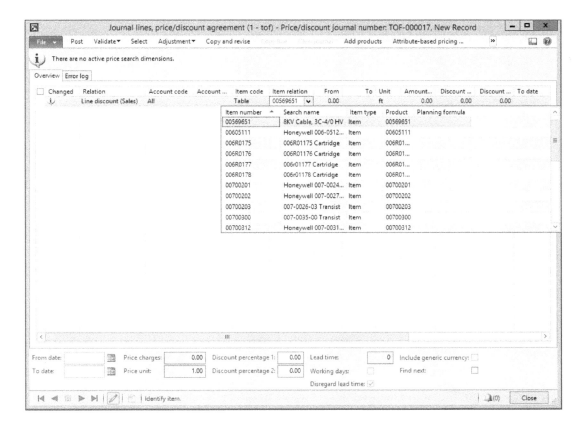

When the **Journal Lines** maintenance form is displayed, set the **Account Code** to **All**, the **Item Code** to **Table** and then from the **Item Relation** table select the **00569651** product.

Creating Tiered Volume Based Line Discounts

Then set the **From** field to **0.00**, the **To** field to **100.00** and the **Discount** field to **1** to set up a discount of 1% for anyone ordering between 0 and 100 ft of the product.

Creating Tiered Volume Based Line Discounts

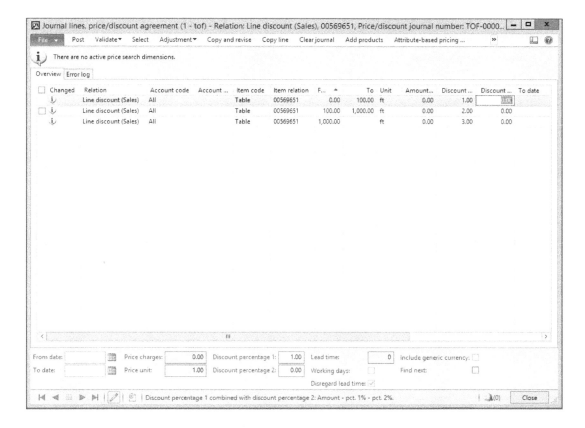

Now click on the New button in the menu bar to add another line for the same customer and product combination but set the second one to be **From 100.00** ft **To 1,000.00** ft and set the discount to **2** %.

Click on the New button in the menu bar once more to add the final line for the same customer and product combination but set the second one to be **From 1,000.00** ft and set the discount to **3** %.

Creating Tiered Volume Based Line Discounts

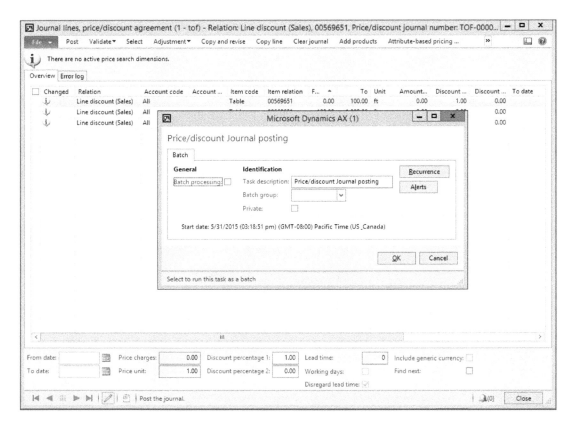

When you have done that, click on the **Post** button in the menu bar and when the **Confirmation** dialog box is displayed, click on the **OK** button to post the journal.

Creating Tiered Volume Based Line Discounts

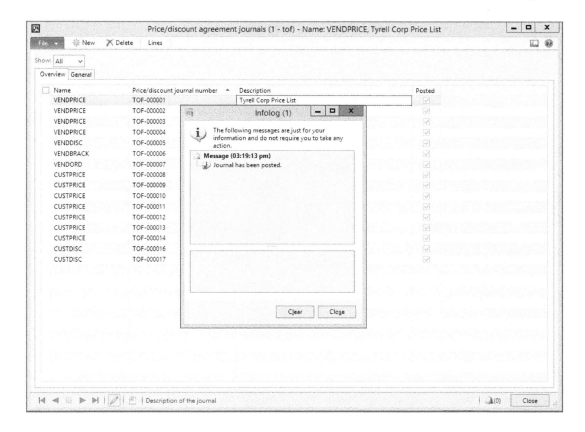

If everything is working right you will get an InfoLog saying so and you can just click on the **Close** button to exit from the form.

Creating Tiered Volume Based Line Discounts

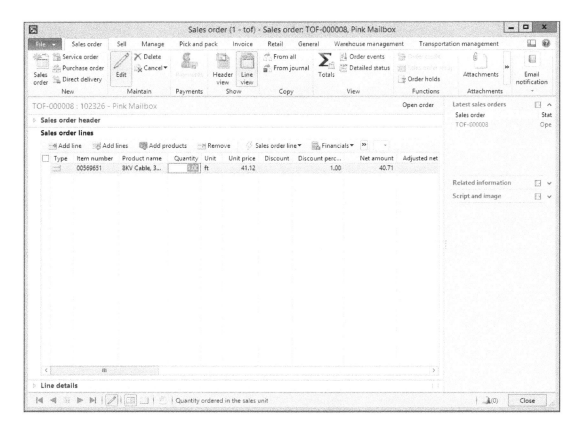

Now if you want to see it in action, just enter in an order for any customer and add the **00569651** product to the line. You will notice that if you have a **Quantity** of **1** then the **Discount Percentage** is **1%**.

Creating Tiered Volume Based Line Discounts

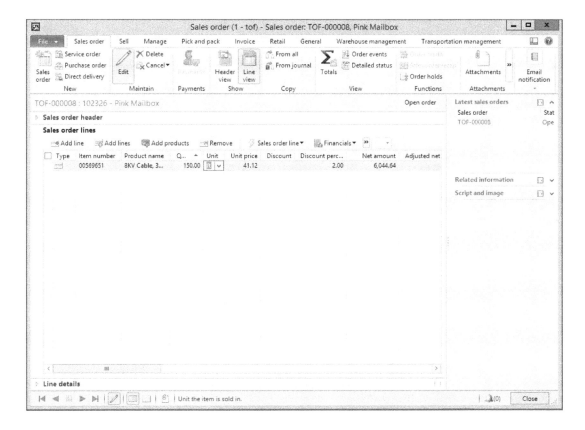

If you order **150** ft of the product then the **Discount Percentage** will change to **2** % because the product is now in a higher discount tier.

Creating Tiered Volume Based Line Discounts

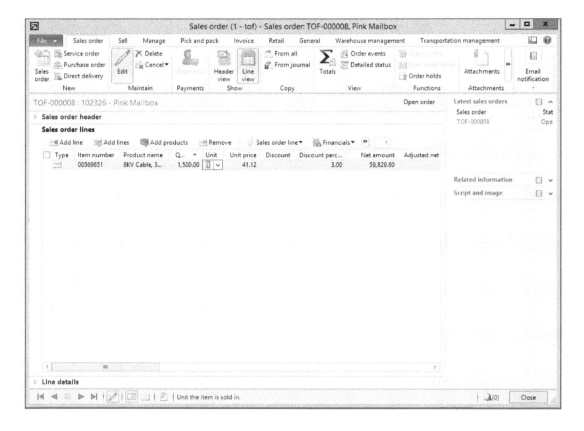

And if you order **1,500** ft of the product then you will be bumped up into the **3** % discount tier.

Creating Product Line Discount Groups

You don't have to set up the discounts individually though for each product like we have been doing so far though. If you have products that you want to assign the same discount structure to then you can create **Line Discount Groups** that you then assign the products to and they will all have the same discounting rules applied to them.

Creating Product Line Discount Groups

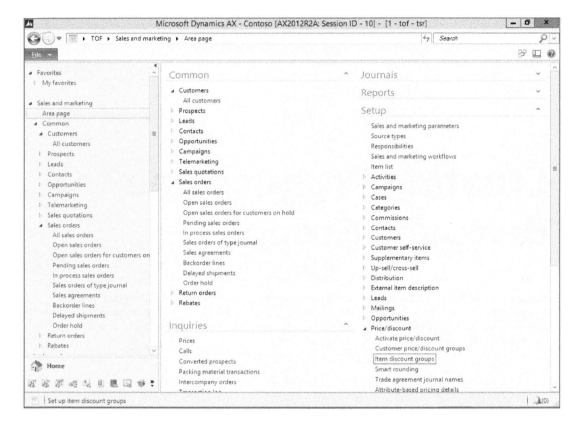

To do this, click on the **Item Discount Groups** menu item within the **Price/Discount** folder of the **Setup** group within the **Sales and Marketing** area page.

Creating Product Line Discount Groups

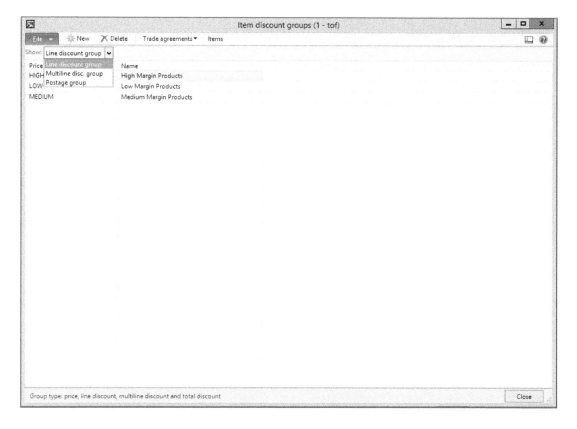

When the **Item Discount Groups** maintenance form is displayed, chick on the **Show** dropdown list and select the **Line Discount Group** option.

Creating Product Line Discount Groups

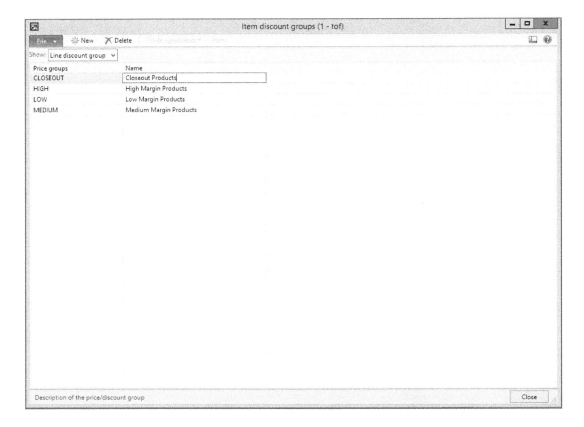

Note: You may notice that there are already some codes defined here. That is because this is the same form that Purchasing uses, and if you are clever enough you can actually reuse the same discount groups if you like.

Just click on the **New** button in the menu bar to create a new record, set the **Price Group** to **CLOSEOUT** and the **Name** to **Closeout Products**.

When you have done that just click on the **Close** button to exit from the form.

Associating Products With Discount Groups

Now that you have your discount groups configured you just need to associate them with the products that you want to apply them to.

Associating Products With Discount Groups

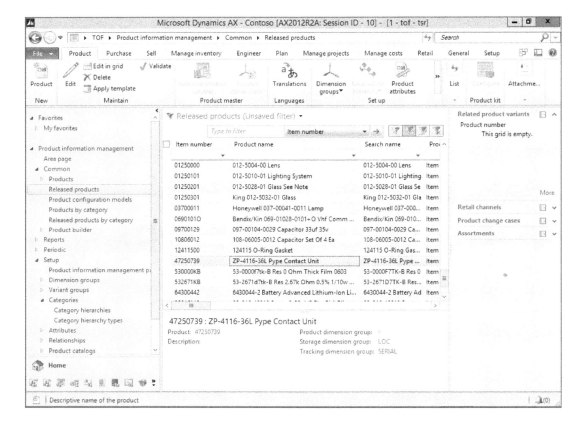

To do this open up the **Released Products** list page and select the product that you want to apply the discount group to.

Associating Products With Discount Groups

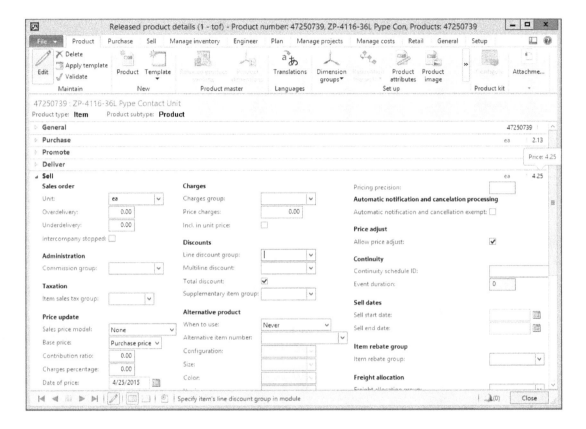

When the **Released Product Details** form is displayed, expand out the **Sell** fast tab and you will see that there are a few discounting fields that we are able to configure within the **Discounts** field group.

Associating Products With Discount Groups

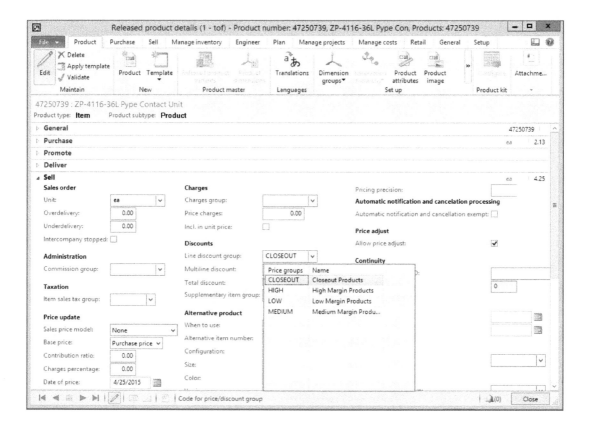

Click on the **Line Discount Group** dropdown list and select the **CLOSEOUT** discount group code.

Associating Products With Discount Groups

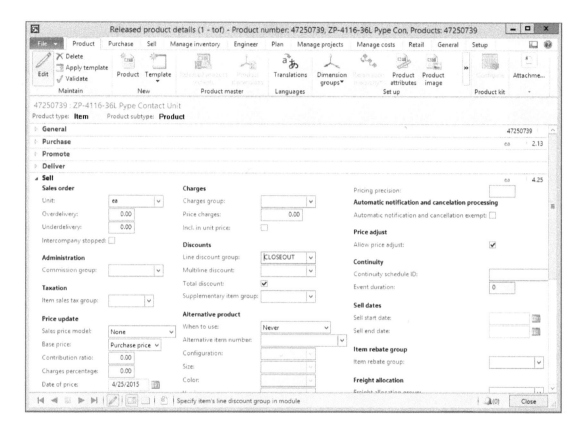

After you have done that you can click on the **Close** button and then repeat the process for any other products that you want to include in the group.

Configuring Product Group Line Discounts

Now we can set up a line discount for the products within the **Discount Groups**.

Configuring Product Group Line Discounts

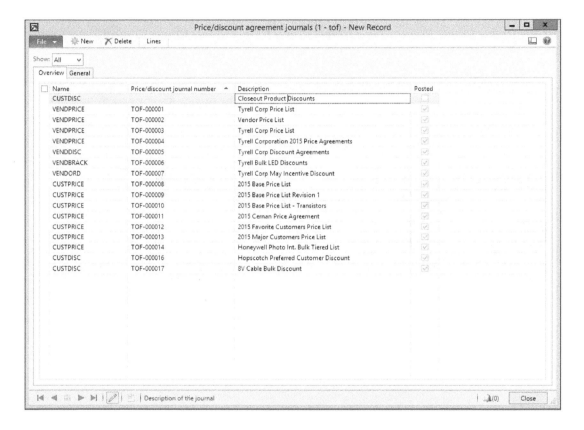

To do this, open up the **Product/Discount Agreement Journals** maintenance form, click on the **New** button in the menu bar, set the **Name** to **CUSTDISC** and the **Description** to **Closeout Product Discounts** and then click on the **Lines** button in the menu bar.

Configuring Product Group Line Discounts

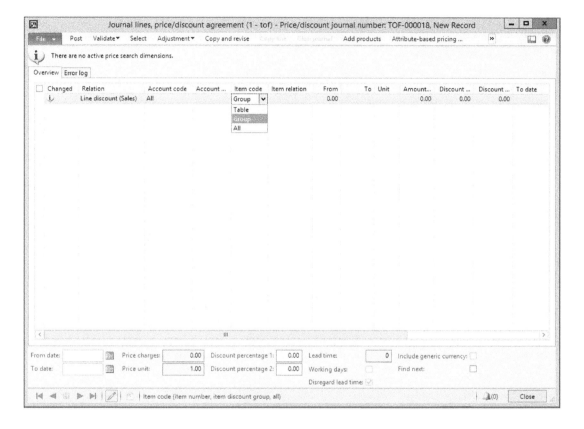

When the **Journal Lines** maintenance form is displayed, leave the **Account Code** as **All**, and then click on the **Item Code** dropdown list and select the **Group** option to apply this discount to a **Product Group**.

Configuring Product Group Line Discounts

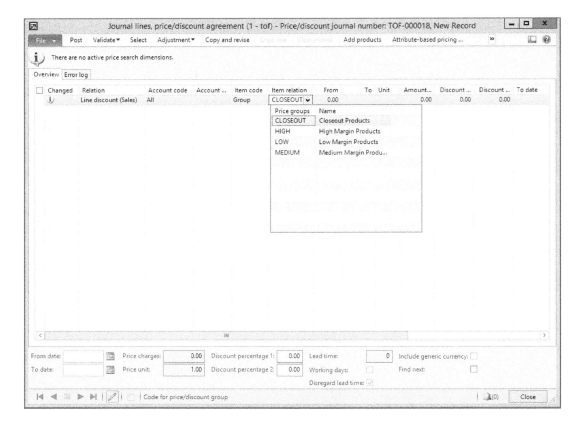

Now click on the **Item Relation** dropdown list and select the **CLOSEOUT** product group to apply the discount to.

Configuring Product Group Line Discounts

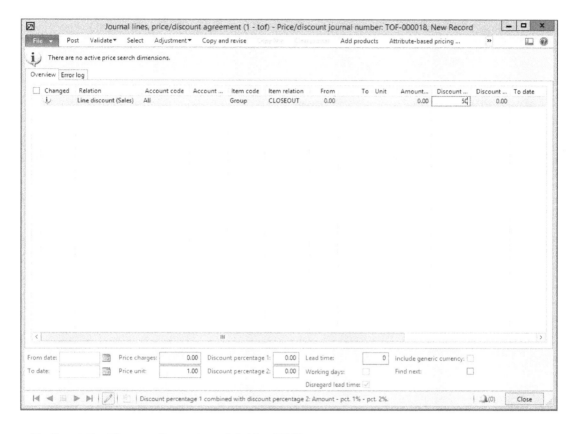

Finally set the **Discount Percentage 1** field to **50** %.

Configuring Product Group Line Discounts

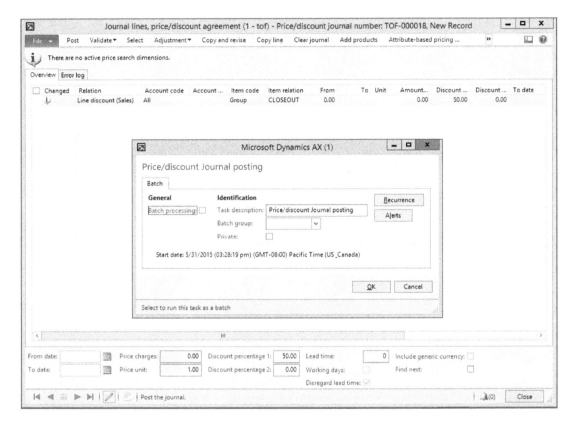

Then click on the **Post** button in the menu bar and click on the **OK** button in the posting confirmation dialog box.

Configuring Product Group Line Discounts

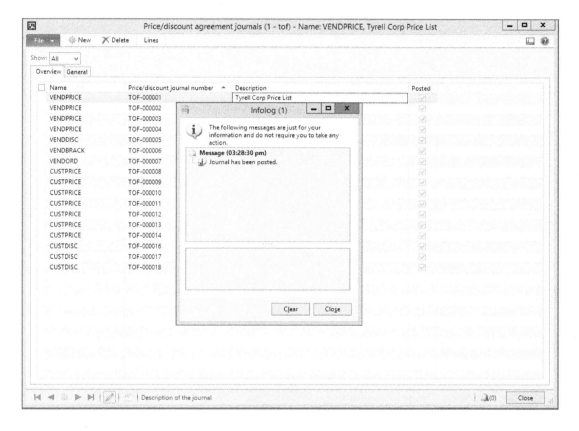

If everything is set up correctly then you will get an InfoLog saying so and you can click on the **Close** button to exit from the form.

Configuring Product Group Line Discounts

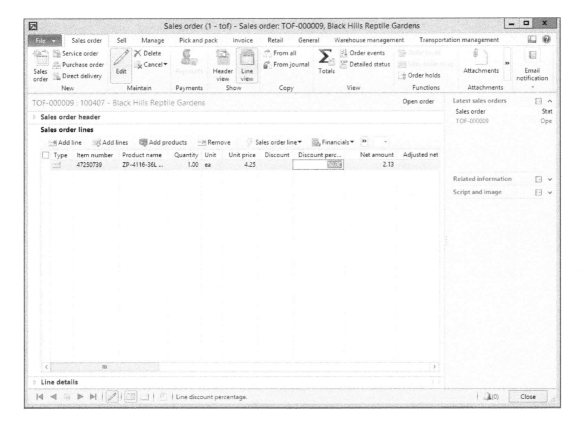

To test this out, just create a sales order for the closeout product and you will see that a 50% discount is automatically applied to that order line.

Creating Multi-Line Product Discount Groups

There is one more variation of the line discounts that we will look at and that is where you have a group of products that you want to give a discount to based on the total sales quantity of all the lines rather than for just the individual line quantities. For this type of discount you will want to use the **Multiline Discount.** The first step in the setup of this type of discount is to set up a **Multiline Discount Group**.

Creating Multi-Line Customer Discounts

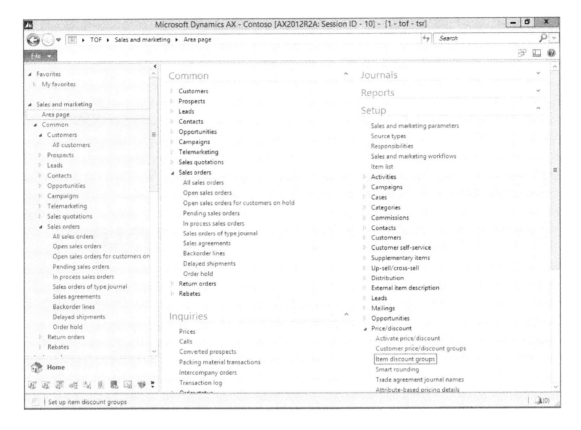

To do this click on the **Item Discount Groups** menu item within the **Price/Discount** folder of the **Setup** group within the **Sales and Marketing** area page.

Creating Multi-Line Customer Discounts

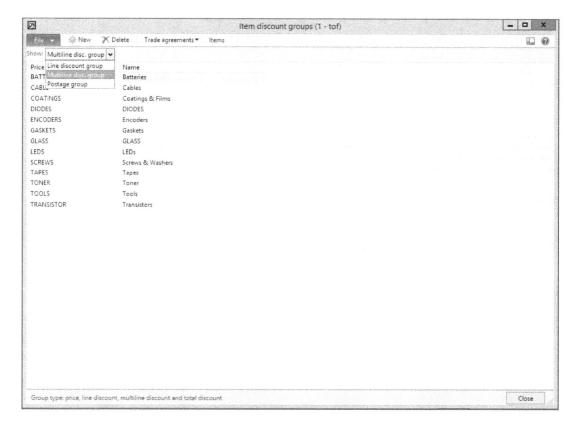

When the **Item Discount Groups** maintenance form is displayed, click on the **Show** and select the **Multiline Disc. Group** option.

Creating Multi-Line Customer Discounts

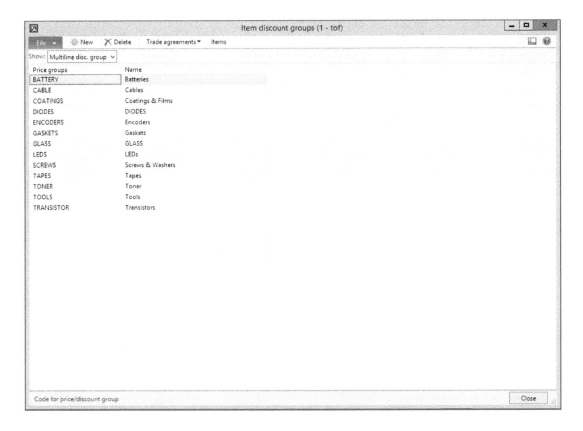

Note: You may notice that there are already some codes defined here. That is because this is the same form that Purchasing uses, and if you are clever enough you can actually reuse the same discount groups if you like.

If you want to add a new group then just click on the **New** button in the menu bar to create a new record, enter the **Price Group** and the **Name**, although in this case we will reuse the **Multiline Discount Groups** that have already been set up.

When you have done that just click on the **Close** button to exit from the form.

Associating Products With Multiline Discount Groups

Now that you have your multiline discount groups configured you just need to associate them with the products that you want to apply them to.

Creating Multi-Line Customer Discounts

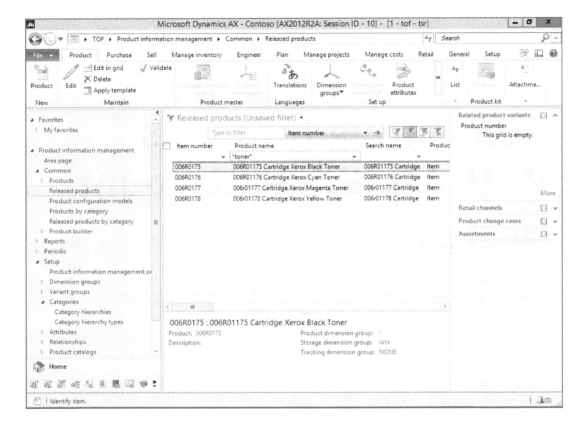

To do this, open up the **Released Products** maintenance form, find the products that you want to group together for the discount, and then open them up.

Creating Multi-Line Customer Discounts

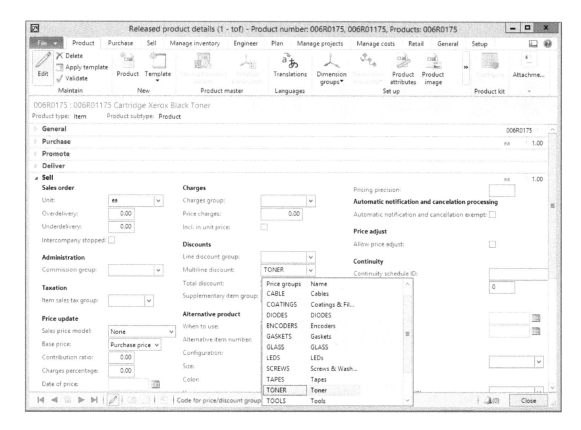

When the **Released Product Details** form is displayed, expand out the **Sell** fast tab, click on the **Multiline Discount** dropdown list and select the **Multiline Discount Group** that you want to assign the product to – in this case **TONER**.

When you have done that click on the **Close** button to exit from the form and then repeat the process for all of the other products within the discount group.

Creating Multiline Order Discounts

Now that we have the codes configured and the products linked to them we can set up a **Multiline Discount** and see it in action.

Creating Multiline Order Discounts

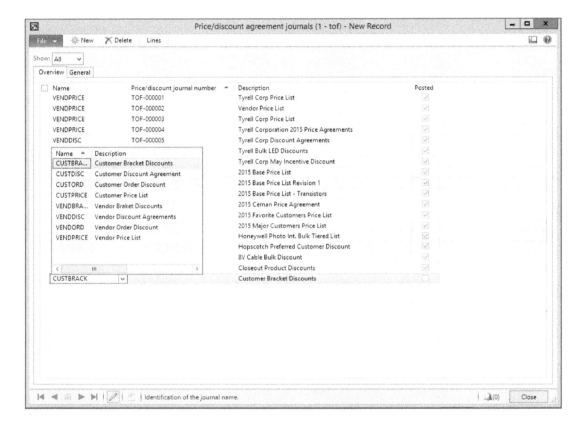

To do this, open up the **Price/Discount Agreement Journals** maintenance form, click on the **New** button in the menu bar to create a new record, and then click on the **Name** dropdown lost and select the **CUSTBRACK** discount journal name.

Creating Multiline Order Discounts

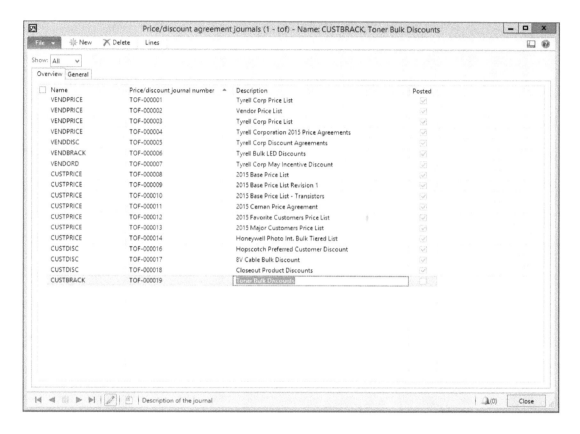

Then set the **Description** to be **Toner Bulk Discounts**.

When you have done that, click on the **Lines** button in the menu bar.

Creating Multiline Order Discounts

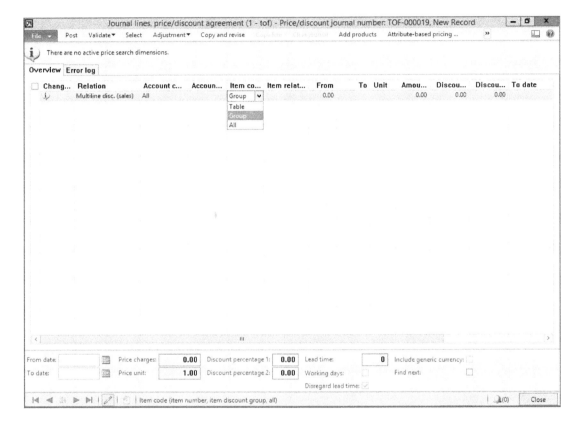

When the **Journal Lines** maintenance form is displayed, leave the **Account Code** to **All** to apply this discount to all of the customers and then click on the **Item Code** dropdown list and select the **Group** option.

Creating Multiline Order Discounts

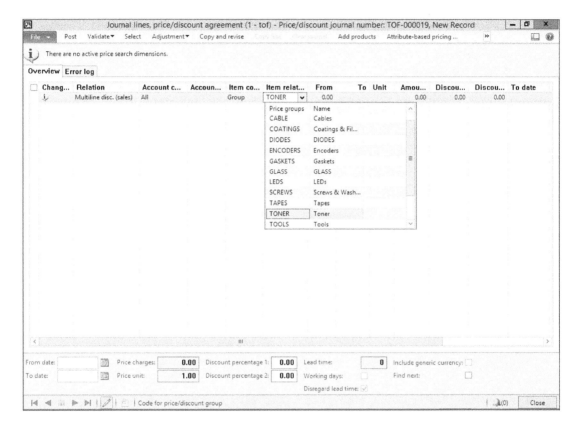

That will allow you to click on the **Item Relation** dropdown list and select the **TONER** multiline discount group code.

Creating Multiline Order Discounts

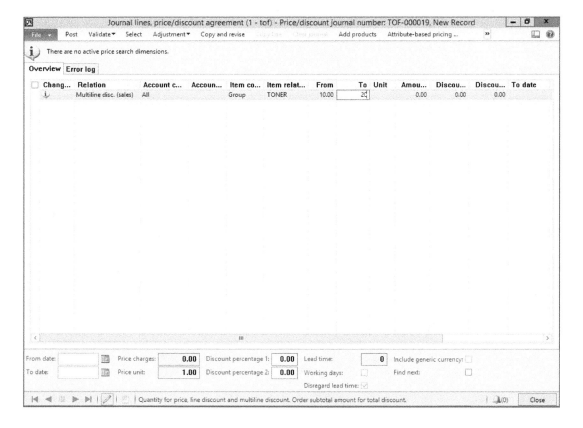

In this example we will create a tiered discount for any sales above 10 units, so set the **To** quantity field to **10** and the **To** quantity field to **20**.

Creating Multiline Order Discounts

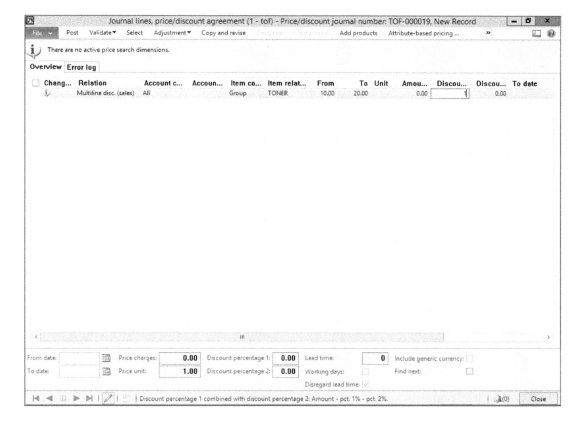

And then set the **Discount** percentage to **1**.

Creating Multiline Order Discounts

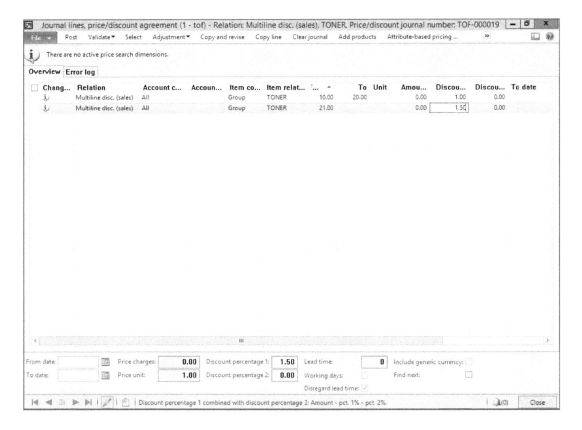

Add another line to the Journal Lines (**CTRL+N**) for the multiline discount group of **TONER**, set the **From** quantity to **21**, leave the **To** quantity field blank to have no upper limit and then set the **Discount Percentage 1** field for this line to be **1.5** %.

Creating Multiline Order Discounts

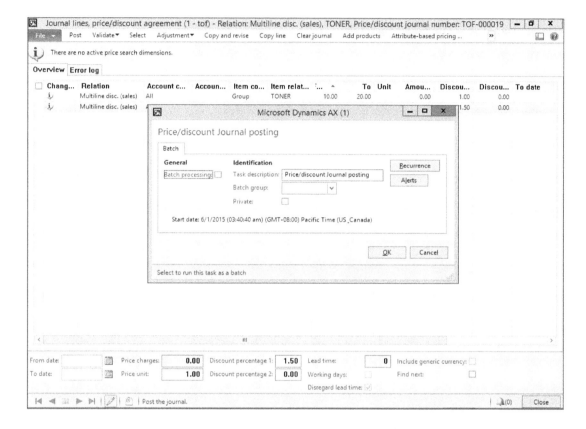

Now click on the **Post** button in the menu bar and when the confirmation dialog box id displayed, click on the **OK** button.

Creating Multiline Order Discounts

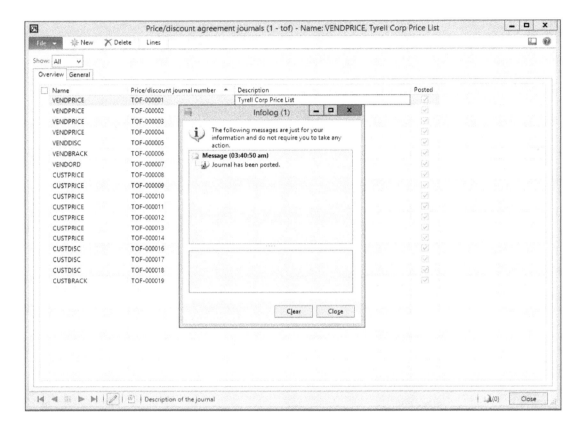

If everything is good then you will get an InfoLog saying that the journal has been posted and you can click on the **Close** button to exit from the form.

Creating Multiline Order Discounts

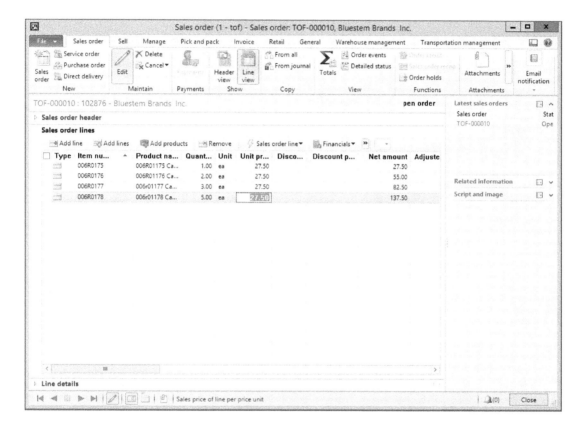

To see the multiline discounts in action just enter in a sales order for the **TONER** products that you set up and make sure that the combined quantity is above 10 units.

Creating Multiline Order Discounts

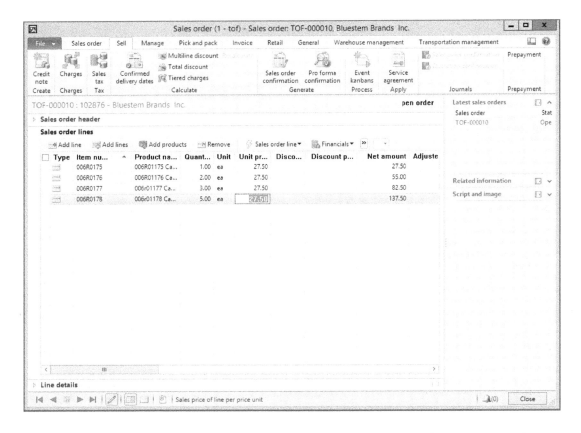

Note: Depending on the setup the multiline discounts are calculated at different points in the ordering process, but you can give them a little bit of a nudge if you like and force the system to recalculate them just by clicking on the **Multiline Discount** button within the **Calculate** group of the **Sell** ribbon bar.

Creating Multiline Order Discounts

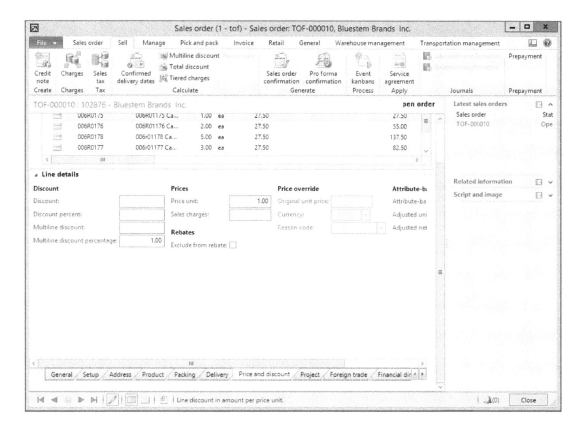

If you want to see the multiline discount that has been applied to the line, just expand the **Line Discounts** tab group at the footer of the order and select the **Price and Discount** footer tab. There you will see that a 1% discount has been applied to all of the lines.

Creating Multiline Order Discounts

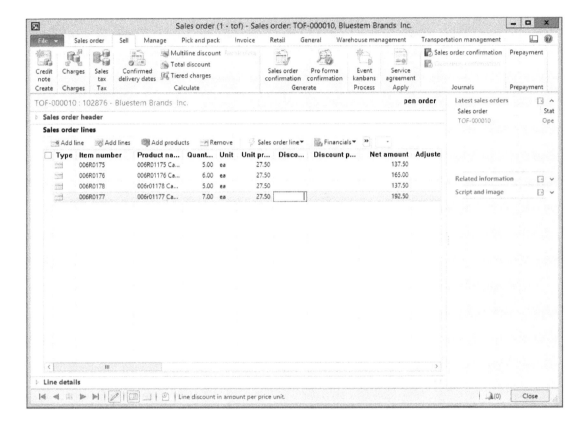

To see the different tiers, just increase the total order about to a quantity of more than 20 units.

Creating Multiline Order Discounts

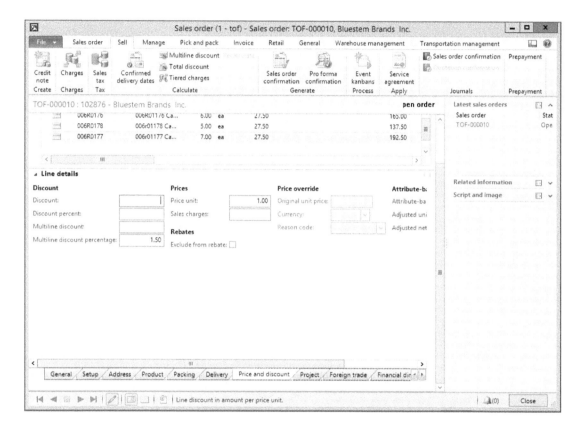

If you return back to the **Line Details** you will now see that the lines have been given a **Multiline Discount** of 1.5%.

How easy is that!

CONFIGURING ORDER CHARGES

Sometimes you just want to add an additional charge or adjustment to your sales orders. These charges could be for things like freight, handling, packaging, penalties, dings & dents markdowns and just because adjustments. And these could be associated with the order in general, or just specific to the individual product lines. But you don't really want to have to create products for them on the to add to the sales order because it's just a maintenance headache to remove these from reports, and it just looks untidy.

Don't worry, Dynamics AX has an additional feature that you can use within the Sales Orders called **Charges** that you can use to make miscellaneous adjustments to sales orders and sales order lines at any time. These can also post to their own main accounts within the ledger so that you can track their costs and they can even be set up as automatic charges that are always applied to the orders.

For anything that you don't want to set up a price or discount structure for, these charges will handle it.

Configuring Charge Codes

To start off we just need to configure some **Charge Codes** that we can use within the Sales Orders.

Configuring Charge Codes

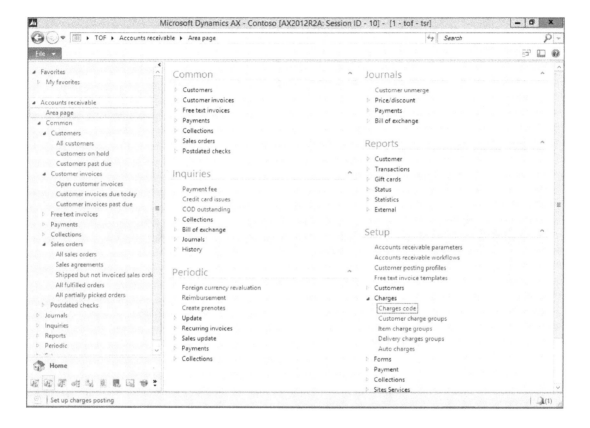

To do this, click on the **Charge Codes** menu item within the **Charges** folder of the **Setup** group within the **Accounts Receivable** area page.

Configuring Charge Codes

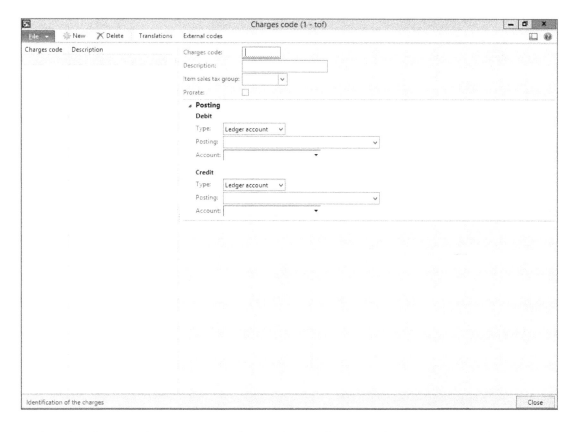

When the **Charge Codes** maintenance form is displayed, click on the **New** button in the menu bar to create a new record.

Configuring Charge Codes

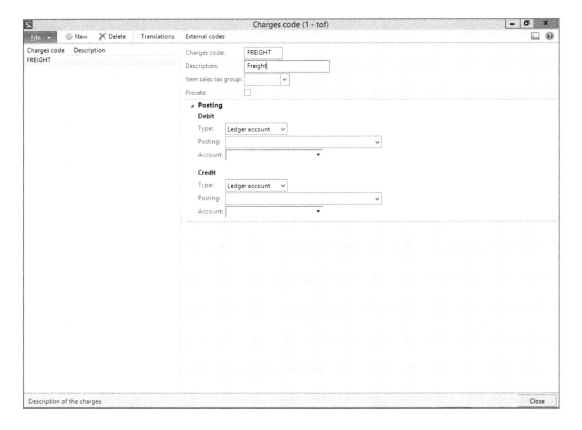

Then set the **Charge Code** to **FREIGHT** and the **Description** to **Freight**.

Configuring Charge Codes

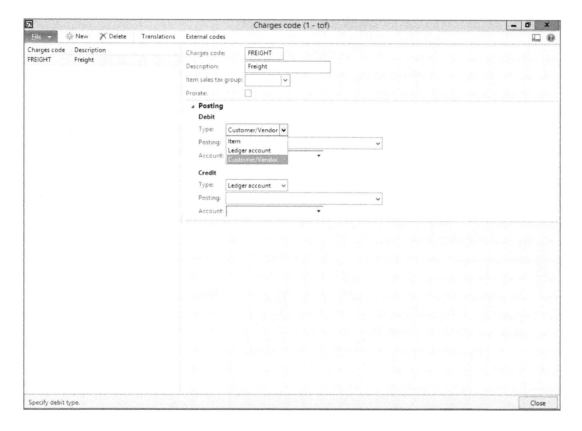

Now click on the **Debit Type** dropdown list and change it to **Customer/Vendor** to post to the account on the Customer/Vendor profile.

Configuring Charge Codes

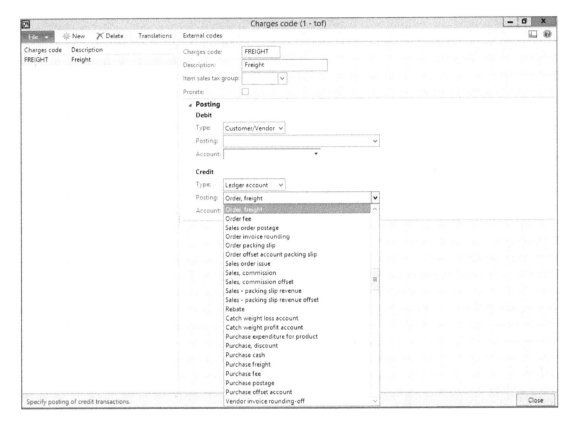

Then leave the **Credit Type** as **Ledger Account** and click on the **Credit Posting** dropdown list and select **Order, freight**.

Configuring Charge Codes

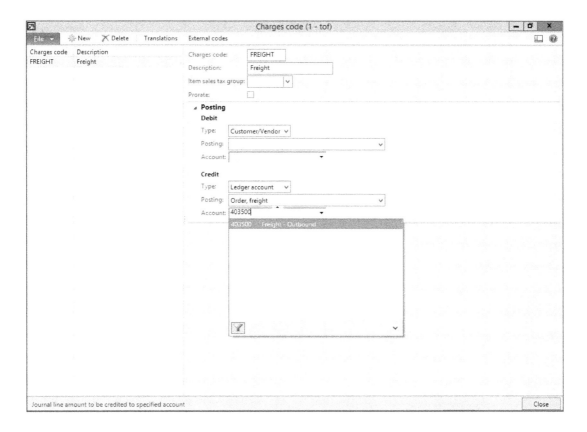

Finally set the **Credit Account** to **401350** to post to the **Freight** main account.

Configuring Charge Codes

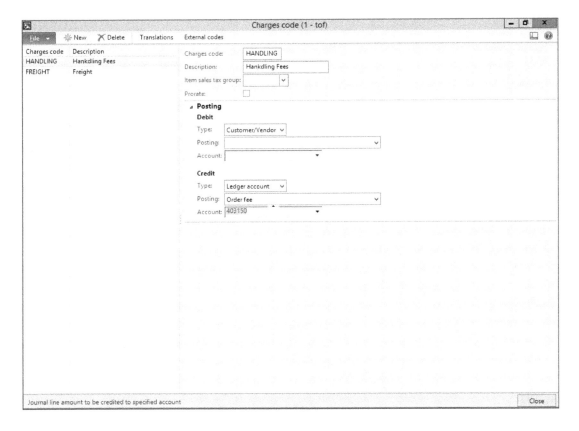

Next we will create another **Charge Code** for miscellaneous handling charges. To do this, click on the **New** button in the menu bar to create a new record.

Set the **Charge Code** to **HANDLING** and the **Description** to **Handling**.

Click on the **Debit Type** dropdown list and change it to **Customer/Vendor**.

Then leave the **Credit Type** as **Ledger Account** and click on the **Credit Posting** dropdown list and select **Order fee**.

Finally set the **Credit Account** to **401350**.

Configuring Charge Codes

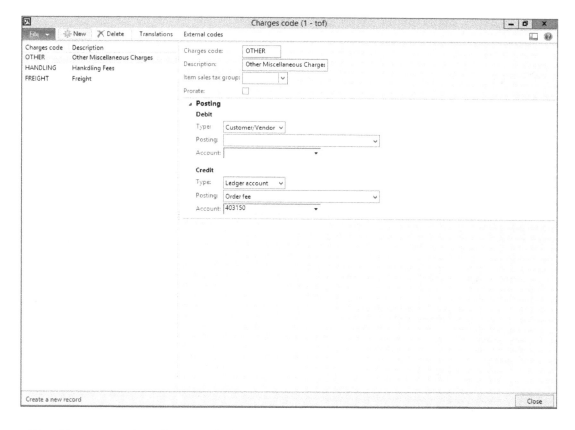

We will create one last **Charge Code** for anything else. To do this, click on the **New** button in the menu bar to create a new record.

Set the **Charge Code** to **OTHER** and the **Description** to **Other Miscellaneous Charge**.

Click on the **Debit Type** dropdown list and change it to **Customer/Vendor**.

Then leave the **Credit Type** as **Ledger Account** and click on the **Credit Posting** dropdown list and select **Order fee**.

Finally set the **Credit Account** to **401350**.

After you have done that click on the **Close** button to exit from the form.

Adding Charges To Orders

Now that we have the **Charge Codes** configured we can start using them on the Sales Orders at either the header level, or at the line level.

Adding Charges To Orders

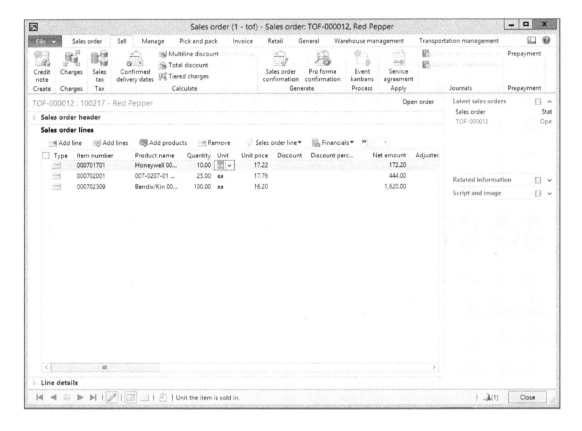

To do this just create a new **Sales Order** with a few lines on it. Then click on the **Charges** button within the **Charges** group of the **Sell** ribbon bar.

Adding Charges To Orders

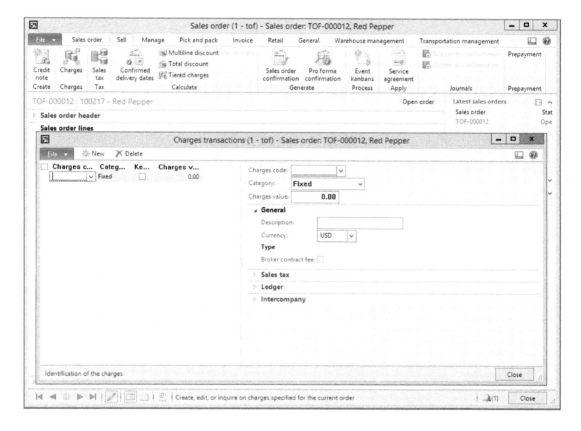

When the **Charges Transactions** maintenance form is displayed, click on the **New** button in the menu bar to create a new record.

Adding Charges To Orders

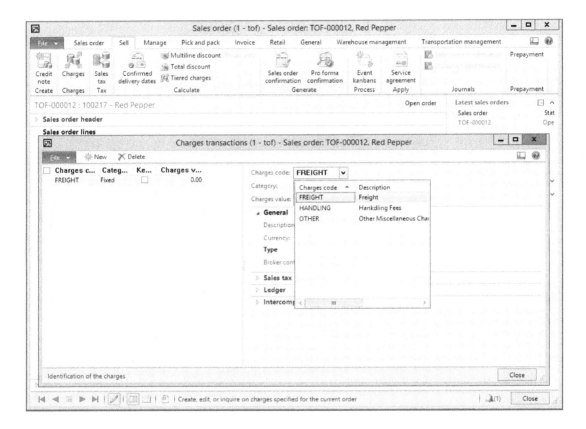

Then click on the **Charge Code** dropdown list and select the **FREIGHT** charge code that you just created.

Adding Charges To Orders

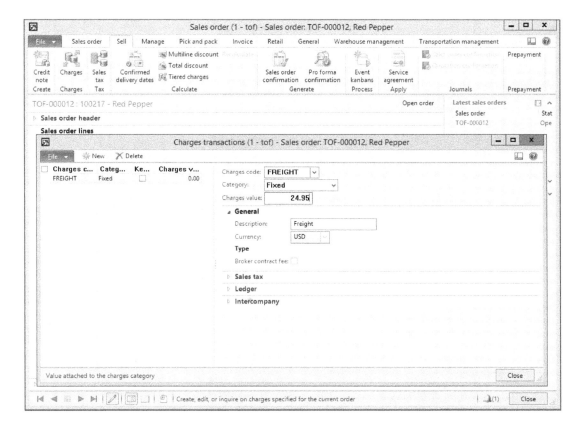

Then type in the **Charge Value** that you want to apply to the order – in this case we are charging **24.99** in freight.

When you have done that just click on the **Close** button to exit from the form.

Adding Charges To Orders

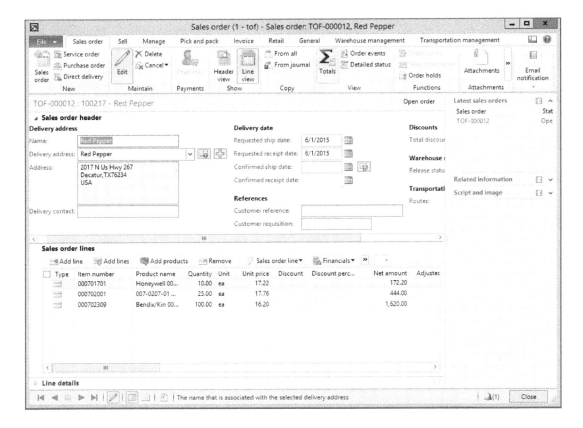

To see all of the total Charges another way, just click on the **Totals** button within the **View** group of the **Sales Order** ribbon bar.

Adding Charges To Orders

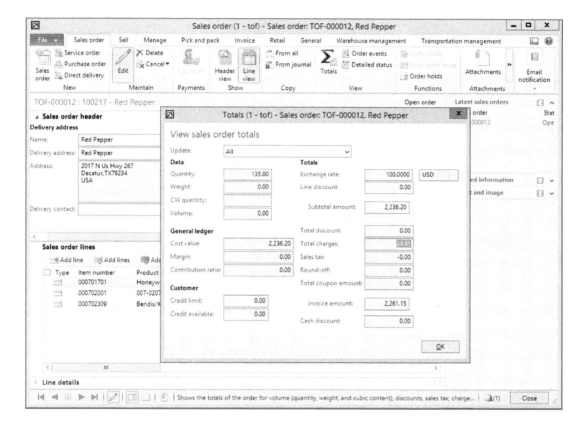

When the **Totals** summary form is displayed you will see that there is is now **24.99** showing up within the **Total Charges** section.

Adding Charges To Orders

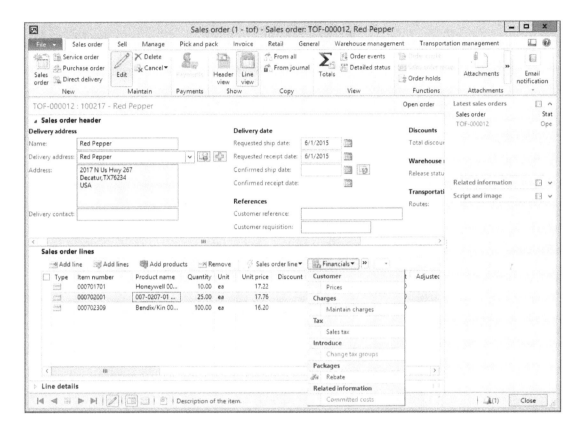

If you want to apply a charge just to one of the lines on the sales order then select the line, then click on the **Financials** menu button within the **Sales Order Lines** tab and select the **Maintain Charges** menu item.

Adding Charges To Orders

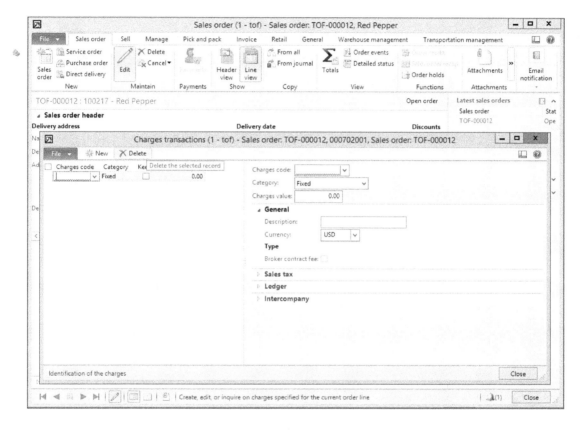

This will open up the same **Charges Transactions** maintenance form that you saw on the header and you can click on the **New** button in the menu bar to create a new record.

Adding Charges To Orders

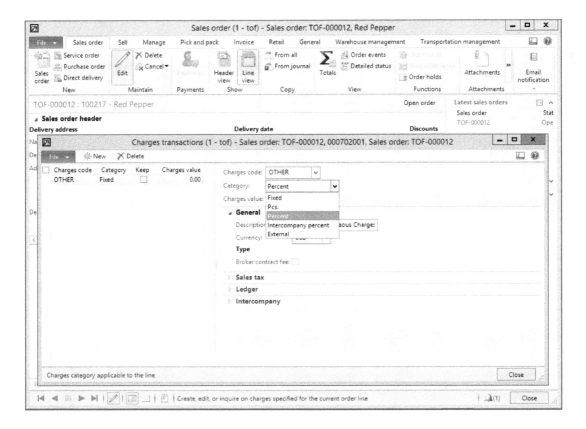

For this charge, set the **Charge Code** to **OTHER** and then click on the **Category** dropdown. You will notice that there are a number of different ways that you can slice and dice the charge. For this example select the **Percent** option to apply a percentage charge to the line.

Adding Charges To Orders

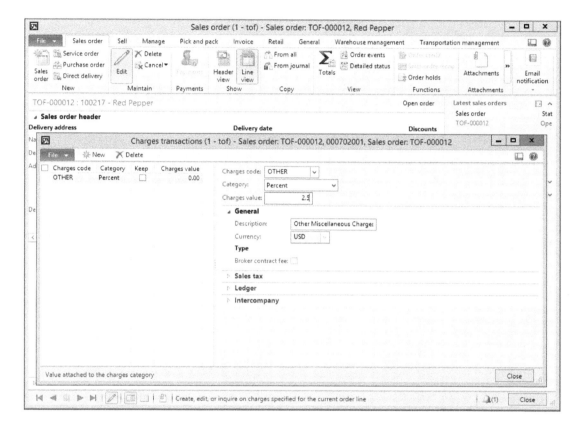

Now set the **Charges Value** to **2.5** % and click on the **Close** button to exit from the form.

Adding Charges To Orders

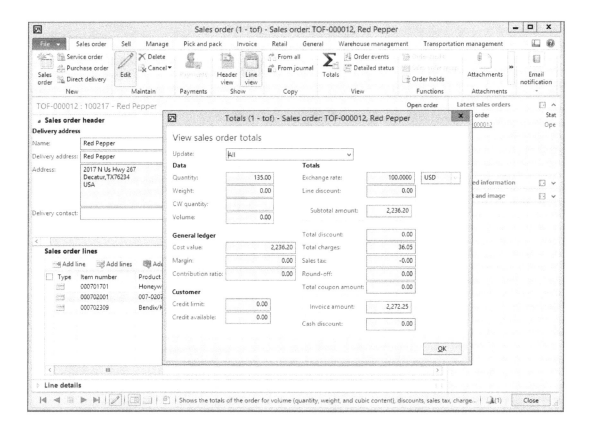

Click on the **Totals** button within the **View** group of the **Sales Order** ribbon bar again to see the summary and you will notice the **Total Charges** has been adjusted to include the line charge.

Creating Customer Charge Groups

If you have charges that should be automatically applied to Sales Orders for groups of customers then you can also set up Automatic Charge rules. Before we set those up though we need to create a group that we can add the customers to in order to tell the system to apply the charges.

Creating Customer Charge Groups

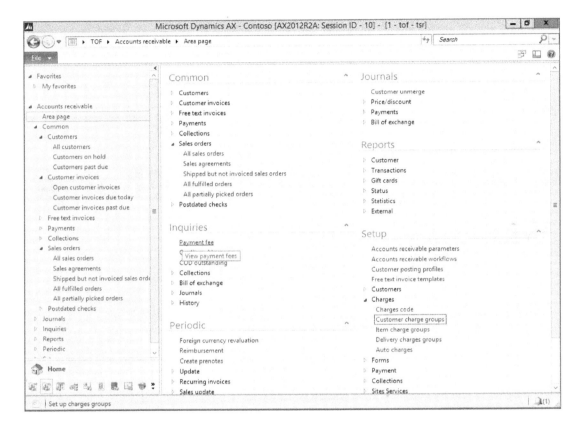

To do this just click on the **Customer Charge Groups** menu item within the **Charges** folder of the **Setup** group within the **Accounts Receivable** area page.

Creating Customer Charge Groups

When the **Customer Charge Groups** maintenance form is displayed, click on the **New** button in the menu bar to create a new record.

Creating Customer Charge Groups

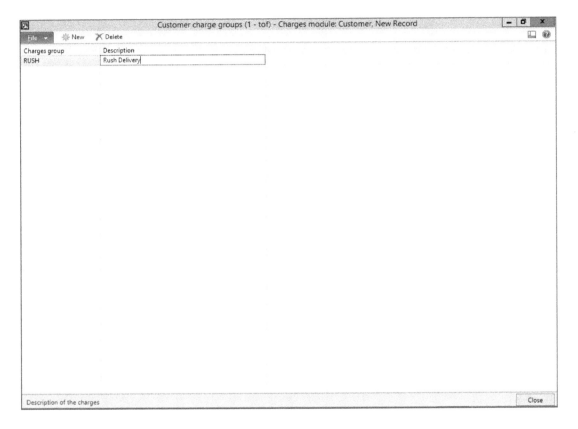

Set the **Charge Group** to **RUSH** and the **Description** to **Rush Delivery.**

Creating Customer Charge Groups

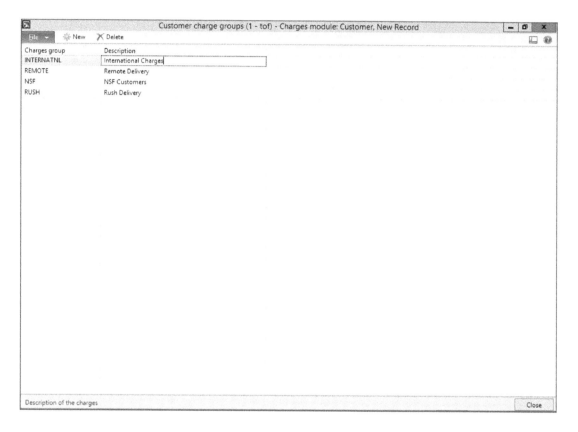

Continue adding any other **Charge Groups** that you like, here are some examples

INTERNATNL	**International Charges**
REMOTE	**Remote Delivery**
NSF	**NSF Customers**

When you have done that just click on the **Close** button to exit from the form.

Assigning Charge Groups To Customers

Once you have configured the **Customer Charge Groups** you then need to assign them to your **Customers**.

Assigning Charge Groups To Customers

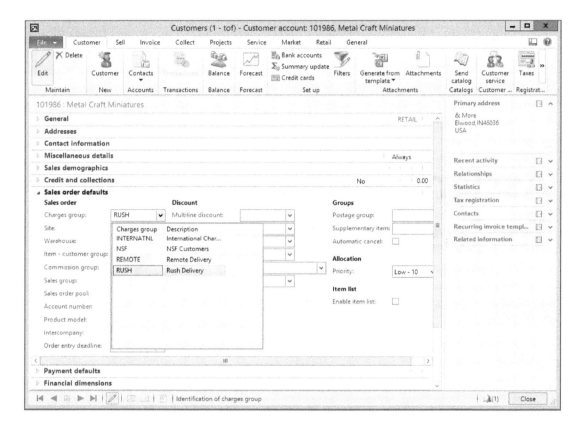

To do this, just open up the **Customer Details** form for the customer that you want to include in the **Charge Group** and open up the **Sales Order Defaults** fast tab. Then click on the **Charges Group** dropdown list and select the **Charge Group** that you want the customer to be included in. In this case we are selecting the **RUSH** option.

Creating Automatic Customer Charge Rules

Now that you have created your **Customer Charge Groups** you can set up an automatic **Charge Rule** that always applies the charge to the customer orders.

Creating Automatic Customer Charge Rules

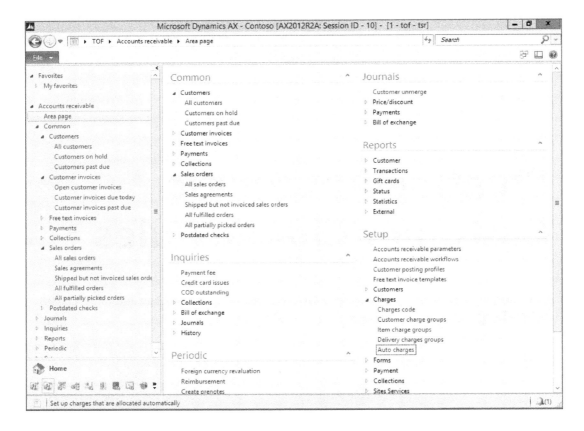

To do this, click on the **Auto Charges** menu item within the **Charges** folder of the **Setup** group within the **Accounts Receivable** area page.

Creating Automatic Customer Charge Rules

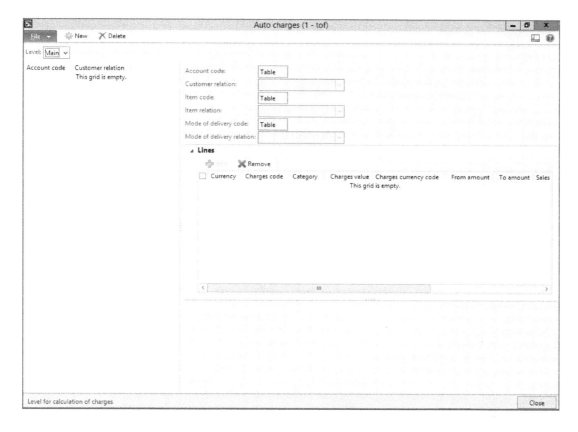

When the **Auto Charges** maintenance form is displayed, click on the **New** button in the menu bar to create a new record.

Creating Automatic Customer Charge Rules

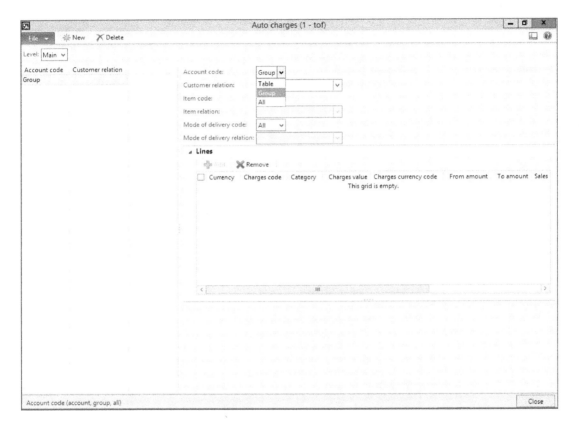

Click on the **Account Code** dropdown list and select the **Group** option to tell the system that this **Auto Charge** will be applied to a group of customers.

Creating Automatic Customer Charge Rules

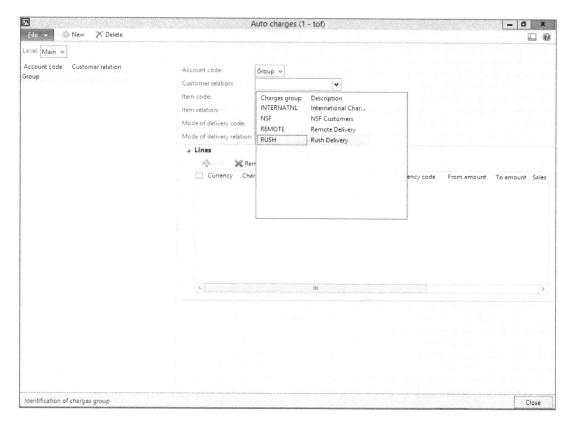

Then click on the **Customer Relation** dropdown list and select the **RUSH** group code that you just created.

Creating Automatic Customer Charge Rules

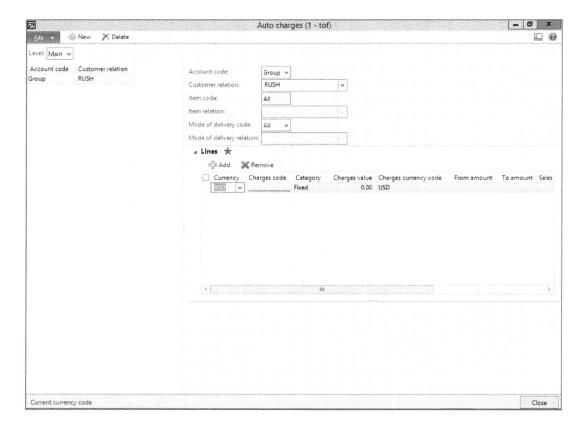

Leave all of the other selection options as they are and then click on the **Add** button in the **Lines** tab to create a new **Auto Charge Line**.

Creating Automatic Customer Charge Rules

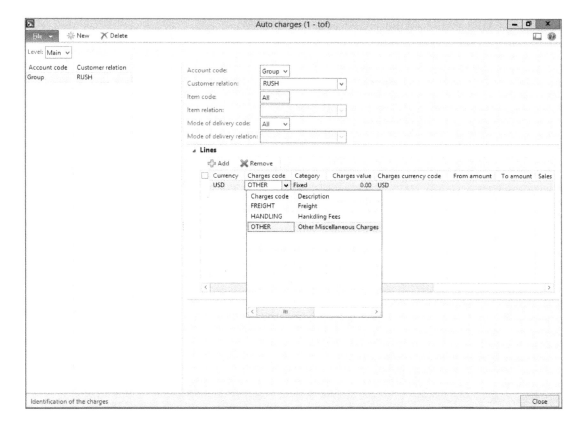

Click on the **Charge Code** dropdown list and select the **OTHER** Charge Code.

Creating Automatic Customer Charge Rules

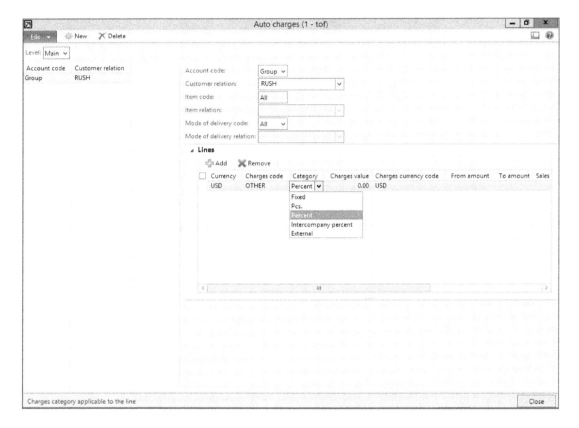

Then click on the **Category** dropdown list and select the **Percent** option.

Creating Automatic Customer Charge Rules

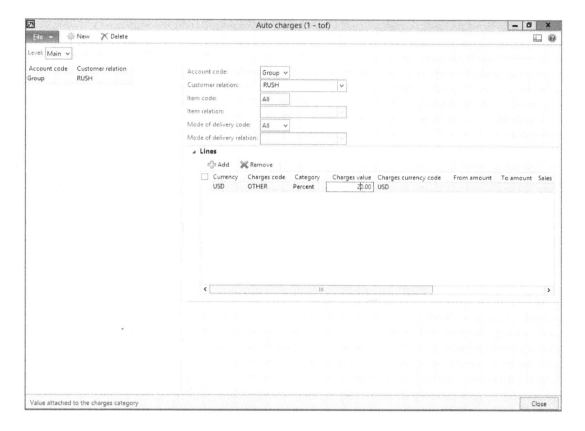

Then set the **Charge Value to** 20 **%.**

After you have done that, click on the **Close** button to exit from the form.

Creating Automatic Customer Charge Rules

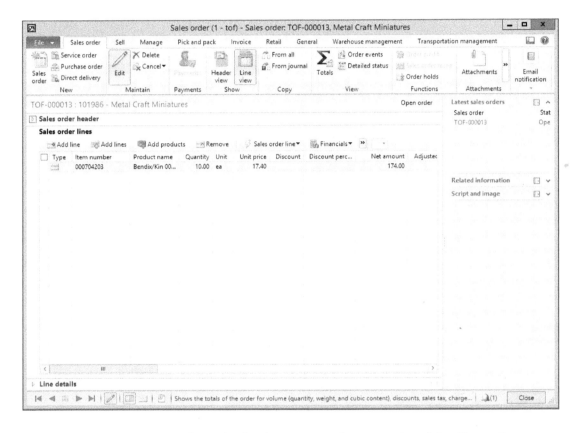

To test it out, just create a Sales Order for the customer that you assigned the **Charge Group** to.

Creating Automatic Customer Charge Rules

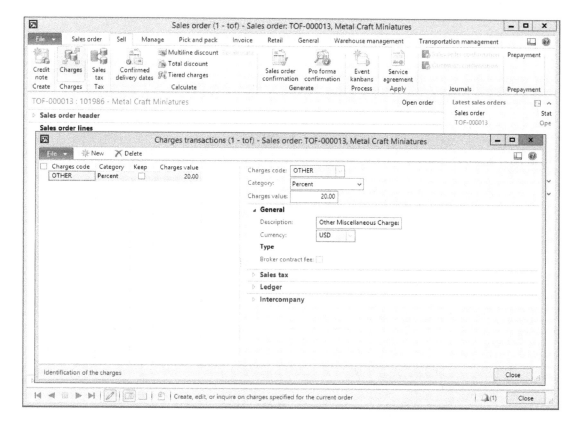

When you click on the **Charges** button in the **Charges** group of the **Sell** ribbon bar to show the **Charge Transactions** you will notice that the **Auto Charge** that you created has automatically been applied to the sales order.

BAM!

Creating Item Charge Groups

You can also create **Auto Charges** at the Sales Order Line level and have them associated with groups of items. In order to do this though you first need to create one or two **Item Charge Groups**.

Creating Item Charge Groups

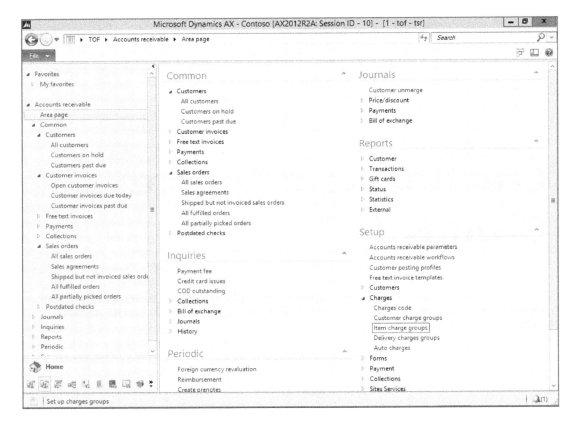

To do this click on the **Item Charge Groups** within the **Charges** folder of the **Setup** group of the **Accounts Receivable** area page.

Creating Item Charge Groups

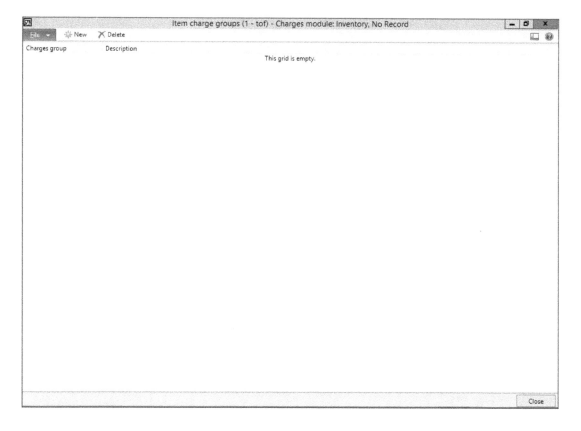

When the **Item Charge Groups** maintenance form is displayed, click on the **New** button in the menu bar to create a new record.

Creating Item Charge Groups

Then set the **Charge Group** to **SPECORDER** and the **Description** to **Special Order**.

Creating Item Charge Groups

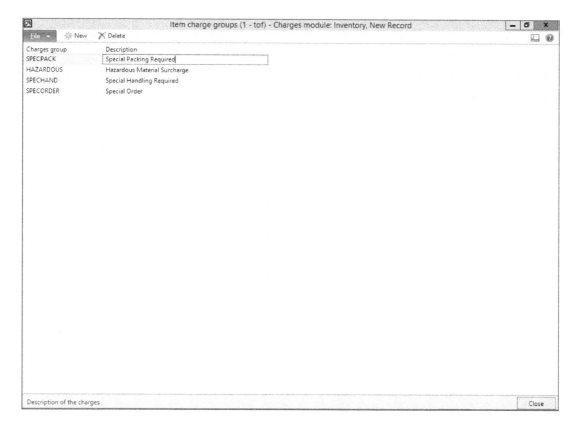

Continue adding any other **Item Charge Groups** that you like, here are some examples

SPECHAND	**Special Handling Required**
HAZARDOUS	**Hazardous Material Surcharge**
SPECPACK	**Special Packing Required**

When you have done that just click on the **Close** button to exit from the form.

Assigning Charge Groups To Items

Once you have configured the **Item Charge Groups** you then need to assign them to your **Items**.

Assigning Charge Groups To Items

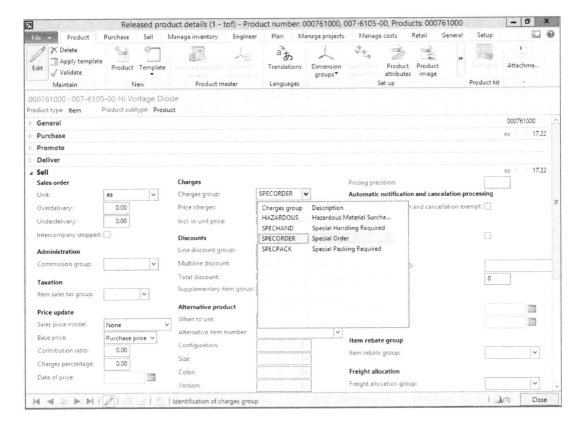

To do this, just open up the **Released Product Details** form for the customer that you want to include in the **Charge Group** and open up the **Sell** fast tab. Then click on the **Charges Group** dropdown list and select the **Charge Group** that you want the customer to be included in. In this case we are selecting the **SPECORDER** option.

When you have done that just click on the **Close** button to exit from the form.

Creating Automatic Item Charge Rules

Now that you have created your **Item Charge Groups** you can set up an **Auto Charge Rule** that always applies the charge to the customer order lines.

Creating Automatic Item Charge Rules

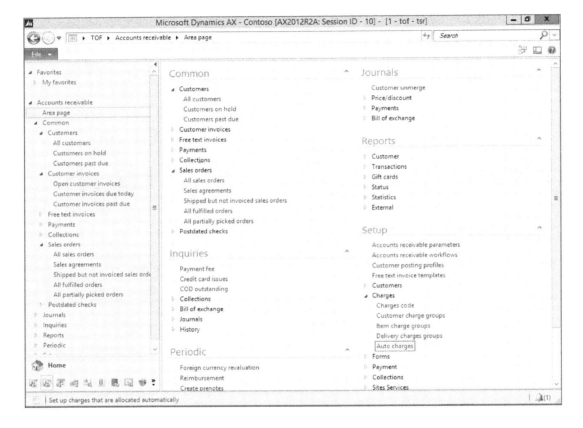

To do this, click on the **Auto Charges** menu item within the **Charges** folder of the **Setup** group within the **Accounts Receivable** area page.

Creating Automatic Item Charge Rules

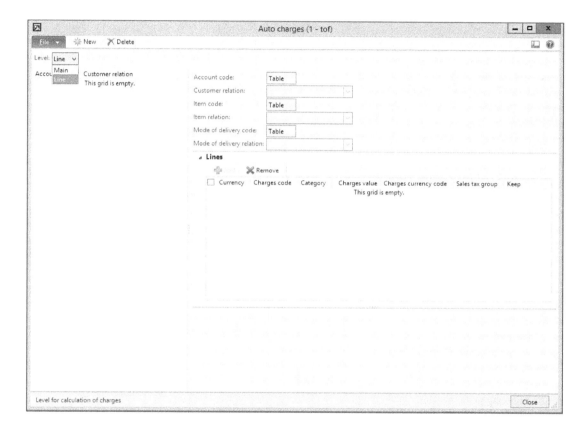

When the **Auto Charges** maintenance form is displayed, click on the **Level** dropdown list in the top right hand corner and select the **Line** option to switch the rules view from the Order Header to the Lines.

Creating Automatic Item Charge Rules

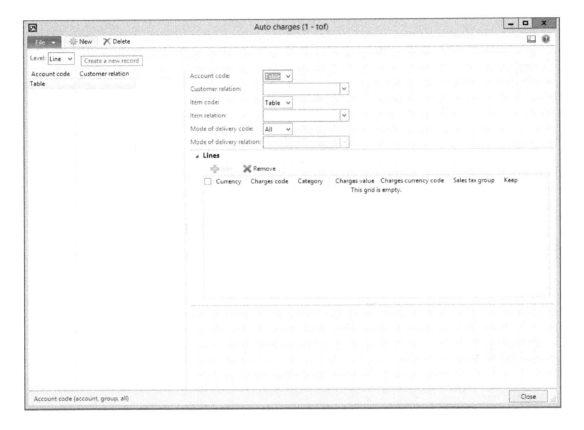

Then click on the **New** button in the menu bar to create a new record.

Creating Automatic Item Charge Rules

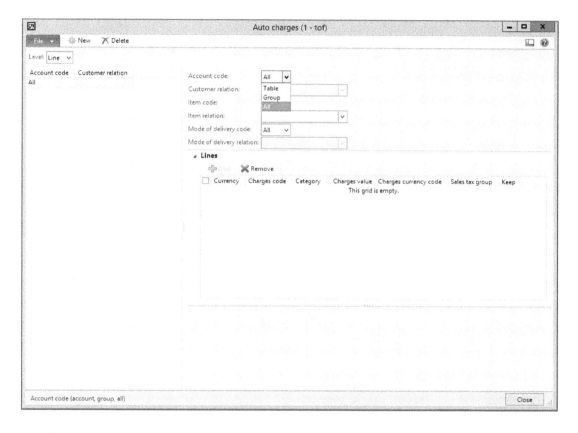

Click on the **Account Code** dropdown list and select the **All** option to apply this rule to all customers.

Creating Automatic Item Charge Rules

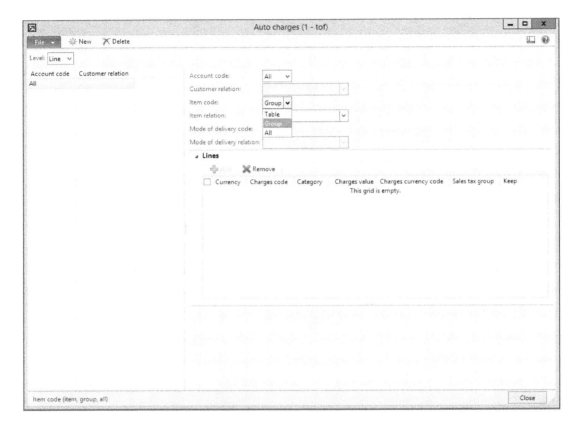

Then click on the **Item Code** dropdown list and select the **Group** option to apply this **Auto Charge** to a **Item Charge Group**.

Creating Automatic Item Charge Rules

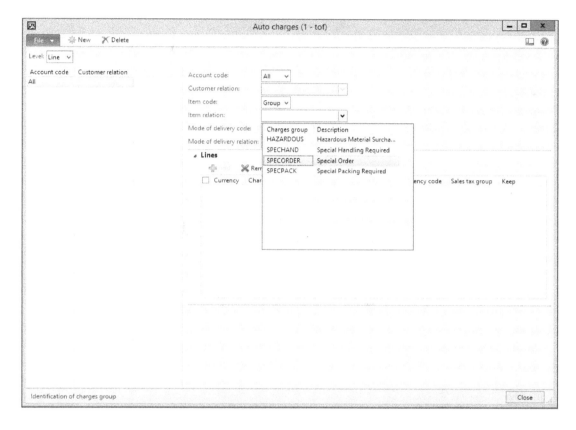

Then click on the **Item Relation** dropdown list and select the **SPECORDER Item Charge Group**.

Creating Automatic Item Charge Rules

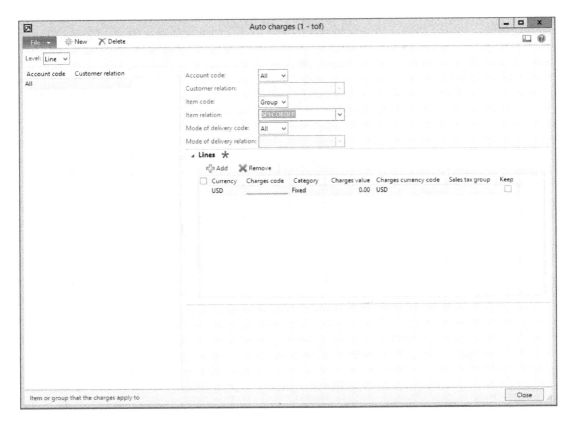

Now click on the **Add** button within the **Lines** tab to create a new Auto Charge Line.

Creating Automatic Item Charge Rules

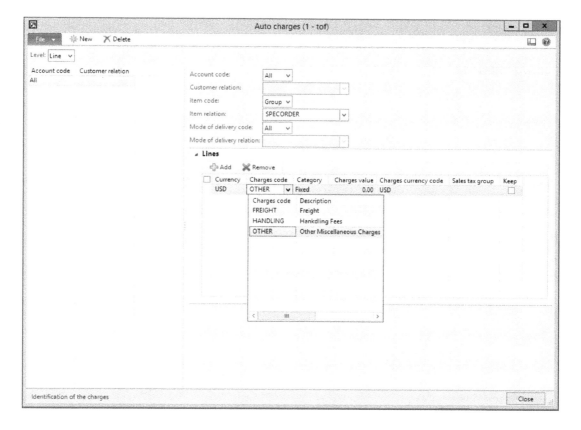

Click on the **Charges Code** dropdown list and select the **OTHER** Charge Code.

Creating Automatic Item Charge Rules

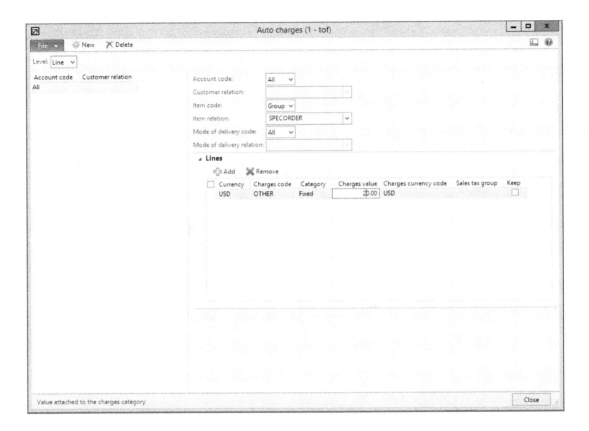

Then set the **Charge Value** to **$20.**

After you have done that just click on the **Close** button to exit from the form.

Creating Automatic Item Charge Rules

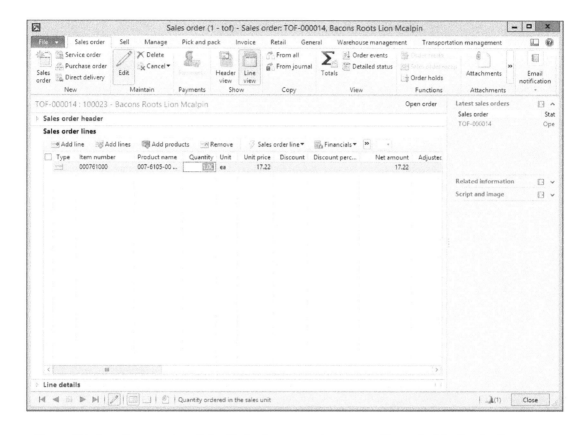

To see this in action, create a **Sales Order** for any customer you like and add a line for the product that you assigned the **Charge Group** to.

Creating Automatic Item Charge Rules

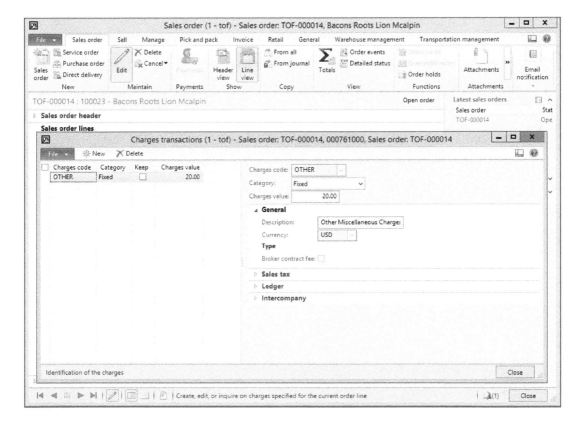

If you click on the **Financials** menu item within the **Sales Order Lines** menu bar and then select the **Additional Charges** menu item then you will see that the automatic charge has been applied for you.

SUMMARY

Hopefully this guide has given you a good foundation of knowledge of how the Sales Order Management area of Dynamics AX works, and also some of the key features that are available for you that allow you to configure and manage your Sales Orders.

We are still just starting you off on your journey through the Sales Order Management module though. There is so much more that you can do including taking advantage of **Return Orders**, **Customer Ordering Templates**, **Customer Credits**, **Customer Holds** and the **Customer Self Service Portal** which we did not have space for in this book, but don't worry, these will be covered in the second volume.

Want More Tips & Tricks For Dynamics AX?

The Tips & Tricks series is a compilation of all the cool things that I have found that you can do within Dynamics AX, and are also the basis for my Tips & Tricks presentations that I have been giving for the AXUG, and online. Unfortunately book page size restrictions mean that I can only fit 50 tips & tricks per book, but I will create new volumes every time I reach the 50 Tip mark.

To get all of the details on this series, then here is the link:

http://dynamicsaxcompanions.com/tipsandtricks

daxc

Need More Help With Dynamics AX?

LUKE SKYWALKER MAY HAVE HAD THE FORCE,
BUT HE STILL NEEDED R2D2 TO PLOT THE
COURSE FOR HIM.
WHO IS YOUR COMPANION THAT WILL HELP YOU
NAVIGATE DYNAMICS AX?

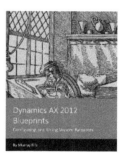

After creating a number of my walkthroughs on SlideShare showing how to configure the different areas within Dynamics AX, I had a lot of requests for the original documents so that people could get a better view of many of the screen shots and also have a easy reference as they worked through the same process within their own systems. To make them easier to access, I am in the process of moving all of the content to the Dynamics AX Companions website to easier access. If you are looking for details on how to configure and use Dynamics AX, then this is a great place for you to start.

Here is the link for the site:

http://dynamicsaxcompanions.com/

daxc

About Me

I am an author - I'm no Dan Brown but my books do contain a lot of secret codes and symbols that help guide you through the mysteries of Dynamics AX.

I am a curator - gathering all of the information that I can about Dynamics AX and filing it away within the Dynamics AX Companions archives.

I am a pitchman - I am forever extolling the virtues of Dynamics AX to the unwashed masses convincing them that it is the best ERP system in the world.

I am a Microsoft MVP - this is a big deal, there are less than 10 Dynamics AX MVP's in the US, and less than 30 worldwide.

I am a programmer - I know enough to get around within code, although I leave the hard stuff to the experts so save you all from my uncommented style.

WEB	www.murrayfife.me www.dynamicsaxcompanions.com www.blindsquirrelpublishing.com
EMAIL	murray@dynamicsaxcompanions.com
TWITTER	@murrayfife
SKYPE	murrayfife
AMAZON	www.amazon.com/author/murrayfife

daxc

www.ingramcontent.com/pod-product-compliance
Lightning Source LLC
Chambersburg PA
CBHW080131060326
40689CB00018B/3748